Critical L

Jennifer L. S. Chandler · Robert E. Kirsch

Critical Leadership Theory

Integrating Transdisciplinary Perspectives

Jennifer L. S. Chandler
Arizona State University
Tempe, AZ, USA

Robert E. Kirsch
Arizona State University
Phoenix, AZ, USA

ISBN 978-3-030-07198-1   ISBN 978-3-319-96472-0   (eBook)
https://doi.org/10.1007/978-3-319-96472-0

This Palgrave Macmillan imprint is published by the registered company Springer Nature Switzerland AG
The registered company address is: Gewerbestrasse 11, 6330 Cham, Switzerland

The authors are deeply grateful to each other for their sustained collegial interdisciplinarity in action. The cliché about the sum being greater than the parts is true and achievable through engaging in the frustrating challenges created in collaborative work. This process was more than just an effort to create a text. We stretched ourselves and the concepts which created thin places and sometimes we tore some tenuous fibrils and had to expand and refashion our own conceptualizations and understandings.

PREFACE

This book is primarily for three distinct, but related audiences. For students who wish to study leadership as an intellectual field of inquiry; for peers who wish to engage in a critical analysis of an emergent field of study to see its interdisciplinary opportunities; and for people in organizations who are in positions designated as leadership, who wish to practice leadership, or understand how leadership is a not an unalloyed good but rather is a problematic concept that needs to be reckoned with.

While we think there is significant overlap in what each audience can get from this text, we also do not claim it is the final word on critical theory or its application in leadership studies. Therefore, there is significant room for any of our audience to find what they need, depart where they may, and find their own intellectual vistas for integrating critical theory into leadership, be that its practice, application, or theory.

Our aim was to begin a conversation to cherish the interdisciplinarity of leadership studies, strengthen its theoretical and methodological pluralism, and find ways of connecting leadership to questions of the good and social goals. The conceptual frame we used to ask these questions was movement and direction. To that end, we looked to other fields of study to see how they understood their undertakings relative to the ways in which societies moved and to what ends. We use these insights to build some non-exhaustive tenets for what critical leadership studies might look like. We welcome any expansion, elaboration, alternatives, or critiques in this conversation.

The beginning of our collaboration started with a critical question: is there a difference between what leadership *is* as opposed to what people who are designated leaders *do*? Feeling discomforted by existing critical leadership texts, we embarked on this collaborative exploratory journey trusting that the classic inquiry process would prove productive. It did.

We express our gratitude to those who read chapters and provided feedback: Engineering: Caitlyn Hall, Kimberly Martin, Wilhelmina Savenye, Jean Larson, and especially Claudia Zapata who lent soil engineering introductory texts and painstakingly explained soil shear strength. Social Sciences: Elizabeth Castillo. Critical Theory: Brandon Kliewer. Animal Science: Emily Mertz and Spencer Stober. Aesthetics: Catherine A. Slye (who also created the cover image). Critical Leadership Tenets: Leigh Fine.

Tempe, USA   Jennifer L. S. Chandler
Phoenix, USA   Robert E. Kirsch

CONTENTS

LIST OF FIGURES

CHAPTER 1

Why Critical Theory Is Important

INTRODUCTION

The importance of a theory being critical may seem so obvious as to almost be glibly affirmed without a second thought. What this chapter aims to achieve is to narrow the scope of what makes a critical theory critical in the first place, as well as the possible effects of critical theory when diagnosing or offering social analysis that is qualitatively different from other theoretical approaches. In other words, we believe that a critical theory is a fundamentally different project than is commonly understood. To achieve this objective, this chapter will lay out the etymological grounding that establishes the urgency of the term *critical*, in a way that differentiates critical theory from non-critical theory, and also the more broadly understood term *critical thinking*. We maintain that critical thinking, while a necessary condition, is not a sufficient condition to build a critical theory of society. To build a robust and narrow conception of what a critical theory can accomplish that is different from normative, empirical, or otherwise traditional theory, we base our analysis on the importance of critical theory on its Frankfurt School originators. Therefore, the analysis will revolve around this school and necessarily involves discussing the role of ideology, totality, and the divergence of facts and norms in contemporary society. We trace a genealogy from the Frankfurt School through its conceptual apparatus to see its evolution into its current theoretical, and indeed, methodological force in the current context for studying current phenomena. We use these concepts to

© The Author(s) 2018   1
J. L. S. Chandler and R. E. Kirsch, *Critical Leadership Theory*,
https://doi.org/10.1007/978-3-319-96472-0_1

build a theoretical frame to assess the current state of leadership theory; is it critical? If not, how might it be and what might we reasonably hope for it to accomplish?

First, an etymology will allow us to distinguish a *critical theory* of society from a broader notion of *critical thinking* as a methodology for assessing the truth value of statements or actions, to say nothing of the reduction of *critical* meaning mean-spirited or spiteful. Showing the social roots and consequences of the concept of *crisis* sets the stage for a theory built around crisis and the resolution thereof. This is different from critical thinking. Critical thinking, while important, is a prescriptive exercise, but can too often obscure the role of crisis in social analysis, so we will draw a sharp distinction that highlights the socially embedded components of a critical theory focused on human flourishing.

Deriving from the term *critical* in a simple sense, the supposition of theory or thought being critical is based on the existence of a crisis. An etymology of the term crisis is therefore appropriate if we wish to flesh out the normative content of critical thought. The term crisis is derived from the Greek *krisis*, which was a medical term that diagnosed a decision point for a physician to determine if the patient's self-healing properties were enough to overcome an illness and if not, at what point an intervention was necessary (Habermas, 1998). From this, we can draw some initial observations behind the concept of crisis. First, that crises are a matter of autonomy that deprives the subjects in crisis their individual capacity for self-governance; the physician is the one who determines the point at which the subject's self-regulation and volition is insufficient, making the outcome of the crisis dependent not on the individual will of the patient. As opposed to say, when a patient has a cold and undergoes a regime of rest and hydration. Rather, the crisis is an objective force that deprives the victim of the capacity for self-determination as they lose their constitutive ability to take meaningful action at the juncture described above (Habermas, 1998, p. 1). That loss of an ability to make a decision for oneself marks the critical juncture, so it acts as a bright line. Before this juncture, the subject has full range of choices, and can exercise autonomous decisions; after this juncture, the subject is incapable and instead must be acted upon. Second, in this medical etymology, a crisis also represents a chance at liberation as a result of the necessary intervention. If the intervention is successful, and proffers a resolution of the crisis, this means the subject's constitutive self-determination as a free subject is restored. While this may seem obvious, this means that recognizing a critical juncture and resolving the crisis means diagnosing the intolerable external conditions on the subject, and that the intervention is normative insofar as the course of action is done on the patient's behalf, or for their own good (Habermas, 1998). The intervention has a certain direction, geared toward human flourishing, so we may then infer that not all interventions are desirable or carry equal weight, but a critical juncture weighs those options and makes an intervention.

This normative dimension is an important carryover when shifting the register of crisis from the individual and the medical into the social and the structural. Before doing so though, the metaphor can be drawn out in an explicit way; the body of the subject can be extended to the body politic.[1] Much in the same way that an ailment can progress to a critical juncture that requires the normative intervention, so can a political society suffer a degradation that requires intervention as well. This ushers in a systems approach that highlights the institutional structures of society in its capacity to sustain the body politic, and a juridical approach that highlights the state's sovereign ability to be the entity that can diagnose the ailment and act in a restorative manner. Habermas (1998) continues that in a systems approach, crises emerge when, "...a social system allows fewer possibilities for problem solving than are necessary to the continued existence of the system" (p. 2). Taken from a medical crisis, the ability of the social system's normal operating procedures to fix what ails it is insufficient. In extension to the structural component of crisis is a juridical one. Much like the individual's subjective sovereign self-determination is impaired at the critical juncture, a society's sovereign apparatus may be unable to fix what ails it through its normal operating procedures.

This shift from individual to social carries the etymology from crisis to critique. Critique is the juridical art whereby problems in the body politic were identified by members of that political society, and through deliberation, offered the restorative means to repair society (Brown, 2005). Again, we see that there is a directional thrust to this social intervention. If society ails, the restorative action is to heal it. We pause to make a provisional observation concerning leadership, that the citizens

---

[1]A rich strain of political theory deploys this metaphor; most notably Augustine (1994), Hobbes (1994), and Locke (1980). The idea behind the metaphor is to prescribe order into the shape and function of the state, civil society, and the economy into a unified and harmonious whole, guided by the head of the sovereign (be that a god, king or representative of the peoples' will).

who step forth to name the problems and to offer restorative action are exhibiting critical leadership. We also note that this shift to critique in crises' social existence, is very different from the way critique or critical thinking is deployed in the current context. Before moving on to what a critical theory of society may entail, it is necessary to distinguish critical theory from critical thinking.

A theory based on critique requires, of course, critical thinking. We will expand on this more below. For now, we only note that the notion of critical thinking is so ubiquitous across so many discourses of everyday life, to say nothing of disciplinary specialties, it would be impossible to catalogue them all. However, as a working concept, we might say that critical thinking is using evidence-based reasoning to determine the truth value of a knowledge claim. Regardless of the strain of critical thinking, it usually revolves around the ability to thoughtfully discern the truth, through the rigorous use of a method. While the ability to discern truth makes this concept share an etymological root with critical theory, it is important to note that the judgment is not necessarily made in the direction of fixing what ails a body, individual or politic. We do not seek to diminish the important role of critical thinking, but putting the strands of critique next to crisis can highlight the importance of the context of critical thinking—what truths are valorized? What methods are appropriate to determine the truth value of statements? In other words, de-linking critical thinking from its social context of intervention for the sake of healing what ails a society can reduce it to an instrument that might otherwise complement domination; in other words, critical thinking is a necessary, but not sufficient, component for a critical theory of leadership specifically or society generally.

To have a critical theory of leadership, or indeed a broader critical theory of society, means fleshing out the contours on which thought is induced, where value judgments are upheld or not upheld, and perhaps most important; to what end the value judgments are working toward an articulated vision of a society. By establishing the role of crisis as a social intervention toward fixing what ails the body (individual or socialized), we may now argue that critical theory must envision, theorize, and set the foundations for an intervention in society that goes beyond the normal operating procedures to fix a problem that has been diagnosed. Our foundation of critical theory will therefore necessarily have to go beyond a conception of theory that relegates it only as a tool for empirical findings and will simultaneously have to surpass the easy affirmations of common sense, since regardless of whether common sense is true, it is essentially a reification of the normal operating procedures under investigation. A critical theory (of leadership or anything else) will instead have to diagnose something that is wrong and offer a restorative course of action to correct it.

CRITICAL THEORY: A PRELIMINARY DEFINITION AND SOME POSSIBLE OBJECTIONS

In many academic disciplines and other fields of study, it is common to come across theories of that field of study, and then a *critical* variety of that same field of study, like a kind of mirror image. We want to address what makes a theory critical as opposed to traditional (be that normative, or formal, or experimental), with the ambiguities and difficulties that come with it that goes beyond a reactionary or mirrored lens of analysis. Our goal is not only to give an overview of what is currently categorized as critical leadership studies, but to show how such categorizations are made in the first place, and then to establish the importance of a critical theory therein. The importance of such a categorization is to uncover the normative foundations as well as direction of a field of study, and opens a vista for that vision and diagnosis, as outlined above. In other words, a critical intervention forces a confrontation with the question, "What is this for?" This exploration of critique and critical theory is therefore not meant to be exhaustive, but rather a basis for determining whether a theory is critical of a body of knowledge as a matter of judgment.

One objection that we anticipate is that if critical is a modifier for an already established body of theoretical literature, does a critical theory have its own content, or is it merely a reaction against an established body of knowledge? This question raises important issues surrounding critical theory, that it is simply negative or pessimistic, refusing to allow for the benefits of certain social arrangements to get their proper recognition for the sake of knee-jerk derision. We will take up a framework of positive and negative theory later, but for now, the consequence of such naysaying is that there is no analytic core to critical theory itself because it is reliant on other cores of knowledge. To that effect, we take the question of critical theory's genealogical and methodological prospects seriously as its own mode of investigation. Answering this question is a matter of critical theory as a methodology of social investigation.

A second objection that one might have is that critical theory does not need to be elaborated separately, as the practice of critical thinking encompasses the goals of critical theory stated above. Critical thinking, while its own vast field of inquiry, can reasonably be described as the use of reasoning faculties to make judgments about the truth value of a statement or situation. The field of study is then concerned with the appropriate skills to make these judgments. We contend that however important these skills are, they are necessary, but not sufficient conditions to engage in a critical theory. Answering this question will show how critical thinking as a skillset can reinforce the oppressive structures of a society, valuing efficient navigation of channels of domination instead of opposing those structures. We will answer these two objections in more detail to sketch a domain of critical theory as a mode of inquiry.

Objection 1: Critical Theory Is Reflective Pessimism, and Lacks an Analytic Core

Answer 1: Critical theory's core is a praxis of immanent critique
While in most empiricist discourses, theory and method are two distinct categories for intellectual investigation, critical theory suggests that it is *in itself* both a theory as well as a method of social analysis. Because it is not, and does not seek to be, a general theory of society, immanent critique and its subsequent critical theory can be understood as a "... method of analysis deriving from a nonpositivist epistemology" (Antonio, 1981, p. 332). This simply means that an immanent critique does not accept the social world as a natural or in place phenomenon, to which the researcher is only left to description. We argue that this understanding of immanent critique is what justifies it is as both theoretical and methodological content to critical theory (Antonio, 1981; Azmanova, 2012; Carrabregu, 2016; Curtis, 2014; Sabia, 2010; Särkelä, 2017). Because it does not seek to describe society from an imagined external vantage, immanent critique is a method of social investigation that focuses on uncovering the internal contradictions in social structures, and how those contradictions are degrading for people subject to those structures (Adorno, 1997). As a result, immanent critique is "... a means of detecting the societal contradictions which offer the most determinate possibilities for emancipatory social change" (Antonio, 1981, p. 332). We think that immanent critique is the most appropriate

basis for the content of a critical theory because it best fulfills the role in the etymological discussion above of diagnosis via highlighting societal contradictions and the restorative role of emancipatory social change from within those social relations.

A frame that we have found most useful for understanding immanent critique is a gap. In this thinking the gap is between the society as discursively presented and the reality of the lived experiences of people within those societies (Wrenn, 2016). Societies offer certain normative statements about its provisions for its members. In a political institutional arrangement, we might think of this as what the state provides for its citizens. Through the institutional arrangements, states putatively offer citizens things like security, equality before the law, and privacy, among others. There is, in other words, a discursive framework of institutional power that generates social relations and practices (Curtis, 2014). If a state decrees, for instance, that there is equality before the law, that power relationship has thus been established and there should be an institutional arrangement to allow for such equality. However, if we were to empirically observe that the institutional arrangement did not provide for such equality due to socioeconomic status, race, or gender, then there is an unsettling conclusion about the inadequacy of subjects in that regime, or something deficient about the institutional arrangement being offered.[2] A critical orientation is thus unsettling because it interrogates those power relations and their deficiencies relative to what is supposedly being accomplished in given social relations (Curtis, 2014). This interrogation exposes a gap between the supposed reality of power relations from its discursive genesis, and the actual lived experience of the social relations.[3] Immanent critique is a method of analysis that is unsettling because it forces people within given institutional regimes that regulate and discipline their behavior to confront the fact that these institutions might not be doing what they have assumed they do.

Much like the notion of crisis itself, we can move between a social and an individual understanding to highlight the importance of critical analysis. At a purely individual level, we may tell ourselves that we have

---

[2] This very concern is the basis for critical race theory, and critical legal studies.

[3] We argue that the pervasiveness of the "bad apples" defense highlights this unsettled reaction to the gap. By assuming the bad behavior of a few individuals as deficient perpetrators of injustice in a system that otherwise works how it is supposed to is a way to ignore the gap.

certain characteristics or traits: we are honest, thrifty, forthright, etc. By the same token, with a bit of self-reflection we may realize the ways in which we fall short of the mark; we sometimes tell untruths, overspend, shirk responsibilities, etc. We see, in other words, that there is a gap between what we proclaim ourselves to be and our behaviors that belie those proclamations. A self-critique is thus an immanent mode of investigation to determine what structural or psychological barriers prevented us from behaving in a way that reflects those qualities, much like critical decision-making is an attempt at restorative action. In other words, we locate the gap, formulate a plan of change, and then try to achieve the qualities we wish to exhibit. Immanent critique simply asks us to perform that same analysis on a social level, noting that the direction is the same; self-critique is toward improvement, and immanent critique of a society is for emancipation and the flourishing of individuals.

While it is true that emancipation and flourishing are normative foundations to build a critical theory, it is important to emphasize that immanent critique, and the resulting critical theory, is not an ethical or moral position (Sabia, 2010). To make sense of this is to reiterate the distinction between individual behavior and system outcomes. Social structures do not fail to live up to their aspirations because people behave immorally, thereby frustrating the capacity for those structures to function, but rather because structures are insufficiently designed to produce the outcomes of those societal aspirations. So instead of making moral pronouncements about the worth of individuals in a society, immanent critique engages the system *as it presents itself and its aspirations* and shows that the internal contradictions present in a system prevent those aspirations from becoming a reality. Resolving those contradiction is vital in order to provide the conditions of free and flourishing people.[4]

---

[4] It is the basis of this immanent critique, and its roots in Hegelian philosophy, that many people assume that critical theory is based on Marxian analysis (Antonio, 1981). This is not an unreasonable assumption, but the role of immanence shows a vital misreading of many of Marx's detractors. His magnum opus, *Capital*, was an immanent critique of capitalist political economy. That is, the internal contradictions of a regime of capital accumulation, which he took as given according to bourgeois political economy's own laws, would necessarily lead to the system's breakdown. His objection was not ethical (in fact he has high praise for capitalism over what it replaced), but structural. Given what we have established about crisis and critique, it is worth noting that *Capital*'s subtitle is: *A Critique of Political Economy*.

Registering critique in a moral or ethical register forecloses avenues of action for restorative action. If the reason for a society not living up to its aspirations is because of some essential moral defect of the people in that structure, then that structure can never live up to its aspirations and will always be frustrated by that essential moral deficit. We find this position incoherent and self-defeatist. It is incoherent because if there were an essential moral character that prevented social progress, then there is no rational basis upon which to articulate those goals in the first place. Further, it is self-defeating because, from the start, it assumes that people cannot fulfill the lofty goals their society sets. It freezes social analysis, and we lose sight of the movement and direction of social dynamism.

The final argument in our answer for immanent critique as a methodology of critical theory is the vantage point from which it is situated. Above, we noted that immanent critique is non-positivist. Without veering off into the depth of Kantian philosophy, positivism suggests that there is an irreducible divide between the subject (the person doing the observing) and the object (that which is under observation), such that the view of logical positivism is an alien one, where a subject that cannot fully apprehend the object tries their best to describe it (DiSalle, 2002). Immanent critique not only denies such an irreducible divide, but it insists that there is no external vantage in the first place, where the subject is not always already a part of the structures, movement, and history of the society that is being studied. Indeed, the feeling of externalization, which Hegel refers to as alienation, is socially produced in the first place; humans are part of structures in which they make things that, because they are not familiar with the entirety of their production as socialized individuals, confront them as foreign (Antonio, 1981). Overcoming that alienation is not to crystallize it in a method, but rather to explain the dynamics, movement, and direction of social activity as it moves around us and as we participate in it and fleshes out our notion of movement and direction as an attempt to overcome that alienation and the domination that comes with it. It is an emancipatory telos that recognizes not only the disconnect or gap between the world as discursively presented and the reality of peoples' lived experiences, but also the ways in which that diagnostic insight provides the tools for overcoming that gap and achieving those same social aspirations (Antonio, 1981). The emancipatory potential is a process, not a break rendered from the outside. A critical theory moves society along in that progressive direction from within, based on an understanding of the facts as we find them; we argue that those who are leaders are the ones who move this internal process. This is clearly not pessimism, but we will take up affirmative and negative theory below when dealing with the Frankfurt School, who give a clear vision of the difference.

Objection 2: The Benefits of a Critical Theory Can All Be Achieved Already in Critical Thinking

Answer 2: Critical thinking is a necessary, but not sufficient, condition for critical theory

We understand that critical theory is inextricably tied up in an investigation for immanent truth; by this, we simply mean a truth that comes from the reality of social relations, and not a transcendent truth from some external vantage. The movement a society takes and in what direction are based on those immanent truths. Without that external vantage, we lose an objective frame from which to assess this movement and direction, and instead are compelled to look at the complex totality of society to draw inferences and make claims about what we ought to do. In the same vein, the immanence of critique and the restorative possibilities are truth claims about what might be done to accomplish societal aims. An important part of this process is the ability to weigh, assess, and understand evidence using critical thinking; or thinking through the crisis. While critical thinking and critical theory share a common adjective, we argue here that in its current context, critical thinking is a necessary, but not sufficient condition to meet the demands of an immanent critical theory. The rationale for this claim is that there is a transformative element to a critical theory that extends beyond assessment for truth value in critical thinking. We just argued in Answer 1 that there is no "outside" or other external vantage point to access to assess or critique a society, hence the importance of critiquing a society on the basis of a gap between what kind of world we ought to strive for and the reality of what is. Any knowledge claim is therefore situated on the position of people within those social structures, making a universal standard outside of that structure impossible. Critical thinking, while an important part of making judgments about the truth value of statements, is not necessarily aware of its own positionality in a given society.

Critical thinking is a broad term with no one definition, but for the purposes of this analysis, it will suffice to suggest that it is a deployment of rational thinking to determine the validity, and therefore truth,

Practice	Virtue		Knowledge	
Skills	*Attitude*	*Disposition*	*Conceptual*	*Disciplinary*
Critical thinking is the ability to: a) assess, b) weigh evidence, and c) identify fallacy	Critical thinking is a habit of mind that cultivates an identity of asking question. It's a matter of character.	Critical thinking carries moral decision-making and requires a critical thinker to be disposed toward the good.	Critical thinking is a sophisticated grasp on epistemology to assess knowledge claims, i.e., critical thinking itself is an epistemological field.	Critical thinking requires advanced knowledge in a particular area beyond general knowledge to assess claims.

Fig. 1.1 Cumulative understandings of critical thinking

of statements (Doddington, 2007; Holmes, Wieman, & Bonn, 2015; Mason, 2007; Mulnix, 2012; Natale & Ricci, 2006; Papastephanou & Angeli, 2007). Mason's (2007) review discusses the continuum along which critical thinking has been presented and we have created this view as a landscape in Fig. 1.1. This cataloging of Mason's argument is cumulative as it moves from left to right. We propose to take each of them in turn, showing how each iteration is a cumulative improvement from the last, but still nevertheless fail to establish critical thinking alone as a replacement for an immanent critique of society.

Practice—Skills
In the current context, critical thinking is often equated with a skill that one can master, like horseback riding, baking, or spinning plates. In fact, a good deal of critical thinking literature even assumes an equivalence with skill, couched in fuzzy terms like being geared toward a desirable outcome or being reasoned (Papastaphenou & Angeli, 2007). Of course, without a clear sense of what outcomes are desirable, or what makes thought reasoned, the strength of this straightforward definition weakens considerably. We believe that without a strong sense of what those terms mean, then the skill that is taught becomes decontextualized from the milieu in which it is practiced and loses its critical reflexivity as a result. Even attempts to place the locus of rationality in a positional framework often relies on the normative strategic rationalities of occidental values, and in so doing can reduce critical thinking to an instrumental technology rather than a mode of thought (Papastephanou & Angeli, 2007). Much like other skills, once they are mastered, the logic behind the skill becomes less important. Our central critique of critical thinking as skills is that while skills can describe certain kinds of thought, they are agnostic toward the ends of that thinking.

The difficulties emerge when investigating the skills in question. Skills-based critical thought seeks to *assess evidence* but falls back on vague categories such as reasonability or rationality, which is begging the question (Papastephanou & Angeli, 2007). That is, evidence assessment is directed toward rationality, but if rationality is a precondition for assessing evidence it is unclear how we are supposed to develop this skill. While it is true that in many areas of life, we may assume an overarching rationality for which everyday decision-making might be guided, it does not get at a critical component of that rationality.

Further, skills-based critical thinking asks thinkers to weigh evidence to know which side of an argument is more persuasive. Our simple question is: Who tares the scale? That is, what are the structures and assumptions around persuasive discourse and what is valued against and above other values, interests, or discourses? We have then yet another example of requiring the result of critical thinking to engage in prior critical thinking, and it does not answer that question. If critical thinking is required to properly understand the criteria that we should use to weigh evidence, then we cannot expect weighing evidence to be a formative element of critical thinking.

Finally, skills-based critical thinking requests an expertise in *identifying fallacies*. This assumes that identifying fallacies leads to some tangible consequence. There are many times when a person confronts fallacies or contradictions, but is able to live happily with them or ignore them for the sake of getting along (Papastephanou & Angeli, 2007). Identifying does not necessarily mean undoing. Further, while we will not dive into the myriad logical constructs, this skill seems to accept that there is one kind of logic, which we suspect is reductive.

In these three instances, skills-based critical thinking seems predicated on the idea that without these skills, one violates rationality itself. If we cannot assess, weigh, or see bad evidence, then we lose our capacity for rational thought. This might sound appealing because it is so stark, and fits in nicely with other arguments from skill.[5]

While this may be the case in a purely technical way that relates to other skills, since the argument from skills is agnostic toward the direction the agent should take after mastering and deploying these skills of critical thought, a paradox emerges. On the one hand, the stakes are so low that there is little compelling reason to enshrine it as rationality, instead noting that this is a just a matter of practice, and can become a performative behavior, without self-reflexivity (Chandler & Kirsch, 2018; Papastephanou & Angeli, 2007). That is, the skills argument assumes that critical thinking is de facto good thought, but there is no

---

[5] This is a rather old argument. Consider Plato's *Republic*, where he essentially argues that a just or good society is when the people who are the most skilled at ruling should rightfully be the rulers. He makes an argument by analogy that the best person to captain is the best sailor. The same question applies here; namely, under what set of assumptions do we measure the "best" sailor, or the best ruler?

normative element to what makes it good or how these skills necessarily lead to good ends. Because they are only skills, it reduces rationality to "...a categorization, not a substantive category of thinking as such with extra-cultural or extra-linguistic existence or objectivity" (Papastephanou & Angeli, 2007, p. 610). On the other hand, however, the stakes are extreme. By conflating the skills argument for critical thinking with rationality itself, then we enshrine the certain sets of skills and assumptions that reinforce certain outcomes with the ability to think and can be reduced to "purposiveness/strategy" (Papastephanou & Angeli, 2007, p. 610). That is, people who have mastered the skill or strategy are good thinkers, and those who deviate from them are not only bad thinkers, they may not actually really be thinking.

None of this is to suggest that there are *no* skilled elements to critical thinking. However, when we frame them in terms of movement and direction, it becomes clearer that paying attention to the social relations behind both rational and critical thought should serve as a de-instrumentalizing force, and rather one that appeals to mutual understanding as opposed to properly executing a set of protocols (Habermas, 2000; Papastephanou & Angeli, 2007). Suffice it to say, building that scaffolding of the social relations behind which thought is accorded its rationality makes skills a barely necessary, but certainly not sufficient, condition for building a critical theory of society.

Virtue—Attitude

We note that these understandings of the content of critical thinking are cumulative. That is, the arguments from virtue are supposed to overcome the argument from skills that critical thought can be reduced to a set of behaviors to be practiced. The argument from virtue proceeds from the insight that it is not just a matter of performing the dictates of critical thinking, but that an individual does it for the right reasons. We will take up two vectors of these right reasons; attitude and disposition. To clarify the discussion, we draw a line of distinction between the two where morality is concerned. That is, attitudes can be shaped along all sorts of lines, but dispositions are moral or ethical orientations that shape a person's praxis. While critical thinking as a virtue is a better variant than as a skill, it still misses the mark to build a critical theory of society.

Defining critical thinking as an attitude is difficult for two reasons. First, it can be used as an essentializing descriptor. That is, some people have this attitude, and others do not. Or some people are more geared toward it and others are not. This is problematic on its face because it overqualifies or disqualifies certain people and this can lead to stratification; not everybody can be a critical thinker because not everybody has the right attitude. Second, and perhaps worse, is that an attitudinal lens values certain attitudes for their own sake and not because of their capacity to engender critical thought. We purport to value people who ask tough questions as a mode of critical thinking, but we pause to note that Socrates was executed for doing just this. So perhaps we are being too generous to ourselves regarding what kind of attitude leads to critical thought. We like question askers, but only certain kinds of question askers—that is, question askers with the right kind of attitude. As a result, critical thinking as an attitude does not avoid the critique of being an instrumental force. We might say that it is essentially a set of skills that one does with a smile on one's face, showing the right kind of attitude.

Still, we should give this attitudinal definition some structure. What this essentially boils down to is an Aristotelian appeal to how virtues are formed: namely, habit (Aristotle, 1999a). Virtue may not be an essentialist characteristic of our identity, any more than other attributes we may find (or not find) desirable. Rather, Aristotle tells us, virtues are done by force of habit. If we tell the truth enough times it becomes habitual, and we are therefore an honest person, and have attained the virtue of honesty. In this sense, virtue becomes a part of a person's identity, not because of constant conscious application, but when it stops being conscious and becomes habitual. All well and good, but Aristotle's vision of virtue as habit is further unique in that he conceives of virtues as *means*, that is, averages between two vices (Curzer, 1996). Vices can be understood as passions, or unreasoned behavior. Attitude thus means that we have balanced ourselves and are able to take a reasoned approach to things.

A common example of an Aristotelian virtue is courage. Between fear and confidence, one finds courage (Curzer, 1996). Quantitatively, this makes sense for certain attributes, and it is easy to conceive of other means. Generosity between miserliness and being spendthrift, for instance. However, as we begin to balance how to behave or what habits to form between these deficiencies and excesses, an element emerges in Aristotle's writing that makes critical thinking or rationality more than simply attitudinal. That is, for Aristotle, finding the mean is a practical exercise in identifying desirous behavior for further moral judgment (Groarke, 2015). We must open a moral dimension if we are to see what attitudes are worth striving for, in other words, and that moral dimension is dispositional. The passions to be weighed, in other words, are not already pre-filled categories waiting out there for us to stumble upon them.

Virtue—Disposition

As just stated, disposition is attitude with a moral or ethical orientation built in. It is better than mere attitude, because attitude can be purely performative or socially pressured into certain modes of expression, and a moral framework has an eye toward the movement and direction of human action. That is, why do we do the things that we do, and to what end? To that end critical thinking requires a disposition toward the good, so moral judgments might be made (Mulnix, 2012). Our objection to this mode of critical thinking as being unable to build a critical theory of society is twofold. First, it changes the focus of the investigation. It conflates moral virtue with intellectual virtue, when these two are quite distinct (Mulnix, 2012). Now instead of fleshing out the intellectual prospects for critical inquiry, we are assessing the character development of individuals, which is not the same thing. Second, virtuous character development does not necessarily lead to critical thought. Virtuous disposition can be achieved in all sorts of structures that neither prompt nor necessitate critical thought. Disposition does not establish how the character development in question encapsulates critical thought. So shifting the emphasis from attitude to disposition is a punt. While consciously developing a virtuous disposition is certainly important, it does not answer the question of what makes for critical thought and how it might relate to the building of a critical theory of society.

Knowledge—Conceptual

Moving into the realm of knowledge builds on the virtues of disposed critical thinkers with an eye toward the actual knowledge claims about which they will purport to think critically. We again note that this is a cumulative effect that builds on the skills and virtues of critical thinkers in order adequately complete the tasks. The argument from knowledge makes an epistemological claim that we have to know something about the content of what is at stake in order to perform the job of critical thinking. We will take up two vectors of these knowledge claims; conceptual mastery of critical thinking as its own epistemology, and disciplinary mastery. We will end our critique of critical thinking by showing how even at its epistemological height, critical thinking is unable to set the foundation for a critical theory of society.

The appeal to epistemology suggests that critical thinkers need to know enough background in order to assess the truth value of statements as a mode of thinking (Mason, 2007). The appeal of this approach is that it fills in the missing gaps that the skills and virtue approaches leave out, namely that it implores thinkers to look at the structures in which knowledge claims are made, and to develop the habit of questioning oneself about one's own knowledge claims (Mason, 2007). It seeks to grasp the world as it presents itself and builds an epistemology of critical theory itself to form an intellectually grounded method of investigation. The upshot to this approach is that it's a portable method. It matters little what knowledge area one applies critical thinking, the epistemological core of critical thinking itself is applicable to all domains of knowledge. In an increasingly complex and fragmented society with myriad knowledge structures and claims, having a kind of key that allows an individual to engage multiple bodies of knowledge for critical thought may certainly seem appealing.

The downside to this approach is that it treats critical thinking like a codex that translates all other areas of thought unto itself. This elevates the knowledge claims of critical thinking itself into its own canon (Mason, 2007). Perhaps unwittingly, this exposes the epistemological claim of critical thinking to the same critique that we built of skills. As we stated with skills, this notion of conceptual apprehension of a body of knowledge is essentially an intellectual skill that, with enough diligence, one can pick up and apply to anything. However, there is a unique element to this critique that is not present in skills; this particular approach crystallizes an approach to critical thought that must be unchanging in order for it to function in its capacity to funnel all other thought. This is because having a stable canon upon which to appeal one's knowledge claims is paramount; and critically investigating the canon means that the codex might not actually work for all fields of human inquiry. If this is true, then it fails as a conceptual anchor and loses its status as a translator of all human inquiry. This creates a perverse incentive not only to maintain but also to calcify the canon to maintain its supremacy, which would ironically violate the dictates of what good critical thinking should aim to accomplish. Claims to the "queen of the sciences" have been made by many fields, at various times. In antiquity, Aristotle claimed it was metaphysics (Aristotle, 1999b), but not too long ago Carl Friedrich Gauss argued that indeed mathematics was the queen science (Waltershausen, 2018). Critical thinking cannot claim to be a meta-knowledge that can translate all others, as that removes it from its own aim of critical engagement.

Knowledge—Disciplinary
The approach of critical thinking as disciplinary mastery avoids the meta-analysis of critical thinking, which deprives it of its codex status, translating all domains of knowledge. What it does instead is situate the ability to think critically in terms of an already defined field of knowledge; a discipline. Critical thinking is then a sophisticated grounding in terms of content, which means epistemological mastery of a field of study is the precondition to do critical thinking. The logic is that in order to determine the validity or truth content to statements, one must have a general sense of the field of study, otherwise there is no baseline on which to even begin to make sense of statements (Yanchar, Slife, & Warne, 2008). This is stronger than the skills or virtue position, because it seeks to comprehend the world as known in as comprehensive a fashion as possible and relies on the corpus of a discipline to anchor that critical engagement.

While this is the most promising standpoint yet, the problem here is that it presumes a canon of content that must be mastered to assess knowledge claims. It further requires that the canon is stable, so it can be used as a benchmark to measure how effective a person is at critical thinking. This means that, as we note above, the canon is unassailable, be it in a conceptual canon of critical theory or the disciplinary canon that anchors inquiry. After all, either a person knows something, or they do not. By tying critical thinking as an emergent feature of a mastery of a canon of knowledge, the canon itself becomes unassailable, which would circumvent critical thinking about the precepts or assumptions of that canon. Perhaps a personal anecdote will illuminate. Facing a daunting job market in academia, one of the authors (Robert) huffed to a mentor that maybe just doing some orthodox political science to get tenure, and then doing the preferred radical work might be the best plan. The mentor advised against such a plan, explaining that regardless of our best intentions, immersing ourselves in canons of orthodoxies changes us. We then adopt and reproduce them. That people are regularly doing this in all the disciplines is the point. People are absorbing, digesting, understanding, and reproducing large bodies of knowledge without ever once critically engaging them. There may be some critical thinking skills developed, but they are rarely, if ever, directed at the norms the person complied with to get what they desired.

We believe we have shown that while critical thinking is desirable, it is not sufficient to build a critical theory of society and have answered these two objections. By looking at the level of skills, virtues, and knowledge we see that each level makes gains in terms of preparing thinkers to engage in a critical theory of society, but we see that it can only go so far as a conceptual or disciplinary approach, but we ask more of a critical theory of society, that does not privilege certain forms of knowledges, nor protects bodies of knowledge from critique itself. In other words, what a critical theory can accomplish, and where critical thinking falls short, is an aversion to *reifying* the status quo (Surin, 2006). Reification here can be understood as a default to the status quo or an assumption that there is nothing fundamentally wrong with a society as such and are not in need of investigation. Reification is a non-reflexive reproduction of social relations, which can perpetuation domination because they are not sufficiently investigated (Gabel, 1978). This concept shows the limits of critical thinking that we detailed above; if the mode of thought depends on the continuation of the status quo, then there is no epistemological room for thought which challenges the status quo. With this in mind, we may now flesh out the particulars of what a critical theory of society can look like, and how it might be integrated into leadership studies.

CRITICAL THEORY IN LEADERSHIP STUDIES

To begin here, we must first distinguish between what *leadership* as commonly used means, and leadership studies as a field of study within science. To make this distinction we do not provide a comprehensive review of leadership because that has been provided by others elsewhere, for example, Harrison's (2018) recent review. To the many reviews that exist, we add our suggestion to engage in the following questions: (1) What does leadership studies do? We argue that charting the organizational dynamics without analyzing the structural foundations of those structures improperly reinforces status quo relations and ignores the cultural, social, and political context of these structures. (2) Where is leadership studies located? We find that leadership studies often exist in schools of business or management, and that relationship can contribute to an instrumentalization of the concept of leadership so that is only understood within the boundaries of capitalistic business and management concerns. (3) Whose interests are served by leadership studies? This question reverberates throughout our text. We argue that instead of providing plans for efficient workplace organization, studying the direction/ teleology of leadership can provide for a better, more democratic society; one that is focused on maximizing citizens' flourishing. This is an ideological debate about what leadership can mean in society; a debate that rarely occurs in the current mode of leadership studies.

Using the insights discussed in the previous sections of this chapter, we can now set the criteria for a critical theory of society, and at that point we can develop how that might fit into studying leadership. There are many theories that claim to be critical, but as we formulate what is appropriate for studying leadership, we must keep in mind that it must be: (1) in keeping with our concept of *crisis*. That is, it is diagnosing a social ill that cannot be worked out through the normal operations of the society itself and offering an intervention that is restorative; (2) the theory is *immanent*. That is, the theory should diagnose and intervene on the basis of what is happening internally within those social structures. This has two main benefits: it avoids arbitrary external standards that may be irrelevant or impossible to achieve given certain structures.[6] It also is able to highlight a gap between the aspirations of a society and what is actually happening, and how to close that gap; and (3) it tries to upset the epistemological foundations of a social body of knowledge that reify the status quo. By avoiding that reification, critical theory can allow a different vision of society to blossom, that is geared toward liberation. Because there are many different variants of critical theory, we believe that these three criteria are best met by the Frankfurt School of critical theory. We will outline the broad goal of the first generation of Frankfurt School thinkers and show how their insights can broadly be applied in the realm of leadership studies.[7]

---

[6]Consider here the relational role of foreign policy. It would be absurd on its face to suggest that every country should simply adopt the United States' (or any other state's) foreign policy. This suggestion simply does not account for the world as we know it exists.

[7]While the generational divide among Frankfurt School theorists can be oversimplified, when we use the term "first generation" we mean Horkheimer, Adorno, and Marcuse. Others were affiliated or involved with the Institute for Social Research, but these three thinkers show the clearest voice and have produced the greatest body of work for a critical theory of society. For an explanation of the generations of the Frankfurt school, see Jay (1996) and Schlembach (2015).

The Institute for Social Research, or as it came to be known, the Frankfurt School, is the most comprehensive attempt at building a critical theory of society (Jay, 1996). What makes the Frankfurt School's attempt at building such a theory noteworthy is that it is far-reaching into multiple disciplines—political science, economics, sociology, cultural studies, anthropology, to name a few—to build a complete vision of a society in crisis. As we outlined above, the function of crisis is to diagnose and offer a vision of restorative action. We will show that the Frankfurt School, through an immanent critique of social crisis, formulates a method that seeks to rupture the foundations of knowledge which can spur social change. The Frankfurt School, because of its interdisciplinary nature and far-reaching works, covered a vast terrain of topics, such as economics, psychoanalysis, and music theory. For the purposes of this discussion, we will center Horkheimer's (1975) work because it sets up a critique of positivism, the need for negativity, and how critical theory is a method of investigation that seeks not only to describe but to change the world. With that groundwork laid, we will investigate contemporary applications of critical theory and what it means to the emerging field of leadership studies to incorporate its insights.

Frankfurt School critical theory laid forth by Horkheimer can be crystallized into the following three arguments against traditional theory for the purposes of our discussion:

1. Traditional theory is inadequate to describe the complexity of social life
2. By relegating theory to description only it does not show a vision for social change
3. It sustains patterns of domination and "technocratic domination" (Bottomore, 2002, p. 28).

Critical theory thus contradicts traditional theory in some important ways. Horkheimer (1975) begins with the notion that traditional theory sees theory as, "...stored-up knowledge, put in a form that makes it useful for the closest possible description of facts" (p. 188). The descriptive function of theory is a corollary of the broader social forces, in particular, the domination of nature in the rise of bourgeois political economy (Horkheimer, 1975). While this version of theory and its method of investigation made great material leaps and bounds, the idea of what theory could do or mean within a society became mechanized, making it for Horkheimer a "reified, ideological" pursuit (p. 194). Returning to our brief discussion of reification above, what makes theory reified as being purely descriptive makes scientific inquiry unable to change the status quo, and perhaps equally importantly, it covers up the assumptions or judgments that go into what scientific discoveries count, how they are used, and by whom. To wit, the movement and direction of the traditional (i.e., noncritical) modes of human inquiry in fields of study reinforce certain assumptions about the society. "Whether and how new definitions are purposefully drawn up depends in fact not only on the simplicity and consistency of the system but also, among other things *on the directions and goals of research*" [emphasis added] (Horkheimer, 1975, p. 196). The challenge is to make those directions more visible in their broader social contexts. As later chapters will show, movement and direction in different fields of inquiry tell us something about, but not the totality of, the complexity of social relations in which research is embedded. Critical theory does not stand in opposition to traditional theory, but it uses the insights of traditional theory through its critical methodology to demand more than traditional theory could deliver on its own (Arato & Gebhardt, 1982). We will take these three claims, in turn, to show how they are needed to build a critical theory of leadership studies.

Traditional Theory Is Inadequate to Describe the Complexity of Social Life

Positivism as a logical construct generally holds that knowledge can only be valid based on empirical evidence (Ayer, 1959; Elias, 2000; Giddens, 1975; Popper, 2002). This notion also generally represents the dominant mode of scientific inquiry that governs knowledge production. The benefit to positivism is that its propositions can be tested, its variables isolated, and as a result, it removes any ambiguity from the validity of knowledge claims. To be sure, in many areas of inquiry, this approach yields specific and workable insight. But let us pause here to reflect on whether we can know if positivism can establish truth. While some might argue that conditions above are the prerequisite for objectivity, establishing a truth outside of the subject's experience, we note that it is simply a method for claiming knowledge and not necessarily for establishing truth. We make this claim on two fronts. First, there are no mechanisms by which positivism can test the desirability or necessity of the observations that the research makes, which limits the ability to posit broad social truth claims (Horkheimer, 1975). Second, positivism cannot actually avoid the subjective experience of the phenomena under investigation. The questions that are asked and the ways in which things are measured are subjective. Perhaps even more importantly, the questions that are *not* asked and the assumptions made at the point of inquiry are all based on a sense-experience that is, at some point, subjective. To wit, these two fronts establish that there is no objective vantage point; no point from nowhere to exclude human experience or social relations.

Regardless of these limitations more generally, in some specific areas of scientific inquiry, positivism may be tolerable or even desirable in some areas of life. Indeed, the appeal of this methodological approach is probably most intuitive in the natural sciences, where experimentation in controlled settings lends itself to the incremental advancement of knowledge (Kuhn, 1970). The ability to derive new capabilities from cataloged and tested facts is powerful, even to a critical theorist, but it simply cannot tell us what kind of world we should collectively build (Horkheimer, 1975). Positivism, nevertheless, also finds some purchase in the social sciences for the supposed soundness of its results. After all, the findings of the natural sciences find their full use only within given social constructs, and the same rigor of findings in a social milieu is certainly attractive. If we could definitively draw the same kind of causal relationships in social sciences that we do in natural sciences, then a great deal of the ambiguities of social life could be resolved, and a roadmap would become visible. Again, while tantalizing, this is impossible. There are no natural laboratories, and the myriad factors that influence human behavior make such claims dubious at best (Bottomore, 2002). We must then take up the question and desirability of objectivity.

Remaining objective is a ubiquity in the current context, and there is of course some intuitive evidence for this strong desire for a certain kind of positivist rigor in society. We do not have to look very far to find stories of how laboratory research yields viable commercial products that make our lives better, more challenging, or somehow different. It is also not a difficult task to find literature about causal relations for why people do the things they do. But we also know the end of the story and remember that these specific instances might not tell us much about the broader context of the movement and direction of society. There is no necessary link between the results of doing research and the useful application of those findings. This is to say nothing of the idea that human behavior cannot be boiled down to one particular stimulus that makes a person behave the way they do. The unasked and unanswered questions remain; why are certain research projects prioritized over others, and why is that model commercial application desirable in the first place. This is the crux of Horkheimer's (1975) critique of positivism; it is unable to describe the complexity of social life. The first consequence we can derive from this observation is that traditional theory tells us little about what a good society looks like, what we ought to do, or why humans do the things they do. Positivist science does an excellent job of isolating variables for analysis and explanation. However, this is impossible in the vast complexity of social settings, where articulation, let alone isolation of atomized variables is difficult, if not impossible (Morrow & Brown, 1994). The second consequence follows from the first; positivism cannot account for the entirety of society because it is based on a logic that is a matter of language, which is itself a social invention (Ruja, 1936). The result is that the validity of claims in that linguistic arena cannot be imported to the broader social realm that produces that arena in the first place and can only highlight knowledge claims given a certain set of linguistic structures (Ruja, 1936). Here the critique of critical thinking elucidated above finds its social impact, and how it cannot form a critical theory. No particular methodology of critical thinking is able to escape the linguistic structures necessary to facilitate that critical thought. These two points also inform the debate about objectivity. If there is no non-socially constructed arena wherein scientific analysis is performed in the first place, then it stands to reason there is no non-social external vantage point through which we might establish objectivity (Wolin, 2016). That is, the researcher is always already enmeshed in the social structures that they are investigating, and there is no outside space where we might enter upon detaching ourselves from our social settings (Macdonald, 2017).

This inability of traditional theory to explain social complexity then falls on the shoulders of critical theory to explain. Here, our emphasis on movement and direction comes clearly into focus. On the one hand, we want to avoid the overspecialization of positivistic methodologies because they lose sight of the broader movements of a society and make no claims on the conscious direction that movement should take. On the other hand, we must avoid overgeneralizing and losing specificity about what is under investigation. This dialectical balance is an age-old question, so we offer a brief genealogy of teleology to see how critical theory is the appropriate lens to examine movement and direction in a society and as a point of departure for intellectual inquiry.

Aristotle used the concept of teleology in a logical framework for what he termed final causes. There is a large volume of literature about this term, but we will narrow our focus to make one particular point. In *The Metaphysics*, Aristotle lays out causes for things that build up from the immanent material that allows for things to exist (Chase, 2011), but we are only concerned here with what Aristotle referred to as final causes, or "that for the sake of which" (Chase, 2011, p. 518).[8] This simply means that for Aristotle, every object, person, and phenomenon had a reason to exist, and that reason is its telos (Aristotle, 1999b). To use a concrete example, the telos or final cause of a house is human shelter, the other causes are precursors to the final one (Chase, 2011). The same is true of human society, for which Aristotle argues the final cause is a state which produces virtuous citizens (Wolin, 2004). We can compare this to a positivist approach to try to answer the same kinds of questions. Using the cataloging or descriptive approaches of traditional theory does not help us understand the answer to the question of what human society is for because it can only tell us discrete facts that are already enmeshed in those questions. It is also important that here we take care not to fall into a positivist frame for asking this question. There is no answer out there that we need to apprehend. Such a frame does not adequately address the social complexity. The telos comes from within; it is immanent. These questions that span the whole of society are an attempt to bring in value judgments about what is good, right, fair, or beautiful. It is, in other words, goal-directed, and are formulated even if there is a lack of strictly empirical evidence behind these claims (Chase, 2011). To phrase it on a quotidian level, if we ask that, against all evidence that a just society has never existed, should we still strive for justice? To nevertheless insist that we should is to have a teleology in mind.

It is against this classical conception of teleology that positivism positioned itself, especially during the Enlightenment and particularly in the works of Descartes and Poincare (Horkheimer, 1975). The radical Cartesian doubt would not permit any musings of what direction a society ought to go because such imaginings were not immediately

---

[8]We also note here that Aristotle's *Physics* also was a forerunner to empirical investigation, but he took pains to say that this area of inquiry could not possibly answer the metaphysical questions of teleology, final causes, or first principles Piccone (1968).

observable so they could only ever be idle speculation (Wolin, 2016). Horkheimer stresses, however, that strict positivism misses the vital human striving for a better world, which is for him an impetus for social change. The attempt to be goal-directed, or to articulate the final causes for undertaking conscious social efforts to guide the movement and direction of society does not rest on a totally cataloged knowledge of all possible facts. Rather, Horkheimer argues, it rests on an articulation of totality. The concept of totality in critical theory rescues the idea of a teleology of society, which achieves both challenges of keeping sight of the broader vision of social movement but also the factual details of traditional theory. Confronting social complexity by analyzing totality is not the same as knowing every single fact that is available. Rather, it is understanding the immanent dynamism of social movement and working for a consciously applied direction to that movement by articulating a goal-driven vision for society as a whole (Horkheimer, 1975; Jay, 1977; Kosik, 1969; Lukács, 1972). In other words, dealing with complexity is not a matter of accumulating ever more facts, but rather understanding how given facts (which are of course contingent) inform a vision of society, and how a vision of society shapes how we come to know and value facts (Kosik, 1969). To illuminate this notion of totality, we highlight the inverse to show how if reality is simply an accumulation of facts, then knowledge of reality is impossible. "If reality is a conglomeration of facts, human knowledge can only be an abstract, systematic-analytic knowledge of the parts, while the whole of reality remains unknowable… If reality is a dialectical and structured whole, concrete knowledge of reality does not consist of a systematic linear fusion of facts with other facts, and of notions with other notions. Rather it is a process of *concretiza-tion*" [emphasis original] (Kosik, 1969, p. 8). Contemplating the concept of totality, we can ask ourselves what we are to do with all these facts, and we can formulate a vision for the movement and direction of society. Concretization of facts helps us consider the totality, and that understanding of totality helps us understand the complexity of facts in a socio-historical milieu (Kosik, 1969; Jay, 1977).

As such, critical theory takes a suspicious view of the current state of affairs and does not accept status quo definitions or attitudes toward things like, "better, useful, appropriate, productive, and valuable, as these are understood in the present order, and refuses to take them as nonscientific presuppositions about which one can do nothing" (Horkheimer, 1975, p. 207). This loops back to our analysis above about being an immanent critique. This skepticism allows a critical theory of society to challenge these concepts and assumptions, and in so doing highlight the gap between a society's stated goals and the actual lived experience of people in that society (Macdonald, 2017). Critical theory keeps our vision clear and helps us avoid the "methodolatry" of uncritical analysis (Macdonald, 2017, p. 520). We want scholars of leadership (and indeed of all fields) to internalize this skepticism, and in so doing formulate a vision for what a good society looks like, and how we are to get there (Wolin, 2004).

Traditional Theory Alone Does Not Envision Social Change

Related to the first point, if positivism is purely descriptive, it assumes the structures surrounding the things it describes, and in so doing reifies those structures. For this reason, traditional theory is unable to imagine the world being a fundamentally different place or even a qualitatively different society. While one might object that scientists are simply describing the change, we would respond that this is insufficient because if that is true, then it cannot account for the underlying causes of that social change, and by the same token, it diminishes the importance of human agency as individuals or collectives who consciously pursue a vision of social change; that is, it might look as if change is happening and being cataloged, but no one individual or group is responsible for it. If the goal of our inquiry is to explain how fields of study understand and explain movement and direction, then social change must be accounted for, not only from a descriptive position but from an active engagement with changing society to show the subjects who pursue this change and the rationale for doing so.

Again, Horkheimer and the first-generation Frankfurt School theorists are instructive. Horkheimer (1975) explains:

> The whole perceptible world as present to a member of bourgeois society and as interpreted within a traditional worldview which is in continuous interaction with that given world, is seen by the perceiver as a sum-total of given facts; it is there and must be accepted. (p. 198)

An inability to imagine other worlds or question the fundamental suppositions of the given order means that traditional theory, while it fits nicely into, and reproduces disciplinary boundaries, it less likely to cross those boundaries or challenge the fundamental assumptions of a given social order. As such, critical theory is necessarily an interdisciplinary endeavor, to the same extent that social change is also accounted for in an interdisciplinary way. It seeks to understand and chart the disruptions of the habitus of everyday life where reality is reified (Bourdieu, 1992, 1994), and challenges the flows of power where such structures and apparatuses of knowledge are produced and fractured (Foucault, 1982). As Bourdieu and Foucault argue, the flows of power, social structure, and apparatuses of knowledge *produce* us as knowing subjects (Luke, 1990a, 1990b; Rose, 2006). As such, produced subjects are conditioned to reproduce the apparatus of their social (re)production. The apparatus is not monolithic, and in fact is dispersed, networked, without a central locus, but at the level of life itself (Deleuze, 1988; Foucault, 2005; Galloway, 2006). This makes the discrete investigations of positivism unable to recognize, let alone change, this architecture of power that is reproduced through knowing subjects of a particular social life. Against this backdrop, the call for interdisciplinarity takes on a more holistic, and perhaps fraught, calling. The vocation of the interdisciplinarian, within this critical theory of society, is to link fields of study to offer an understanding of the social totality, but also to trace vectors of power, and then give a vision for how we might consciously change those vectors. Here, movement and direction take on a more concrete vision than the teleological discussion above. We ask how researchers in various fields of inquiry might engage self-reflexively about how their fields of inquiry have understood the consciously directed social change that is a result of their research.

On the one hand, grappling with the dynamism of the social world as it develops seems like a self-evident research paradigm, but on the other, the dictates of positivism value a snapshot, or static moment to perform research, and the result is an inability to account for that dynamism (MacKenzie, 2008). Instead, the critical theorist positions themselves as a participant in that dynamism, not only to explore the potential causes of the dynamism, but to consciously direct it toward progressive ends (Horkheimer, 1975). In this way, engaging in a theory of social change also opens up the normative element for the social theorist. None of the social dynamism that we observe happens in a vacuum. Some aspects of social change are desirable; other less so. Some move social relations in a direction that enhances human flourishing, and others impede it; but there is no necessary direction or inevitable progress toward the good for everyone. The ability of the researcher to judge whether the movement of society is in a direction of being more emancipatory or more oppressive brings research questions to life and asks for judgment, which is a more humane mode of inquiry in the first place (Horkheimer, 1975). To make Horkheimer's point of humaneness clear: if a researcher only limits themselves to pure description, then describing oppressive social relations, while refusing to judge them as such or issue a call to do anything about them can only reinforce those oppressive relations.

On the other hand, as well as refusing to take the world as a static place to be described, because of this dynamism, critical theory's recognition of movement and direction of society is only a starting point. That is, just because a researcher adopts a critical method of investigation does not mean that the more just or progressive world comes to pass. Injustice must be confronted, social strategies for change must be devised, and there are as a matter of dialectical development, more concerns that come to light as ends are pursued (Horkheimer, 1975). Critical theory is, therefore, critical of itself and there also must be a push to continue recognizing and developing praxes to resolve, injustices. This self-critique with an eye toward praxis keeps critical theory's vitality. We do not offer it to be a Rosetta Stone that unlocks and explains the whole world, as that would belie the social dynamism in which the researcher operates. Rather, by having an orientation toward social change as the milieu of investigation, and paying attention to the totality, teleology, movement/direction in a society, a critical theory of society seeks to understand, interpret, and be cognizant of the researcher's participation in these flows of change. Part of that undertaking is by a thorough skepticism of institutions, power relations, and social structures. There is an element of common sense to this notion of dynamism; if we accept that critical theory produces prescriptive results to change things for a better or more just world, then pointing out where the current context fails to reach those goals necessitates building a theory that changes, abolishes, or avoids whatever injustices or oppressions lead to these gaps that critical theory points out in the first place. On top of that, as social change occurs, a critical orientation will then expose new injustices, or new immanent gaps where society fails to live up to its goals. In other words, it establishes that the end point (or teleology, to borrow language from the last section) of inquiry is a better world. If nothing else, that can provide an excellent baseline for assessing the movement and direction of a society.

Traditional Theory Sustains Patterns of Technocratic Domination and Instrumental Rationality

As traditional theory is unable to, on its own, cope with the totality of social analysis and cannot account for, let alone engage, with social dynamism, the final area of critical theory's methodology of social analysis has to do with the effects of these limitations on the researcher, and highlights the challenges that must be overcome to engage the world in a critical theory framework. This critique penetrates into the subjectivities that are produced in contemporary society and how they, in turn, reproduce the structures of contemporary society.

We turn to another first-generation Frankfurt School theorist. In *One-Dimensional Man*, Herbert Marcuse argues that a devastating symptom of contemporary society is a flattening out of the very possibility of critique, and therefore, a critical theory of society (Kellner, 1984; Marcuse, 1968). As we laid out at the beginning of this chapter, critique is the basis by which society is held to its own standards and where demands for a better world can be made based on the necessity of intervention. The flattening out is thus a metaphor to describe a lack of alternatives; society becomes a monolith. For Marcuse, the vision with which one critiques a society is an alternative dimension where we envision a better world for which to strive, but we are unable to formulate a vision due to the overwhelming instrumental rationality where modes of thought, culture, and politics are all subsumed to reify the existing world (Farr, 2009; Marcuse, 1969; Rovatti, 1968). It gives an account for the direction and movement of society throughout history, which shows the stakes of the flattening out of critique; without a critical theory that gives an alternative vision, it becomes practically impossible for a society to qualitatively or fundamentally change (Marcuse, 1971). It is not enough to merely *say* that things ought to be different or better, we must be able, as critical theorists, to provide a *praxis* whereby those different or better social relations might be attained.

Just because a vision is formed through critical theory does not mean that a better world necessarily emerges.

> To strive for a state of affairs in which there will be no exploitation or oppression, in which an all-embracing subject, namely self-aware mankind, exists, and in which it is possible to speak of a unified theoretical creation and a thinking that transcends individuals – to strive for all this is not yet to bring it to pass. (Horkheimer, 1975, p. 241)

Of course, the hard work of changing society only begins when a compelling vision takes shape and can be acted upon, but what Marcuse warns us about contemporary society is that vision does not take shape, because in a one-dimensional society, the only coherent forms of knowledge, culture, politics, language, science, or actions are ones which reify the existing order (Marcuse, 1968). Consider a student who gets a question wrong on a standardized test because they used a logic to arrive at an answer that was different than the logic of the test-writer; only the test-writer's logic is correct.[9] At a social level, the stakes are much higher, but the idea is the same. We then live in, what Marcuse calls, "a society without opposition" (1968, p. xxxix). In such a society, attempts to oppose the existing order actually affirm that order, or offer mere tweaks or reforms. That is, even though we may form what at first glance seem like critical or alternative formulations of social relations, they often mask a reification of the same social relations they might seek to critique, and alternative arrangements, logics, or knowledges are precluded for not fitting the status quo.[10] If the institutions and power structures in a society were not oppressive, this might be acceptable, but the structures in a society are producing domination, so a critical theorist cannot simply accept reforms to structures which produce bad results, especially when what is required is to change those structures entirely.

This loops back to the first two critiques of positivism and adds even more dire consequences. Because of its inability to understand totality and account for change, positivism alone reinforces the existing power structures, even if we realize that they are producing bad results. This is the condition of the one-dimensional society where positivism is the only acceptably scientific thought, and results in what Marcuse refers to as technological rationality (Marcuse, 1968). Technological rationality is itself a mode of thought that limits the scope of what is possible to be those things which only improve already existing modes of social

---

[9] Much has been examined about standardized tests and the education system in maintaining oppression in societies. See, for example, Ballantine, Hammack, and Stuber (2017).

[10] Environmentalism is an example to understand what Marcuse means. If it is true that environmental degradation is, at least in part, due to overconsumption, then changing consumption habits is important. However, if changing consumption habits is to simply replace consuming one commodity with consuming another "green" commodity, then the logic of overconsumption remains in place, even though we might think that we are doing our part to forestall environmental degradation (Luke, 1997).

reproduction, but in ways that have no political or social impact on the underlying structures. The resulting technocracy makes a fetish of certain kinds of technologies, both in terms of the technology's potential to make our lives different or better, but also in terms of how technology determines what is feasible in a society, which immediately delegitimizes critical voices that are fundamentally different (Marcuse, 1968, p. 162). The resultant attitude that only technological advances will save us is both simultaneously wrong and excuses people from the work of changing their society for the better (Kirsch, 2016; Luke, 1990a, 1990b). The baseline assumption here is that, apart from some fine tuning at the margins or when things do not work the way they are supposed to, the organization of society is unchangeable, and the best we can hope for is a wise administration.

The inability to critically envision alternative social relations within the current condition is what Marcuse calls the "affirmative character of culture" (1969, p. 65). In a society of technological rationality, the only acceptable culture is one which affirms the social order; with the inverse notion that a critical one is irrational or otherwise out of bounds. This affirmative character means that we need to be thoughtful about how we choose to cultivate our critical rationality; to link back to the discussion about critical thinking, it is easy to see how critical thinking has become affirmative in that it is not meant to fundamentally question the foundations of social relations. In a broader sense, this tells us that something is not critical just because we insist that it is, which further reinforces the idea that critical theory needs to be critical of itself. Being a critical theorist is therefore not an identity that one decides to be or a fixed identity that can never change, but rather it is a practice, that is kept alive through constant reinvestigation of the research and researcher.

The Difficult But Vital Need for Critical Theory in Fields of Inquiry

While these three critiques of traditional theory are undoubtedly daunting, it may further seem like the cure is worse than the disease. That is, if attempts at thinking critically are so often co-opted, and even the attempt at critical theorizing is foreclosed upon by a society without opposition, how is it possible to defend a critical theory of society? It is certainly true that the challenges are daunting, but we hold firm to the idea that a critical theory is formable. No society is ever totally without the possibility of opposition. The more a society rationalizes itself to prevent opposition, the more fissures appear that show where the potential for opposition is ripe (Adorno, 1997).

Still, the task is large, and certainly beyond the scope of one single text to investigate every area of society to cultivate a comprehensive critical rationality to resist all avenues of oppression. However, because we have highlighted the importance of an interdisciplinary approach to building a critical rationality within research, we will shift our attention to disciplinary modes of inquiry. We believe that this fulfills the demands of critical theory because we will: (1) *upset the assumptions behind disciplines*. That is, we investigate how disciplines understand their own knowledge claims and how that fits into our broader framework of social movement and direction. Disciplinary knowledge does not happen in a vacuum, nor outside of a given social milieu, so the questions that fields of study ask, and how they research the world around them reflects that position; (2) *give a vision of an alternative*. In this case, we will make the case for a critical theory of leadership studies. Much in the same way that Horkheimer insists that critical theory builds on the insights of traditional theory and expands it into a normative realm, so too will we argue that the insights from our exploration of fields of inquiry can help set the normative basis to show what a critical theory of leadership studies could look like. Also, much like Horkheimer, our goal is not to undercut or dismiss the important findings of the positivist findings of leadership studies, but we wish to pull them into their broader social and normative dimensions; and (3) *argue that leadership is a potential fissure point for critical engagement*. Leadership studies is a relatively new field. While studies of leadership go back long before the first academic unit took the name leadership studies, this field of study as it exists goes back only some decades. As such, it is already an interdisciplinary endeavor, pulling insights from psychology, political science, business, economics, sociology, anthropology, and others. This interdisciplinary assemblage of this field of study belies the idea of disciplines and discrete units of certain kinds of knowledges and can readily absorb a critical view of its place in the academy.

With that in mind, because we are not simply overlaying a critical thinking component onto an already existing discrete field of knowledge production, we will now venture into other fields of study to see how they deal with their own situatedness in broader social relations, understand their contribution to movement and direction, and show the possibility of a critical rationality. We want to keep the notion of a teleology of leadership in mind as we believe that a critical rationality can orient leadership studies to being in the service of human flourishing.

REFERENCES

Adorno, T. W. (1997). *Negative dialectics*. New York, NY: Continuum International Publishing.
Antonio, R. J. (1981). Immanent critique as the core of critical theory: Its origins and developments in Hegel, Marx and contemporary thought. *The British Journal of Sociology, 32*(3), 330–345. https://doi.org/10.2307/589281.
Arato, A., & Gebhardt, E. (Eds.). (1982). *Essential Frankfurt School reader*. New York: Continuum.
Aristotle. (1999a). *Nicomachean ethics* (T. Irwin, Trans.) (2nd ed.). Indianapolis: Hackett Publishing Company.
Aristotle. (1999b). *The metaphysics* (H. Lawson-Tancred, Trans.) (New ed.). London and New York: Penguin Classics.
Augustine. (1994). *Augustine: Political writings* (E. L. Fortin & D. Kries, Trans.). Indianapolis: Hackett Publishing Company, Inc.
Ayer. (1959). *Logical positivism*. Glencoe, IL: Free Press.
Azmanova, A. (2012). Social justice and varieties of capitalism: An immanent critique. *New Political Economy, 17*(4), 445–463. https://doi.org/10.1080/13563467.2011.606902.
Ballantine, J. H., Hammack, F. M., & Stuber, J. (2017). *The sociology of education: A systemic analysis* (8th ed.). New York, NY: Routledge.
Bottomore, T. (2002). The high tide of critical theory. In *The Frankfurt School & its critics* (pp. 27–54). London and New York: Taylor & Francis.
Bourdieu, P. (1992). *The logic of practice* (1st ed.). Stanford, CA: Stanford University Press.
Bourdieu, P. (1994). *The field of cultural production: Essays on art and literature* (New ed.). New York, NY: Columbia University Press.
Brown, W. (2005). *Edgework: Critical essays on knowledge and politics*. Princeton and Oxford: Princeton University Press.
Carrabregu, G. (2016). Habermas on solidarity: An immanent critique: Habermas on solidarity: Gent Carrabregu. *Constellations, 23*(4), 507–522. https://doi.org/10.1111/1467-8675.12257.
Chandler, J. L. S., & Kirsch, R. E. (2018). Addressing race and culture within a critical leadership approach. In J. L. Chin, J. E. Trimble, & J. E. Garcia

(Eds.), *Global and culturally diverse leaders and leadership: New dimensions and challenges for business, education and society.* Bingley: Emerald.

Chase, M. (2011). Teleology and final causation in Aristotle and in contemporary science. *Dialogue: Canadian Philosophical Review/Revue Canadienne de Philosophie, 50*(3), 511–536. https://doi.org/10.1017/s0012217311000527.

Curtis, R. (2014). Foucault beyond Fairclough: From transcendental to immanent critique in organization studies. *Organization Studies, 35*(12), 1753–1772. https://doi.org/10.1177/0170840614546150.

Curzer, C. (1996). A defense of Aristotle's doctrine that virtue is a mean. *Ancient Philosophy, 16*(1), 129–138.

Deleuze, G. (1988). *Foucault.* Minneapolis: University of Minnesota Press.

DiSalle, R. (2002). Reconsidering Kant, Friedman, logical positivism, and the exact sciences. *Philosophy of Science, 69*(2), 191–211. https://doi.org/10.1086/341049.

Doddington, C. (2007). Critical thinking as a source of respect for persons: A critique. *Educational Philosophy & Theory, 39*(4), 449–459. https://doi.org/10.1111/j.1469-5812.2007.00350.x.

Elias, N. (2000). *The civilizing process* (2nd ed.). Hoboken, NJ: Wiley Blackwell.

Farr, A. L. (2009). *Critical theory and democratic vision: Herbert Marcuse and recent liberation philosophies.* Lanham, MD: Lexington Books.

Foucault, M. (1982). *Archeology of knowledge.* London and New York: Pantheon Books.

Foucault, M. (2005). *The hermeneutics of the subject: Lectures at the college de France 1981–1982.* New York: Picador.

Gabel, J. (1978). *False consciousness: An essay on reification* (1st Torchbooks Ed. Publ. 1978 edition). New York, NY: Harper Torchbooks.

Galloway, A. R. (2006). *Protocol: How control exists after decentralization* (New ed.). Cambridge, MA: MIT Press.

Giddens, A. (1975). *Positivism and sociology.* London: Heinemann.

Groarke, L. (2015). Aristotle's contrary psychology: The mean in ethics and beyond. *Review of Metaphysics, 69*(1), 25.

Habermas, J. (1998). *Legitimation crisis.* Beacon Press.

Habermas, J. (2000). *On the pragmatics of communication* (M. Cooke, Ed.) (1st ed.). Cambridge, MA: MIT Press.

Harrison, C. (2018). *Leadership theory and research: A critical approach to new and existing paradigms.* Basingstoke: Palgrave Macmillan.

Hobbes, T. (1994). *Leviathan* (E. M. Curley, Ed.). Indianapolis: Hackett Publishing Company.

Holmes, N. G., Wieman, C. E., & Bonn, D. A. (2015). Teaching critical thinking. *Proceedings of the National Academy of Sciences, 112*(36), 11199–11204. https://doi.org/10.1073/pnas.1505329112.

Horkheimer, M. (1975). *Critical theory: Selected essays* (M. J. O'Connell, Trans.) (1st ed.). New York: Continuum Publishing Corporation.

Jay, M. (1977). The concept of totality in Lukacs and Adorno. *Telos, 1977*(32), 117–137. https://doi.org/10.3817/0677032117.

Jay, M. (1996). *The dialectical imagination: A history of the Frankfurt School and the institute of social research, 1923–1950.* Berkeley: University of California Press.

Kellner, D. (1984). *Herbert Marcuse and the crisis of Marxism.* Berkeley: University of California Press.

Kirsch, R. (2016). The "digital revolution" reconsidered. *New Political Science, 38*(1), 100–115. https://doi.org/10.1080/07393148.2015.1125635.

Kosik, K. (1969). The concrete totality. *Telos, 1969*(4), 35–54. https://doi.org/10.3817/0969004035.

Kuhn, T. S. (1970). *The structure of scientific revolutions* (2nd ed.). Chicago, IL: University of Chicago Press.

Locke, J. (1980). *Second treatise of government* (C. B. Macpherson, Ed.). Indianapolis: Hackett.

Lukács, G. (1972). *History and class consciousness: Studies in Marxist dialectics* (R. Livingstone, Trans.) (MIT Press edition). Cambridge, MA: MIT Press.

Luke, T. W. (1990a). *Screens of power: Ideology, domination, and resistance in informational society* (Reissue). Urbana and Chigago: University of Illinois Press.

Luke, T. W. (1990b). *Social theory and modernity: Critique, dissent, and revolution.* Newbury Park: Sage.

Luke, T. W. (1997). *Ecocritique: Contesting the politics of nature, economy, and culture* (1st ed.). Minneapolis: University of Minnesota Press.

Macdonald, B. J. (2017). Traditional and critical theory today: Toward a critical political science. *New Political Science, 39*(4), 511–522. https://doi.org/10.1080/07393148.2017.1378857.

MacKenzie, D. (2008). *An engine, not a camera: How financial models shape markets.* Boston: The MIT Press.

Marcuse, H. (1968). *One-dimensional man* (6th ed.). Boston, MA: Beacon.

Marcuse, H. (1969). *Negations: Essays in critical theory.* Boston, MA: Beacon Press.

Marcuse, H. (1971). The concept of negation in the dialectic. *Telos, 1971*(8), 130–132. https://doi.org/10.3817/0671008130.

Marcuse, H. (1999). *Reason and revolution* (100th Anniversary Ed.). Amherst, NY: Humanity Books.

Mason, M. (2007). Critical thinking and learning. *Educational Philosophy & Theory, 39*(4), 339–349. https://doi.org/10.1111/j.1469-5812.2007.00343.x.

Morrow, R. A., & Brown, D. D. (1994). *Critical theory and methodology* (1st ed.). Thousand Oaks, CA: Sage.

Mulnix, J. W. (2012). Thinking critically about critical thinking. *Educational Philosophy & Theory, 44*(5), 464–479. https://doi.org/10.1111/j.1469-5812.2010.00673.x.

Natale, S., & Ricci, F. (2006). Critical thinking in organizations. *Team Performance Management: An International Journal, 12*(7/8), 272–277. https://doi.org/10.1108/13527590610711822.

Papastephanou, M., & Angeli, C. (2007). Critical thinking beyond skill. *Educational Philosophy & Theory, 39*(6), 604–621. https://doi.org/10.1111/j.1469-5812.2007.00311.x.

Piccone, P. (1968). Towards a socio-historical interpretation of the scientific revolution. *Telos, 1968*(1), 16–26. https://doi.org/10.3817/0368001016.

Popper, K. (2002). *The logic of scientific discovery* (2nd ed.). New York, NY: Routledge.

Rose, N. (2006). *The politics of life itself: Biomedicine, power, and subjectivity in the twenty-first century.* Princeton, NJ: Princeton University Press.

Rovatti, P. A. (1968). Marcuse and the crisis of the European sciences. *Telos, 1968*(2), 113–115. https://doi.org/10.3817/0968002113.

Ruja, H. (1936). The logic of logical positivism. *The Journal of Philosophy, 33*(15), 393–408. https://doi.org/10.2307/2015867.

Sabia, D. (2010). Defending immanent critique. *Political Theory, 38*(5), 684–711. https://doi.org/10.1177/0090591710372864.

Särkelä, A. (2017). Immanent critique as self-transformative practice: Hegel, Dewey, and contemporary critical theory. *The Journal of Speculative Philosophy, 31*(2), 218–230. https://doi.org/10.5325/jspecphil.31.2.0218.

Schlembach, R. (2015). Negation, refusal and co-optation: The Frankfurt School and social movement theory. *Sociology Compass, 9*(11), 987–999. https://doi.org/10.1111/soc4.12321.

Surin, K. (2006). The Frankfurt School, the marxist tradition, culture and critical thinking: Max Horkheimer (1895–1973), Herbert Marcuse (1898–1979), Theodor Adorno (1903–1969), Jurgen Habermas (1929–). In J. Wolfreys (Ed.), *Modern European criticism and theory: A critical guide.* Edinburgh: Edinburgh University Press.

Waltershausen, W. S. V. (2018). *Gauss: A memorial.* Sacramento, CA: Sagwan Press.

Wolin, S. (2004). *Politics and vision: Continuity and innovation in western political thought* (Expanded ed.). Princeton, NJ: Princeton University Press.

Wolin, S. (2016). *Fugitive Democracy: And Other Essays* (N. Xenos, Ed.). Princeton, NJ: Princeton University Press.

Wrenn, M. V. (2016). Immanent critique, enabling myths, and the neoliberal narrative. *Review of Radical Political Economics, 48*(3), 452–466. https://doi.org/10.1177/0486613415605074.

Yanchar, S. C., Slife, B. D., & Warne, R. (2008). Critical thinking as disciplinary practice. *Review of General Psychology, 12*(3), 265–281. https://doi.org/10.1037/1089-2680.12.3.265.

CHAPTER 2

Interlude: Prepare for Exploring Movement and Direction Through Transdisciplinary Vectors

INTRODUCTION

We confess that we did not want to call this a chapter. The way that the book is laid out makes a hard pivot after arguing for a critical theory of society, and *interlude* was the most appropriate term for a metatextual interruption to prepare the reader for what follows the theory section. As such, think of this as a perhaps a welcome pause after the dense theory section, where we lay out our roadmap for what to expect in the next four chapters. This will be less of a chapter than a conversation with you. It is perhaps odd, but we hope it will nevertheless prove helpful.

To get practical matters out of the way, if you are expecting several, "leadership of (x)" or "leadership in (x)" chapters, such as leadership in physics, leadership of biology, medicine, education, etc. then you have probably already figured out that this is not that book. However, if you have a particular disciplinary background you might be well served by skipping to your disciplinary chapter, and then to the final chapter, then return to the disciplinary chapters that you are less familiar with keeping in mind that our selection of these four disciplines is not meant to be exhaustive. We invite leadership scholars engaged in critical work to join the interdisciplinary exploration by adding their ventures. If you are a leadership scholar, our approach might provide a holistic understanding of how our field of inquiry fits into broader questions of intellectual production of knowledge. If you are a student, you have probably already resigned yourself to reading what was assigned.

© The Author(s) 2018   39
J. L. S. Chandler and R. E. Kirsch, *Critical Leadership Theory*,
https://doi.org/10.1007/978-3-319-96472-0_2

KEEP CRITICAL THEORY CENTERED

Throughout this book, our guiding rationale is that a critical theory is not simply an *addition* to an already complete body of knowledge and that means there is a lot more work to do. A critical approach essentially breaks down fields of knowledge production into their component parts, and the exciting upshot of this is that looking at these pieces of knowledge production, we can reassemble them in a way that integrates, rather than overlays, critical theory into a field of study. We hope then that not only can we provide a rationale for what studying leadership critically might look like, but even more generally how to critically investigate the structures of knowledge production.

There are three standout ideas that we ask you to take with you from the detailed Chapter 1 examination as you focus on the overall objective of critical theory which is to resolve crisis:

1. Upset or disrupt the assumptions. While our goal is to fuel the reader with abundant examples through our explorations and discussions in the next four chapters that can be used to assist in the disruption of existing assumptions in leadership studies, we have not provided those arguments for the reader because assumptions vary across people and the common assumptions shift over time. Rather we leave it for readers to create their own such arguments by integrating insights gleaned from the remaining chapters with their already existing leadership understandings applied to their own experiences. To do that there are two equal tasks. First, the reader must explicate the assumption. Then the reader must demonstrably disrupt it.
2. Contribute to a vision of an alternative. In Chapter 7, we arrange and explain our tenets that contribute to an alternative. We acknowledge that our tenets also draw from others' critical theory work with race; specifically, Delgado and Stefancic (1997), Hill (1997), Kimberle, Gotanda, Peller, and Thomas (1995), and Lynn and Dixson (2013). So, when we describe our tenets as novel, we mean that they will be novel to some within leadership studies, but they are by no means novel ideas for many who have already invested in critical work. In any case, contributing to a vision of an alternative for the reader means that they can, practicing within their existing sphere of influence, prepare and share alternative

visions that are more than technical improvements. Such changes are like shifting the lens of a kaleidoscope which offers a tantalizing new array of shapes, patterns, and colors, but does not alter the thing itself. What we encourage readers to do in this area is to develop alternative visions that noticeably disrupt the oppression created in their spheres of influence.

3. Use leadership as a fissure point for critical engagement. The term and the concept *leadership* conveys many meanings in organizations and that variety can be employed strategically if one prepares for the opportunities. Recall Robert's conversation years ago with a mentor pondering a strategy for achieving professional goals by adhering to the dominant social norms within the field of political science until achieving a safe position from which to return to disrupting those norms. Robert's mentor counseled that one cannot collude with the dominant norms without also being molded by them. This means that whatever our intentions are, when we go along to get along, we are investing in those habits and being rewarded for doing so. Expecting to, at a later date, begin dismantling the very structures that have provided material rewards for years is not reasonable. This is not because the person who does this is a bad person or an unethical person. This is something that recurs over and over in critical work and was also addressed in Chapter 1. When using a critical perspective, we must always remember that the goal is not to apply simplistic categorization rules labeling some people as inherently bad and some as essentially good. Rather, we must focus on the diffuse and ubiquitous social processes operating that encourage and reward some behaviors just ever so slightly more than others. Those behaviors will be performed more because of those rewards and we are all involved in the creation and allocation of those rewards because the behaviors we choose repeatedly become our habits, and our habits are things we do not readily critically analyze because they are just part of who we are. Continued collusion with the dominant social norms means reaping the repeated tiny rewards for such collusions, those accumulate, and they tie one ever tighter to the perpetuation of those dominant social norms. Tools like the model and exercises that are part of *Examining Interactions with Dominant Social Norms* (Chandler, 2017) for recognizing dominant social norms

that perpetuate oppression for analyzing the ways in which people interact with those norms can increase one's skills but more work is needed because as we discussed in Chapter 1, skills are necessary but not sufficient to disrupt the epistemological foundations of business as usual.

ATTEND TO MOVEMENT AND DIRECTION

The next four chapters adopt spacious interpretations of movement and direction within each field and as such, we do not, and could never, claim disciplinary expertise in every field of study. And you can choose to read these chapters in any order that suits you. As you progress through the text, in whatever way works best for you, we should clarify a few things. First, we know that we will not exhaustively cover every aspect of every field of study. Not only is that on its face hubristic, it would be impossible to do. Rather, what we wish to investigate are the notions of movement and direction in four selected broad fields of study. You may be wondering at this point why we do this, and that question deserves an answer. We decided to shatter the cluttered, confounded, and conglomerated thing that *leadership* is and pick through the resulting mess to select less encumbered constructs to serve as our lens while we trekked into other disciplines for knowledge. We have selected the notions of *movement* and *direction* for our journey. We selected these components because they persist—no matter how broad or confined the definition of leadership employed, and regardless of the organizational or societal context, or the historical relevance—these constituent pieces of leadership remain embedded in the meaning of leadership. Leadership entails some things (be they concrete things or abstract concepts) or some beings moving and the direction of the movement matters. The meaning of *movement* that we use in the next four chapters is simple; it is the one that conveys the idea of motion or changing physical location. We do not use the word in the sense that it is people working in groups to achieve a goal in the way it is used in the expression, the civil rights movement. Granted, there were other components of leadership that we could have selected instead of movement and direction. For example, we could have chosen one of the detailed skills that leadership includes from one of the sources like the list of competencies prepared by Hiller, Novelli, and Ponnapalli (2016) or Simonet and Tett's (2012) list which compares leadership and management competencies. But we wanted to avoid those arrangements that leave leadership intact, so we could unravel leadership itself. Selecting from its fundamental strands to feed an innovative exploration across multiple knowledge domains is itself a critical project.

Secondly, we are not claiming to be content matter experts in the fields addressed in the coming chapters. Rather, we are reading them as embedded social scientists who study questions of leadership (and in sometimes quite different ways between the two of us). While we certainly aim not to misrepresent our cases from fields of study, the insights that we reveal are not always from the content itself, but again, their positionality in the field of broader intellectual inquiry. And yet, we did not select our cases from these different fields arbitrarily. Nor are we over-relying on using *movement* and *direction* as keyword search terms. For those in need of a formal method of investigation, we would characterize what we are doing as boundary work. That is, how do fields of study understand their aims, and how is that manifested in the research that is being done? We believe this is particularly salient for a field that is emerging, as being conscious of how boundaries are created, guarded, or crossed is an important part of knowledge production. Consequently, our selection of movement and direction as the generative birthplace for our explorations across the selected disciplinary fields affords us more freedom and our resulting boundary transgressions are therefore a manifestation of a critical investigation.

Lastly, we caution the reader that while reading Chapters 3 through 6 and intently focusing on movement and direction in each discipline, do not lose sight of why we drew your attention to movement and direction. While it might be tempting to get lost in the fascinating particulars of any of the research explored and wander off exploring more of those particulars, bear in mind that we invoked the concepts of movement and direction as a mechanism to assist us in realizing the three items emphasized in the section above: (1) upset or disrupt the assumptions, (2) contribute to an alternative vision, and (3) use leadership as a fissure point for critical engagement.

ANALYZE LEADERSHIP IMAGERY

As you embark on your journey through the next four chapters, we request that you consider the imagery used within leadership studies. The imagery we refer to includes cartoons, photos, and drawings you have seen in books, assignments, movies, videos, advertisements, and social media memes. It also includes the images you create for yourself that never materialize outside your mind. All those images include many embedded assumptions. We expect that some of those assumptions will be contested by what you will read in the following chapters.

To set off moving in that direction, descriptions of images appearing on leadership book covers are provided below. These arose from a recent search for *leadership* within the books section on Amazon.com which displayed thousands of books. Surveying the first 500 cover images revealed the following repeated themes:

- Going somewhere—These images included: steering a ship, climbing a mountain, follow-the-leader type figurines or lines or arrows, bike riders in a line, locker room/sports, line charts indicating up, viewpoints that are looking up, mountains, whitewater rafting, gazing at a lake, open doors, empty forward pointing roads, lighthouses, and compasses.
- One of many—These images included: lines of objects all the same except for one a distinct color, balls, chairs, etc., and the hand of an orchestra conductor.
- Ordered complexity—These images included: geometric perspectives images, chess pieces, puzzle pieces, fractals, stones piled atop one another, steps, tree rings, building foundations, buildings, close-up of a leaf, close up of a drop of water on water, concentric circles, and circles with arrows.
- Vision—These images included: sunrise, planet eclipse, light bulbs, arrows, pendulum, key, and magnifying glasses.
- Animal Metaphors—These images included: flying birds and schooling fish.
- People—These images included: cartoons of people, images of dead people, such as presidents, photos of the person who wrote the book or who the book is about, photos of people in meetings, falling/kick in the rear end, heads with gears inside, stylized photoshopped images like a person standing on a rock in water, hands and gears, and blurry images of people at work.
- Unique and symbolic for the book—These images were unique and represented something unique about the specific book. Images included; umbrellas, coffee cups, serving platter, surfboard, campaign buttons, pen on paper, clipboard, folded up dollar bill, tied piece of string, cards and gambling chips, an arrow into a prescription bottle with a dollar bill around it, awards/trophies, and a paper airplane.

Our final words of advice as you read on is do not expect packaged take-aways at the end of the next four chapters. These chapters are exploratory, not explanatory. That means you should not expect summarized conclusions that condense facts into attractive nuggets from the terrain covered. Each chapter closes with a *final thoughts* section offering more questions and challenges rather than wrapping things up with a tidy bow. So, after reading these chapters, you may have more questions. If you do, we will consider one of our objectives met. Your questions, we hope, will linger and perhaps amalgamate to guide some of your movement or influence your directions within your own leadership work.

REFERENCES

Chandler, J. L. (2017). Examining interactions with dominant social norms. In *Teaching Resources and Innovations Library for Sociology.* Washington, DC: American Sociological Association.

Delgado, R., & Stefancic, J. (Eds.). (1997). *Critical white studies: Looking behind the mirror.* Philadelphia, PA: Temple University Press.

Hill, M. (Ed.). (1997). *Whiteness: A critical reader.* New York: New York University Press.

Hiller, N., Novelli, S. Ö., & Ponnapalli, A. R. (2016). *Leadership competency builder.* Miami, FL: FIU Center for Leadership. Retrieved from: http://lead.fiu.edu/the-leadership-competency-builder.

Kimberle, C., Gotanda, N., Peller, G., & Thomas, K. (Eds.). (1995). *Critical race theory: The key writings that formed the movement.* New York, NY: The New Press.

Lynn, M., & Dixson, A. D. (Eds.). (2013). *Handbook of critical race theory in education.* New York, NY: Routledge.

Simonet, D. V., & Tett, R. P. (2012). Five perspectives on the leadership-management relationship: A competency-based evaluation and integration. *Journal of Leadership and Organizational Studies, 20*(2), 199–213. https://doi.org/10.1177/1548051812467205.

CHAPTER 3

Exploring Movement and Direction in Aesthetics

INTRODUCTION

Readers keenly interested in aesthetics specifically within organizations are encouraged to explore reviews such as those produced by Minahan and Cox (2018) or by Bouilloud and Deslandes (2015) as this chapter explores movement and direction broadly understood within the realm of aesthetics. Aesthetics addresses the nature and appreciation of beauty; thus, it does not concentrate solely on art. Nevertheless, "humans appear to be the only animals to have developed the practice and culture of art" (Calvo-Merino, Urgesi, Orgs, Aglioti, & Haggard, 2010, p. 447) and "neurally speaking, art moves us by harnessing a key system with extraordinary resources, a system that not only helps make us who we are but also helps us be aware of who we are" (Starr, 2013, p. 66). But beauty is not limited to the realm of art. Aesthetics live within math, science, and engineering too. "A powerful, scientific understanding (similar to an artistic understanding) puts one in close personal contact with ideas that can (and should) change the way we think, feel, and act" (Girod, Rau, & Schepige, 2003, p. 577). Science, math, and engineering are often portrayed as unfeeling, unmoving, and analytical realms and yet, repeatedly researchers report that their discoveries occurred after they let go of orthodox frameworks and allowed themselves to get into their raw materials and play with them (Girod et al., 2003). Additionally, through the realm of aesthetics, scientists can generate the connections that allow people to make sense of their new discoveries and concepts. For example,

© The Author(s) 2018
J. L. S. Chandler and R. E. Kirsch, *Critical Leadership Theory*,
https://doi.org/10.1007/978-3-319-96472-0_3

in mathematics, the concept of beauty and the designation as beautiful or ugly has long been applied to theorems, proofs, and theories (Rota, 1997). Labeling a mathematical component as beautiful is not simply a designation of its aesthetic value to mathematicians, it is a designation of quality because beautiful theorems and proofs are the ones that are included in curricula or are imitated by others (Rota, 1997). Thus, referring to them as beautiful indicates something about their overall value. Of course, this chapter focuses a great deal on art because much of the attention within aesthetics research focuses there.

The last introductory element that requires an introduction here is the concept of being moved. Cova and Deonna (2014) argued that "being moved" is an emotion distinct from sadness or joy or any other emotion. They explained that it is an experience in which the person recognizes one of their core values being emphasized within a contrasting background and subsequently, they emphasize that core value in their life in a way that is meaningful for them.

> Being moved operates first as a powerful reminder of the values that we hold most dear and take ourselves to be governed by. It attracts our attention to things that are important to us but which we have come to take for granted and no longer notice or appreciate. This role is not confined to the function of validating our current beliefs, for it might also trigger conversions or reconversions by bringing to light important values which we were no longer sensitive to, at least at an explicit and personal level. (Cova & Deonna, 2014, p. 458)

This aspect of movement and direction occurring within individuals is only one area explored in this chapter as a kind of movement and direction related to the content of beauty. The movement and direction in the creative process are explored in this chapter as well.

Experiencing Beauty

Human Faces

This section starts by focusing on the beauty of the human face because "the human face plays a key role in human interactions" (Sheehan & Nachman, 2014, p. 1) and a great deal of research has been invested in understanding the complex ways in which human faces factor into human experiences. For example, Okumura, Kanakogi, Kanda, Ishiguro, and Itakura (2013) found that learning differed between infants observing human faces compared to those observing robot faces. Another example is Ambron and Foroni's (2015) research measuring the change in movements caused by the sudden appearance of a face that was irrelevant to the task at hand. And while the search for a universal understanding of beauty in human faces has driven much research, some researchers argue that all human faces are beautiful, for example, Perrett (2012) while others, for example, Chatterjee (2014) argue that there are predictable components of attraction regarding human faces that persist across time and cultures which can be measured.

Pallett, Link, and Lee (2009) used four experiments to test the hypothesis that "facial attractiveness can be optimized when the spatial relations between facial features approximate those of the average face" (p. 149). They used images of real people's faces and they altered the images using software resulting in the original image and its related altered images. All the images used were White females who appeared to be in their 20s and only their faces were clearly visible as their hair was obscured. The majority of the participants in the study identified themselves as female, but no racial or age data was reported for them. Across the four experiments conducted, Pallett et al. (2009) found that observers preferred faces with an eye-to-mouth distance that was 36% of the face length and a distance between the eyes that was 46% of the face width. Pallett et al. (2009) referred to these percentages as the "new" golden ratio referring to the mathematical expression of two quantities whose ratio is the same as the ratio of their sum to the larger of the two quantities. That irrational number was referred to as the divine proportion by Pacioli (1509) and since then has been referred to as the golden ratio, golden mean, or golden rectangle and Livio (2002b) argued that it had been used to create architecture and art. Devlin (2011) explained that those stories are appealing but inaccurate. In the final analysis, Devlin (2011) and Livio (2002a) seem to agree that while the golden ratio appears in fractals, regular solids, and many other mathematical components like pentagons as well as in many natural forms, the golden ratio as a universal rule in aesthetics is not helpful:

> In spite of the Golden Ratio's truly amazing mathematical properties, and its propensity to pop up where least expected in natural phenomena, I believe that we should abandon its application as some sort of universal standard for 'beauty,' either in the human face or in the arts. (Livio, 2002a, p. 1)

Additional investigations of the utility of the golden ratio in facial beauty include the research conducted by Alam, Mohd Noor, Basri, Yew, and Wen (2015) among Malaysian people. They focused on the three main ethnic groups in Malaysia to determine the frequency of faces whose measurements conform to the golden ratio and they were also interested in ascertaining whether there was a relationship between self-satisfaction with one's face and the degree to which their face represented the golden ratio. Alam et al. (2015) found that only 17.1% of the 286 faces conformed to the golden ratio and yet all the participants were generally satisfied with their own facial appearance.

Another approach in facial beauty research focuses on developing technologies that can evaluate images according to universal facial beauty and provide rankings or scores that match groups of expert human raters. Chiang, Lin, Huang, Lo, and Wan's (2014) work is an example of this research using three-dimensional images. Much of the previous research relied on only two-dimensional images and the golden ratio had been applied to those images. In the realm of three-dimensional images which demands a focus on the contours of faces, the golden ratio would be challenging to apply. Chiang et al. (2014) claimed that their work demonstrated:

> that the facial beauty is a universal concept, in general, and can also be learned by machine through supervised learning techniques. The high accuracy achieved by the proposed [algorithm/tool] proves that it can be used as a general, automated tool for objective classification of female facial attractiveness. Its potential applications also include autonomous system of human-like aesthetic judgment, cosmetic industry for assessing the effectiveness of cosmetic intervention, virtual worlds for morphing real face under aesthetic criteria, and/or attractiveness evaluation for a post-plastic-surgery face. (Chiang et al., 2014, p. 1258)

Another similar project was Liu, Fan, Guo, Samal, and Ali's (2017) recent work proposing a computational model that they refer to as 2.5 dimensional. Their aim was to produce a "computational model to gain a more comprehensive understanding of how face geometry affect[s] its attractiveness" (Liu et al., 2017, p. 177). While not a perfect correlation, they too were able to produce a model that correlated with human scores on facial attractiveness. Both these examples of more than two-dimensional facial beauty research projects focused on still images of expressionless faces. In Laurentini and Bottino's (2014) compiled review of research on the computer analysis of human beauty, one of the research areas they argued had received scant attention is in the area that examines beauty and facial movement and they argued that "human attractiveness is also related to movements, since static and moving stimuli convey different types of information that can lead to different attractiveness ratings" (Laurentini & Bottino, 2014, p. 196). Indeed, Hughes and Aung (2018) discovered from their study that greater facial symmetry while speaking was correlated with higher attractiveness scores even when still images of the same person received lower attractiveness ratings. Likewise, moving faces that were less symmetrical were rated as less attractive even when the still image of the same face was rated more attractive. Thus, Hughes and Aung's (2018) research results can be interpreted to maintain that because we see moving faces in our real lives, it is moving faces that should be the focus of the research on facial beauty not still images.

It is not surprising that human faces occupy as much research space as they do given that the "human face represents the most richly informative and pervasive social stimulus we encounter in our daily lives" (Adams & Nelson, 2011, p. 394). University research labs like the Langlois Social Development Lab in Texas, United States (The University of Texas at Austin, 2018) and the Face Research Lab at the University of Glasgow (Face Research Lab, 2018) funded by European, UK, US, and Canadian federal and private grants are just two of the organizations researching facial attractiveness. And despite Foo, Simmons, and Rhodes's (2017) recent research that found only "weak links between attractive facial traits and health" (p. 1) as long as attractive people are judged more positively and treated more positively as found in meta-analyses like that of Langlois et al. (2000), research investments into human facial beauty are likely to continue.

Paintings and Photos

Graham, Pallett, Ming, and Leder (2014) examined preferences when people viewed painted human face portraits compared to photographs of real faces. The researchers selected 16 color frontal portraits of individuals they categorized as White and female from art books and created high-resolution scans of those images. Then, using software for this purpose they took each original photo and averaged it with another original photo. Then they repeated the process to result in 31 images (16 original, eight two-portrait averages, four four-portrait averages, two eight-portrait averages, and one sixteen-portrait average). They completed the same type of manipulation on images of painted portraits of human faces. They concluded that "artistic representations of frontal female faces have representational properties that broadly match those of the natural face, but also [found] properties unique to artworks" (Graham et al., 2014, p. 75). They found that like other facial beauty research using still photos, averaged faces were rated as more attractive and the more face images averaged together increased the attractiveness scores. However, they also found that the averaged images of photographed human faces were preferred over the averaged images of painted portraits from art books. Investigating the possible causes for this difference, they discovered differences between the width and height dimensions of faces in the portrait images they created and the images they created from actual photos. So, they manipulated those dimensions and generated new images from the paintings and again the study participants rated those images similarly to the averaged photos previously. They concluded that "despite the demonstrated differences between artistic representations and natural faces, fundamental properties of natural faces are preserved in artistic representations of the face" (Graham et al., 2014, p. 75).

The notion that images averaged from unique and distinct images to achieve a universally appealing image seemed to also underlie Vitaly Komar and Alexander Melamid's project investigating democracy in art appreciation. Attempting to determine the art tastes and desires of people democratically, they commissioned several nation-wide polls conducted by The Nation Institute (Wypijewski, 1999) collecting data about landscape image preferences in the USA, China, Denmark, Finland, France, Germany, Holland, Iceland, Italy, Kenya, Portugal, Russia, Turkey, and the Ukraine. From each set of results, they painted pictures for each nation representing the dominant preferences (Dia Center for the Arts, 1997; Wypijewski, 1999). There was a great deal of similarity across the resulting paintings and the artists argued that humans seem to have an innate preference for a certain kind of landscape image. Dutton (2009) continued this argument that all humans prefer similar landscape images in his review of Komar and Melamid's work tracing it through the subsequent related research. Dutton (2009) sketched a landscape of his own, so to speak, of the research describing human evolutionary benefits of preferring such landscapes.

Approaching the universally appealing image issue from another direction, Joshi et al. (2011) argued that algorithms that can scan and select digital images based on their beauty "can help find exciting and appealing photographs from large collections while sorting out unappealing ones" (p. 95). Indeed, there are several such algorithms in use today and Tan et al. (2017) recently set about comparing their method with six other state-of-the-art methods demonstrating that their method for doing so was right 87.10% of the time. Getting it right in this context requires some explanation of the process applied. The images selected for the test were from an online database that included photographers' subjective ratings allowing scores from 1 to 10. Tan et al. (2017) averaged those scores for the images they selected and categorized scores above 5.5 as high quality and below 5.5 as low quality because the algorithm they developed only classified images using the binary choice of high quality or low quality. Then, their algorithm was right 87.10% of the time. While Tan et al. (2017) demonstrated that their algorithm is incrementally better than the others produced to date, the existing mathematical approaches to assessing the beauty of an image may not be taking all the contributing parameters into account.

Friedrich and Elias (2016) conducted research examining directional aesthetic preferences in humans. They also provided a cogent summary of related research with humans and other vertebrate animals that supports the argument that an underlying neurological mechanism is responsible for asymmetric leftward biases and left-to-right ordinal preferences across species. Fourteen individuals whose first language learned was Hindi and 17 individuals whose first language was Urdu participated in Friedrich and Elias's (2016) study in Canada. Their study examined preferences that could be related to a person's writing customs since Urdu is written right-to-left and Hindi is written left-to-right. The participants viewed looping two second videos of moving animals, natural phenomena like clouds, or moving vehicles and still photos captured from those videos. The researchers manipulated the images to result in paired sets that were duplicates of each other flipped horizontally so that there were equal numbers moving from left-to-right as there were moving right-to-left. The image pairs were presented to the participants in sequence and the participants were required to indicate their preference for each pair. As a group, the Hindi speakers demonstrated a preference for all the images related to movement from left-to-right, but the Urdu speakers showed no overall preferences. Friedrich and Elias (2016) explained that these results are similar to previous research and that researchers had not yet agreed on the "exact underlying neurological mechanisms responsible for the increased salience of features located in the left hemispace" (p. 131).

Addressing the internal mental processing that humans engage in when they experience art, Pelowski, Markey, Forster, Gerger, and Leder (2017) recently presented their "Vienna Integrated Model of top-down and bottom-up processes in Art Perception (VIMAP)" which they described as a "comprehensive theory explaining… the multiple ways by which people respond to art" (p. 80). Their model consists of seven linear stages beginning with the state a person is in before they experience art and five possible cognitive outcomes from an experience. A flurry of comments on their work included praise and doubts expressed by Ayala and Cela-Conde (2017) who questioned the validity of VIMAP based on the technologies used to collect relevant brain responses during experiences with art because "neither the PET technique nor the fMRI can provide temporal series adequate for detecting functional connectivity and, thereby, brain networks in the perception of art" (p. 133). Others, such as Jacobsen (2017), chimed in with recommendations to incorporate their previous work. Still others, such as Brattico, Brattico, and Vuust (2017) bring attention to the aesthetic value of nothingness or rather "non-appearance properties" (p. 128) as they refer to them because the ways in which the absence of stimuli contributes to beauty, as well as the artist's intentions, must be addressed in a model that attempts to comprehensively address the human experience with art. Lastly, criticisms from Nadal and Skov (2017) focus on the presentation of bottom–up and top–down brain processing which they argued "disregards evidence and current thinking on brain function" (p. 148). This criticism cited research about how human brains constantly predict experiences rather than trying to make sense of them after the fact. This state-of-the-art understanding of how the human brain operates is explored further in the next chapter.

Addressing the argument that there are images humans universally experience as beautiful, Vessel, Starr, and Rubin (2013) conducted a study in which participants were "asked to base their ratings on how much each artwork 'moved' them" (Vessel et al., 2013, p. 1). Using what they classified as little-known artworks, Vessel et al. (2013) zeroed in on the unique aesthetic experience for each individual. Sixteen individuals participated in their study in which they rated, on a scale from one to four indicating how much the image moved them, 109 color images shown in random order while their brains were being scanned using fMRI. As Vessel et al. (2013) hypothesized, there was no overall consensus on the images that were highly moving. Without detailing the intricate details of brain regions, their functions, and the layered brain scan results, suffice it to say the fMRI results indicated that when participants rated images as highly moving, their brains were involved in self-relevance processing which occurs in what is called the default mode network.

> Such processing is, of course, ubiquitous in everyday life and is undoubtedly important for normal functioning. In experimental settings it can occur spontaneously (e.g., as "mind wandering" during periods of rest) but it can also be triggered in structured tasks, by external stimuli that cause observers to draw on self- referential information (intentionally or automatically), or to engage in inwardly focused attention. (Vessel et al., 2013, p. 6)

Their work relates to the explanation that being moved is a unique and separate emotion as argued by Cova and Deonna (2014).

Dance, Music, and Movies

Reason et al. (2016) investigated the experiences of people watching dances to determine the impact of the auditory stimulation on the kinesthetic and the aesthetic experiences of the spectator. Their research investigated the effect when music was present and when music was absent, and spectators only heard the sounds the performers made. This mixed methods research combined a qualitative approach with one group of participants and functional brain imaging (fMRI) scans with another group of participants. The qualitative portion included 15 people who participated in workshops immediately after watching live dance performances. The workshops consisted of structured exercises for collecting data from the participants in which they wrote their responses and then participated in an open discussion which was audio recorded. The fMRI scans were conducted on 22 other participants who only viewed videos while being scanned. The videos were of the same dances that the live audience participants watched. Reason et al. (2016) concluded that hearing audible breathing and footfalls as part of watching dance leads to increased embodiment for spectators, regardless of whether the spectators enjoyed that experience. For some spectators, the kinesthetic properties of the experience increased their enjoyment and for others it seemed to interfere with their enjoyment because they preferred to hear music controlling the emotional experience rather than focusing on the performers' physical exertions.

A different approach in investigating emotions in music was taken by Castellano, Mortillaro, Camurri, Volpe, and Scherer (2008) who were interested in verifying whether emotional expression could be interpreted from the movements of the musician by trying to determine which motion cues were most emotion-sensitive. They concluded that an automated system could produce usable results by only attending to two motion cues, that is, the quantity of movements made by the upper body and the velocity of head movements. Home-Cook (2015) provided a more expansive description of the human experience of music:

> the sense in which listening entails movement in and through environmental space challenges the notion of an aural immersion as straightforwardly conceived. We are not statically 'immersed' in sound, any more than we are detached or removed from the world of vision; sound does not intrude upon a passive subject, any more than the visual world is 'taken in' by the objectivizing activity of a detached, disembodied eye. Whilst the listener resides in the medium of sound, equally this medium must be attended, explored, and travelled through. (pp. 168–169)

Thus, Home-Cook's likening experiencing music to experiencing visual art reflects the similarities across the ongoing work by those who aim to develop automated means of recognizing beauty in images that was explored above, and those who seek to develop automatic emotion recognition in music. In a review of such work compiled by Kim et al. (2010) the researchers concluded that "recognizing musical mood remains a challenging problem primarily due to the inherent ambiguities of human emotions" (p. 264). Another of their conclusions seems to echo Vessel et al. (2013) findings presented above because they emphasized that "it is clear that individuals perceive emotions within music differently" (p. 264). These and other research avenues will undoubtedly benefit from the continued flow of results produced in the young field of enquiry called neuroaesthetics which uses neuroscience as the "method of enquiry [into] how aesthetic behavior is underpinned by brain processes" (Skov & Vartanian, 2018, p. 2).

Interested in the experiences of people far from their homes who were moved to travel to those places, Reijnders (2016) conducted 15 in-depth interviews with acquaintances, friends, family, and colleagues to examine the phenomenon of people who traveled to places that they read about in novels, or saw in a televised program, or in a movie. Reijnders (2016) admitted that this approach restricted the dataset to people in the Netherlands who were highly educated, middle-aged White people which means the results will reflect the WEIRD problem that is mentioned in the next chapter. At any rate, Reijnders (2016) concluded that:

> every human being has a small treasure trove of stories which they love and which are considered part of their identity... [and] there is a strong relationship between the recollection of beloved stories and tourist practices – in terms of both destination decision making and tourist experience. (p. 672)

Reijnders (2016) further argued that the travelers used the stories they brought with them to ascribe the meanings they created before traveling onto their experiences once they were there. Additionally, their stories carried embedded structures delineating self from other that the travelers used to reinforce their stories. Reijnders (2016) did not mention that any of the travelers interviewed had experienced overwhelming emotions while experiencing some great beauty of the place, a condition referred to as Stendahl syndrome. Palacios-Sánchez et al. (2018) recently provided a historical and clinical review of the very rare condition which can cause chest pain, rapid heart rate, excessive sweating, and loss of consciousness. This condition is not commonly experienced by people other than Europeans and little research has been conducted on it within medical communities. Palacios-Sánchez et al. (2018) described the common cause of the syndrome as "the experience of finding oneself in a city or a building that allows the visitor to behold wondrous works of art, the greatness of the past and its historical perspective" (p. 122). Risk factors were identified as: educational level, marital status, age, stress over traveling, living alone, reaching the end of a journey, and a religious upbringing (Palacios-Sánchez et al., 2018). The authors speculated that reaching the end of one's journey triggers a profound sense of sadness and loss as the person then contemplates returning home where their surroundings lack the magnificent beauty that they have experienced on their travels. The syndrome is considered a psychiatric condition, so the authors referred to those exhibiting its symptoms as patients. "Affected patients are overwhelmed by beauty and are forced to remove themselves from the experience, due to their inability to tolerate the passionate connection [with] art" (Palacios-Sánchez et al., 2018, p. 123).

Schubert, Zickfeld, Seibt, and Fiske (2018) also investigated the emotion of being moved with 909 participants in the United States who were recruited and paid very small sums through Amazon's online work marketplace. Each participant watched two videos and provided feedback online indicating their changes in feelings as soon as they noticed them. Participants also rated how close they thought the people in the videos were. The videos used have been available on social media for some time. One is called Unsung Hero and it is a commercial for Thai Life Insurance. Another tells the story about Christian the lion who recognized his owners after he was released in the wild when they came to visit. Several of the videos have text in English on the screens telling the story and they have heartfelt music as well. Schubert et al. (2018) acknowledged that the music likely amplified the experiences for the participants. One of their hypotheses for this study was that the participants would notice an increase in closeness among the people in the videos and the closeness of the people in the videos would precede their feeling moved by the video. However, that did not occur; the participants' reports of the closeness and feeling moved tended to occur at the same time. The researchers speculated on possible reasons for their results. Oddly, even though Schubert et al. (2018) cited Cova and Deonna's (2014) work, one possible emotion that may have played a role they did not address was one that Cova and Deonna (2014) discussed thoroughly. That is sentimentality.

Cova and Deonna (2014) described sentimentality as indulging in experiences of being moved without genuinely caring about the core value presented in the experience. Applying this to the videos used in Schubert et al. (2018) study to derive examples gives us the person who gets teary-eyed watching the Thai Life commercial video, but who never helps the people in their life. Another example is feeling touched by the Christian the lion video and yet continuing to support the killing of big cats for sport. Cova and Deonna (2014) explained that these people are generating the emotion, but there is no corresponding action. Perhaps because the participants' experiences examined in Schubert et al. (2018) study were while they were watching the video before they had any opportunities to take action, sentimentality was all they could muster. Another factor that Schubert et al. (2018) discussion failed to address was that the participants who found their study in among solicitations to perform actual work were not seeking out psychological studies to participate in; meaning that they likely carried their reasons and dispositions with them when they entered the study and those factors likely impacted their performances during the study.

CREATING BEAUTY

Performance

Zaidel (2016) explained that the human process of creating art is a fundamental process of human sense-making and perhaps this mirrors some of what Joseph Beuys meant by his words, "every human being is an artist who – from [their] state of freedom – the position of freedom that [they] experience at first-hand – learn to determine the other positions of the total art work of the future social order" (Beuys, 1974, p. 48). It could be interpreted that Beuys was referring to a wide variety of creative productions as art. Furthermore, it can be argued that much unintentional beauty also exists in life, and it could be that unintentionality that some artists seek to emulate with exhibits that require audience participation.

Art exhibits can explicitly invite observers to participate in the creation of the art they are observing. For example, the exhibit *Moving Creates Vortices and Vortices Create Movement* "comes to life and transforms under the influence of visitors' movement" (*Designboom*, 2018). This digital art installation responds to the people walking through the space by reflecting lines on the floor that represent the vortices and velocities of their movement (teamLab, 2017). When seen by the participants, the vortices can then influence their movement and thus the display constantly changes. But the resulting display might be predictable because according to Bejan (2013), humans have a predictable comfortable and desired walking speed and cooperativity [is] perceived as pleasant.... For humans, these feelings are of the same nature as the pleasure derived from beauty, and from understanding something easily and fast, in order to get moving to safety and better life in general. (Bejan, 2013, p. 199)

Therefore, the resulting patterns would likely have a repetitive and predictable pattern to them that would not be recognizable to the individual participants who might participate thinking they are creating something entirely original and unpredictable.

A very different kind of performance is created by Theo Jansen's (Jansen & Sheil, 2008) kinetic sculptures called *Strandbeests* that are powered by the wind on the beach. He described his lifelike creatures, made mostly out of polyvinyl chloride tubing, as eating wind for energy. Granted, they are also powered by visitors to the Exploratorium who are allowed to interact with the beests that live there after their brief lives on the beach (Exploratorium, 2016). What Jansen refers to as the beests' evolution is an intriguing aspect of the creative process as each one is designed to be better adapted to the beach environment based on the results of the previous generation's experiences there.

Another participatory art piece came to the fore during the development of this chapter. One of the authors (Jennifer) had the opportunity to "receive the gift of song" (Ureña, 2018, p. 2) in the participatory performance, *Sonic Blossom*, at the National Portrait Gallery in Washington, DC. Conceived by artist Lee Mingwei, the performance was commissioned in 2013 for the inauguration of South Korea's National Museum of Modern and Contemporary Art and it has since toured New Zealand, Germany, Canada, Taiwan, and Japan (Ureña, 2018). The performance consists of a singer wearing a custom-designed gown who approaches patrons in the museum and asks one "May I give you the gift of song?" The acquiescent patron is guided to a chair and sits. The singer stands about 20 feet in front of the lone seated patron, then sings a Schubert solo accompanied by recorded music while other museum patrons gather and watch. The performance at the National Portrait Gallery did not take place in a performance hall; it occurred in a large open space between galleries where patrons were moving from one gallery to another and moving up and down stairs. Patrons murmured as they moved from one area of the museum to another and many of them came upon the performance unexpectedly. The piece was designed by Lee to provide the selected patron with "a moment of catharsis, joy and connection" (Ureña, 2018, p. 2). He designed the piece after finding solace in Schubert's solos with his mother whom he cared for after her surgery and he wanted to give others a similar gift. As the seated patron, I was keenly aware of being part of the performance and that role felt quite different than the previous song I listened to while someone else sat in the receiving chair. The performance could be classified as a mixed reality performance as discussed by Benford and Giannachi (2011) which are performances that often combine or span different environments, sliding the performance into real life. Expanding this notion by drawing from Goffman (1959), all people are performers in the sense that they are aware of and attending to their actions as they believe they are seen by others. Or as Bleeker, Sherman, and Nedelkopoulou (2015) put it, "both performance and phenomenology engage with experience, perception, and with making sense as processes that are embodied, situated, and relational" (p. 1). That human experiences creating art are always embodied, situated, and relational is not always evident in the research frames discussed in this chapter.

Cancienne and Snowber (2003) also argued against such artificial distinctions of mind from body. They explained that "integrating the choreographic process as central to research begins to shift the perception that we have bodies to the reality that we are bodies" (Cancienne & Snowber, 2003, p. 239). They argued that the choreographic process is similar to the writing process in that it is a process of "sorting, sifting, editing, forming, making, and remaking; it's essentially an act of discovery" (Cancienne & Snowber, 2003, p. 237).

Writing

Ardila (2004) emphasized that the human brain does not have a specialized area for writing like it does for speech. Furthermore, the process we refer to as writing is actually a complex amalgam of basic abilities that differs wildly depending on whether one is grasping a pen to write on a piece of paper or if one is using a keyboard to generate words on a screen or one is speaking into a device that captures them as text (Ardila, 2004). Furthermore, the variety of movements involved in the mechanics of writing are not at the heart of the creative process of stringing words together to convey meaning. Others, such as Spry (2011), have produced rich texts plumbing the intricate ways in which lived experiences can be autoethnographically explored and shared through iterations of performance and writing.

Recognizing, of course, that creative processes are not all concerned with creating beauty, a glimpse of what the human creative process is understood to be can add to our exploration here. Lubart (2000) described and explained the existing models of the creative process starting with the classic model that has four-stages: preparation, incubation, illumination, and verification. This model has been critiqued and argued over and has had many modifications and refinements proposed. Lubart's (2000) review included a discussion of the possibility that the human process is the same across individuals, but the results can differ drastically based on the knowledge each uses in the process. Another intriguing conundrum addressed is how to differentiate the process of being creative from the problem-solving process that is declared not creative. In other words, who decides whether there is actual creativity occurring?

Liu et al. (2015) argued that their research was one of the first to examine all facets of the creative process in action simultaneously: multiple phases of the creative process, quality of the creative product, and the impact of expertise. They examined individuals creating poetry and their participants were 27 right-handed individuals for whom English was the language they learned as children. These individuals were also skillful typists which was necessary for they were required to type their responses during the experiments. Fourteen of the participants were designated as experts because they had completed at least one year of a Master of Fine Arts program and had published in poetry journals and the thirteen individuals designated as novices had not. These participants completed two verbal fluency tests to classify their verbal skills before performing six tasks while having their brains scanned with fMRI. To prepare for their brain scans all the participants were provided the same two short poems to memorize and a list of ten single-sentence facts to memorize. They were tested before their brain scans to demonstrate that they had indeed, memorized these items. The tasks they performed while being scanned were: recite the poems they memorized, generate their own poems, revise those poems, complete random typing movements, recite the facts they memorized, and generate their own facts that were not part of the memorized ones.

Expectedly, the poems produced by the group designated as experts were rated more favorably than those produced by the novices by the panel who reviewed the resulting work. However, their fMRI scans revealed similar brain activity in both experts and novices which Liu et al. (2015) argued supported "a single neuroanatomical model to explain both process and the impact of expertise" (p. 3367) and they provided such a model. Their final cautions included the acceptance that their study artificially defined the creation processes as entirely distinct from the revision process, when in reality, these processes are uniquely inseparable for each individual performing them. Interestingly, they mentioned the default mode network, but they did not investigate its role in the same way that Vessel et al. (2013) did as the site where being moved occurs in the brain. To the layperson, there can seem to be a connection between being moved by beauty and attempting to create such beauty, but maybe the work of creating beauty is just that—work. And as such, the brain processes involved in creative generation are vastly different than the ones involved in appreciating beauty and being moved.

Fürst, Ghisletta, and Lubart (2017) recently employed an experimental manipulation of the classic staged creative process in a writing task to determine which subprocesses led to higher creativity: generation or selection. The participants were 174 undergraduate psychology students who were informed that the experiment was about creativity who also filled out a personality questionnaire after they completed the writing task. The participants were asked to write 3000 characters maximum prose or poetry, fiction or nonfiction, about the season they were randomly assigned: spring, summer, fall, or winter. Before the participants began writing, the following was explained to them:

> Research has shown that the creative process consists of two main subprocesses: (a) Generation, which consists of searching for many ideas, having wild ideas, making original associations of ideas, trying various options, exploring unusual possibilities. In summary, Generation is a warm, chaotic, divergent kind of thinking. (b) Selection, which consists of evaluating, sorting and selecting ideas, criticizing one's own work, developing and formalizing ideas, searching for improvements. In summary, Selection is a cold, thorough, convergent kind of thinking. (Fürst et al., 2017, p. 206)

The participants used computers for the experiment and instructions were provided multiple times. The text above that addressed generation was displayed in red and the text addressing selection was displayed in blue and this convention was used throughout the experiment. Participants were told there were time limits for completing each stage, but those were not enforced and there were ten different sets of instructions that participants were provided along the way to test various conditions and one of those was the control group. The test conditions were the researchers attempts to increase the intensity during the creative sub-processes. The written results of the participants were evaluated on their quality and their originality and of the ten groups there was only one whose end products were rated as a little more original but not higher in quality, and there was one group who writing was rated as higher quality but much lower in originality than the control group. This result surprised the researchers because the control group was "told about the existence of the two subprocesses, but was not instructed on how to use them during the task" (Fürst et al., 2017, p. 212).

One common myth about artists that we have not yet addressed in this chapter is the belief that mental illness is the source of artistic creativity. Kaufman (2014) provided one of the reviews that has addressed theories, historical frames, and accumulated research on mental illness and creativity. In it, Nusbaum, Beaty, and Silvia (2014) compiled investigations that have demonstrated that within certain creative fields, such as poetry and fiction writing, there tended to be more individuals with mental illnesses when compared to scientific creators. Having surveyed the evidence across the broad spectrum of creativity, Kaufman (2014) concluded that "creativity and mental illness are less related than common stereotypes would have us believe....[However,] for some severity levels, of some disorders, and for some domains, one can reasonably conclude that creativity and mental illness are linked" (pp. 398–399). But the connection is tenuous at best Kaufman (2014) cautions.

Movies

Representing movement in a still image has always been a challenge (Cutting, 2002) and movies, as we know them today seem like a twentieth century invention. However, Wachtel (1993) argued that people painted in caves tens of thousands of years ago because the conditions there allowed them to produce moving images. The techniques used included superimposed images and the use of curved and straight lines over images. Both these techniques when viewed in darkness with only flickering burning lamps produced the illusion of movement (Wachtel, 1993). Cutting (2002) argued that the function of pictures that convey movement is "not to trick the visual system into seeing motion; instead, it is merely to suggest to an observer, sometimes a well-informed one, that motion has occurred" (p. 1190). Cutting (2002) further argued that brains are looking for motion, that is they are ready for it and so it is easy for brains to interpret many things as motion. In still images, our brains can readily interpret, for example, squiggly lines or multiple blurred or repeated images as motion. Combining this notion with conclusions from Clark's (2016) work, which will be explored more fully in the following chapter, the human brain as a predictor seems to bend toward expecting movement.

Apart from our brains' tendency to expect movement, what is it about movies that fascinate and move people? This question, of course, assumes that people are moved by movies. Psychocinematics is the field of research that addresses this question as it refers to the scientific analysis of humans' aesthetic response to movies explained Shimamura (2013) who also reiterated that movies are a type of storytelling, which is a very old universal human activity (Boyd, 2009). Moreover, movies, according to Carroll and Seeley (2013) are but one genre of motion pictures. Motion pictures:

> is a broader term that refers to the medium as a whole and includes movies, art films, experimental films, flip books, hand-etched animations made frame by frame with an Exacto knife from a loop of celluloid, and whatever else under the sun that can be fit into the category. (Carroll & Seeley, 2013, p. 53)

As collaborative products, movies include all the previously discussed artistic forms. Attempting to identify the key contributors, Simonton (2002) analyzed 2323 movies that were nominated for Academy Awards from 1928 through 2000 to decipher which contributions from all those collaborations mattered most. They analyzed 16 categories that movies were nominated for: direction, female lead, male lead, screenplay, cinematography, art direction, female supporting, male supporting, film editing, visual effects, costume design, score, sound, sound effects editing, and makeup and correlated those data with whether the movie was selected for best picture and what its movie guide ratings were. Unsurprisingly, they found that a movie nominated for best director had the most predictive value for determining whether it was likely to receive the best picture honors. Similarly, the best original screenplay nomination had the most predictive value for the movie guide ratings. They found that several of the nomination categories were not instrumental in predicting the rating outcomes for a movie. Conceivably, we can consider the rankings a movie receives contributes to moving people into theaters to spend their money to watch the movie. But is there more; do movies make a difference?

Lumet (1996) described his directorial work on films such as *12 Angry Men* and *Murder on the Orient Express*. Lumet (1996) referred to directing as the best job in the world and narrated some of the fiscal management challenges of directing films as well as his personal creative intentions and choices.

> I don't mind limitations. Sometimes they even stimulate you to better, more imaginative work. A spirit may develop among the crew and cast that adds to the passion of the movie, and this can show up on-screen. On certain pictures, I've worked for union minimum, and so have the actors. We did *Long Day's Journey Into Night* that way. We did it because we loved the material and wanted to see the picture made no matter what. (Lumet, 1996)

Reading Lumet's (1996) description of the challenges of shooting the scene in *Murder on the Orient Express* when the train leaves the station and re-watching that scene provides a deeper appreciation for the creative investment especially considering current movies employ a fair amount of computer graphic imagery. Lumet's (1996) descriptions portray a sense of camaraderie, excitement, and fun among those contributing creatively to the creation of movies that belies the reality revealed by recent investigative reporting, assault charges, and mass media surveys like the one conducted by *USA Today* in collaboration with The Creative Coalition, Women in Film and Television and the National Sexual Violence Resource Center that "nearly all of the women who responded to the survey (94%) say they have experienced some form of harassment or assault, often by an older individual in a position of power over the accuser" (Puente & Kelly, 2018). And that is just the commercial movie making industry in Hollywood. 2011 numbers indicate that India and Nigeria both produce more films than the USA with China, Japan, the UK, France, and South Korea following behind (Fellows, 2015).

Creating beauty in movies through systemic practices that perpetuate and coverup sexual assault contrasts sharply with Emma Sulkowicz's performance-art project called *Carry That Weight* which consisted of her carrying a fifty-pound mattress around the Columbia University campus for a year and even carrying it with her during her graduation (Bauer-Wolf, 2017) and *The Hunting Ground*, a documentary about rape culture on college campuses. *The Hunting Ground* was produced by Amy Ziering and after premiering at the 2015 Sundance Film Festival it was presented by New York Governor Cuomo in conjunction with efforts there to pass new legislation. Complicating the field further, *The Hunting Ground* was distributed by CNN and The Weinstein Company (TWC) and more recently, Ziering and her collaborator encouraged the Academy to rescind Weinstein's membership and distribute the proceeds from their documentary to sexual assault victim support organizations and encouraged everyone to:

> examine in what ways they can work to change our culture so that these crimes are no longer normalized and tolerated. This means no longer mass-producing narratives that are sexist, misogynistic and traffic in rape myths. There are more diverse stories to be told. Start telling them. (Dick & Ziering, 2017)

Documentaries are about real people and real events and indeed, many documentarians are created by driven filmmakers passionate about sharing their truth with an audience through film (Nichols, 2017) and several organizations evaluate such works, give awards such as the Doc Impact Award (Doc Impact Award, 2018), and also provide resources for those interested in developing documentaries. Interestingly, there are increasing numbers of documentaries investigating obsession with human beauty as well as the cost to individual psychological health and to society of acquiring beauty. Some recent documentaries have been criticized and labeled propaganda. Are they propaganda? Jowett and O'Donnell (2015) argued that it is surprising that:

> Of all the mass media, the motion picture has the greatest potential for emotional appeal to its audience, offering a deeper level of identification with the characters and action on the screen than found elsewhere in popular culture. The motion picture can also make audiences laugh, cry, sing, shout, become sexually aroused, or fall asleep; in short, it has the ability to evoke an immediate emotional response seldom found in the other mass media. Yet, systematic attempts by governments or other groups to use the motion picture as a major channel for the delivery of deliberate propagandistic messages have not, on the whole, been very successful. (pp. 110–111)

However, Jowett and O'Donnell (2015) further contended that movies do "succeed as propaganda vehicles in a much subtler way by presenting one set of values as the only viable or attractive set" (p. 111) and in this way movies, whether or not they are beautiful, continue to steer prevailing public attitudes.

FINAL THOUGHTS

While all human cultures have art, not all cultures practice the same art forms (Dutton, 2009). Expanding on that, Eisner (2008) explained that "the idea that art can be regarded as a form of knowledge does not have a secure history in contemporary philosophical thought" (p. 3) and then made a cogent argument for just that—art as a legitimate form of knowledge. As the scope of this chapter was limited by what was available and practical to cover, we could seize but a few glimpses. Nevertheless, this chapter served as an apt entrance to the explorations of movement and direction because it thrust the conceptual doors wide open to explore movement and direction down many corridors.

In addressing human experiences with art, Dewey (1934) long ago distinguished between experience in general and an experience with art clearly demarking the second as the highly valued one. Dewey (1934) explained that an experience with art is recognizable, it takes time, and that active engagement is what impacts or moves a person. For the interaction to qualify as an experience in Dewey's (1934) parlance, the interaction must include rhythm, the person contributes to the creation of this rhythm, and it must proceed to culmination. This is one type of movement and direction embedded within Dewey's (1934) explanation of an experience with art. It would be enlightening to read an analysis of Dewey's theories on experiencing art aligned with results compiled from recent studies employing fMRI.

But beauty is not confined to art. A century earlier, Emerson (1836) encouraged people to recognize beauty in the transitory ordinariness of nature. "To the attentive eye, each moment of the year has its own beauty, and in the same field, it beholds, every hour, a picture which was never seen before, and which shall never be seen again" (Emerson, 1836, p. 14). Recommendations echoing Emerson (1836) to enjoy the simple beauty of nature that surrounds us are abundant. For example, a series of short videos titled *Gratitude Revealed* by Louie Schwartzberg described as:

a series of 15 film shorts, [in which] we explore what gratitude is, why it's important and what we can all do to live more gracious lives. From wonder and curiosity, to courage and generosity, we'll examine different components of emotional wellness as we connect our community with tools and resources to help them along the way. Some of these tools will come from leading experts, some will come from the community itself. But all of us will benefit from this shared experience. (Moving Art, LLC., 2016)

Overflowing with beautiful scenes and accompanied by lilting music, these short films deliver succinct affirmations about love, mindfulness, forgiveness, curiosity, wonder, patience, connection, happiness, energy, purpose, generosity, focus, and creativity (Moving Art, LLC., 2016). These exhortations to recognize and appreciate the beauty, wonder, and bounty that surround us are meant to improve our well-being because compiled research results (e.g., Komter, 2004) examining the impact of such actions and emotions have explained the many ways in which they are beneficial to human physical and psychological health. Those appeals to express gratitude and appreciate beauty in the mundane also echo Cova and Deonna's (2014) explanation that the emotion of being moved is when our attention is captivated by something that is "important to us but which we have come to take for granted and no longer notice or appreciate" (p. 458). Refocusing on a specific core value and acting on it can be seen as movement in a particular direction so that one returns to a previous position or re-centers oneself. Such movements can also be interpreted as acceptance that movement away from one's focus on one's core values is also a normal part of the overall process, for how can one return to something if one never leaves it? An absolute and unchanging focus cannot be maintained on all the core values one possesses; people have many core values—not just one. Thus, fluctuating movements away from followed by returning to one's core values resulting in a kind of movement back and forth that can achieve an equilibrium over time comes to mind. Perhaps those movements are related to movement toward one' goals as studied by Vazeou-Nieuwenhuis, Orehek, and Scheier (2017) for example. They investigated what they called locomotion and assessment related to one's sense of living a purposeful life with different types of samples based on the theory that "to attain our goals, we must identify what it is that we want to accomplish and how best to get there (assessment), and then follow through and actually do this (locomotion)" (Vazeou-Nieuwenhuis et al., 2017, p. 115).

They found that an "emphasis on locomotion was associated with greater perceptions of life as purposeful, while an emphasis on assessment was associated with lower perceptions of life as purposeful" (Vazeou-Nieuwenhuis et al., 2017, p. 120). Again, it is exciting to contemplate forthcoming theory and research integrating conceptualizations of beauty like Dewey's (1934) and Emerson's (1836) through constructs like being moved as explained by Cova and Deonna (2014) and finally linked to things like appreciation, gratitude, and a sense of purpose in life. Because, on balance, we all create beauty and observe beauty in our lives as we make sense of our lives and its purpose.

REFERENCES

Adams, R. B., & Nelson, A. J. (2011). Intersecting identities and expressions: The compound nature of social perception. In J. Decety & J. T. Cacioppo (Eds.), *The Oxford handbook of social neuroscience* (pp. 394–403). New York, NY: Oxford University Press.

Alam, M. K., Mohd Noor, N. F., Basri, R., Yew, T. F., & Wen, T. H. (2015). Multiracial facial golden ratio and evaluation of facial appearance. *PLoS One, 10*(11), e0142914. https://doi.org/10.1371/journal.pone.0142914.

Ambron, E., & Foroni, F. (2015). The attraction of emotions: Irrelevant emotional information modulates motor actions. *Psychonomic Bulletin & Review, 22*(4), 1117–1123. https://doi.org/10.3758/s13423-014-0779-y.

Ardila, A. (2004). There is not any specific brain area for writing: From cave-paintings to computers. *International Journal of Psychology, 39*(1), 61–67.

Ayala, F. J., & Cela-Conde, C. J. (2017). Which brain networks related to art perception are we talking about? "Move me, astonish me…" by Matthew Pelowski et al. *Physics of Life Reviews, 21*, 133–134. https://doi.org/10.1016/j.plrev.2017.04.009.

Bauer-Wolf, J. (2017, July 24). Mattress protest and its aftermath. *Inside Higher Ed.* Retrieved from: https://www.insidehighered.com/news/2017/07/24/media-circus-surrounding-mattress-girl-case-changed-conversation-sexual-assault.

Bejan, A. (2013). Constructal law: Pleasure, golden ratio, animal locomotion and the design: Comment on "the emergence of design in pedestrian dynamics: Locomotion, self-organization, walking paths and the constructal law" by A. Miguel. *Physics of Life Reviews, 10*, 199–201. https://doi.org/10.1016/j.plrev.2013.04.010.

Benford, S., & Giannachi, G. (2011). *Performing mixed reality*. Cambridge, MA: MIT Press.

Beuys, J. (1974). *Art into society, society into art.* London: Arts Council England.

Bleeker, M., Sherman, J. F., & Nedelkopoulou, E. (Eds.). (2015). *Performance and phenomenology: Traditions and transformations.* New York, NY: Routledge.

Bouilloud, J.-P., & Deslandes, G. (2015). The aesthetics of leadership: Beau Geste as critical behaviour. *Organization Studies, 36*(8), 1095–1114. https://doi.org/10.1177/0170840615585341.

Boyd, B. (2009). *On the origin of stories: Evolution, cognition, and fiction.* Cambridge, MA: Belknap Press of Harvard University Press.

Brattico, E., Brattico, P., & Vuust, P. (2017). The forgotten artist: Why to consider intentions and interaction in a model of aesthetic experience comment on "move me, astonish me…" by Matthew Pelowski et al. *Physics of Life Reviews, 21*, 128–130. https://doi.org/10.1016/j.plrev.2017.06.014.

Calvo-Merino, B., Urgesi, C., Orgs, G., Aglioti, S. M., & Haggard, P. (2010). Extrastriate body area underlies aesthetic evaluation of body stimuli. *Experimental Brain Research, 204*(3), 447–456.

Cancienne, M. B., & Snowber, C. N. (2003). Writing rhythm: Movement as method. *Qualitative Inquiry, 9*(2), 237–253. https://doi.org/10.1177/1077800402250956.

Carroll, N., & Seeley, W. P. (2013). Cognitivism, psychology, and neuroscience: Movies as attentional engines. In *Psychocinematics: Exploring cognition at the movies* (pp. 53–76). New York, NY: Oxford University Press.

Castellano, G., Mortillaro, M., Camurri, A., Volpe, G., & Scherer, K. (2008). Aautomated analysis of body movement in emotionally expressive piano performances. *Music Perception, 26*(2), 103–120.

Chatterjee, A. (2014). *The aesthetic brain: How we evolved to desire beauty and enjoy art.* Oxford: Oxford University Press.

Chiang, W.-C., Lin, H.-H., Huang, C.-S., Lo, L.-J., & Wan, S.-Y. (2014). The cluster assessment of facial attractiveness using fuzzy neural network classifier based on 3D Moiré features. *Pattern Recognition, 47*, 1249–1260. https://doi.org/10.1016/j.patcog.2013.09.007.

Clark, A. (2016). *Surfing uncertainty: Prediction, action, and the embodied mind.* New York, NY: Oxford University Press.

Cova, F., & Deonna, J. A. (2014). Being moved. *Philosophical Studies, 169*, 447–466. https://doi.org/10.1007/s11098-013-0192-9.

Cutting, J. E. (2002). Representing motion in a static image: Constraints and parallels in art, science, and popular culture. *Perception, 31*, 1165–1193. https://doi.org/10.1068/p3318.

Designboom. (2018). *Teamlab's ocean vortices-inspired installation makes waves at the national gallery of victoria.* Retrieved from: https://www.designboom.com/technology/teamlab-national-gallery-of-victoria-vortices-installation-12-27-2017/.

Devlin, K. (2011). The golden ratio & the Fibonacci numbers: Fact versus fiction. In *Math encounters—Fibonacci & the golden ratio exposed—Keith Devlin (Presentation & Workshop)*. Stanford, CA: National Museum of Mathematics.

Dewey, J. (1934). *Art as experience*. New York, NY: The Berkley Publishing Group.

Dia Center for the Arts. (1997). *Komar & Melamid: The most wanted paintings*. Retrieved from: http://awp.diaart.org/km/index.html.

Dick, K., & Ziering, A. (2017, October 12). Filmmakers of sexual assault doc call on academy to oust Harvey Weinstein. *The Hollywood Reporter*. Retrieved from: https://www.hollywoodreporter.com/race/filmmakers-sexual-assault-doc-call-academy-oust-harvey-weinstein-guest-column-1048412.

Doc Impact Award. (2018). *Doc Impact Award*. Retrieved from: http://www.docimpactaward.org/.

Dutton, D. (2009). *The art instinct: Beauty, pleasure, and human evolution*. New York, NY: Oxford University Press.

Eisner, E. (2008). Art and knowledge. In J. G. Knowles & A. L. Cole (Eds.), *Handbook of the arts in qualitative research: Perspectives, methodologies, examples, and issues* (pp. 3–13). Thousand Oaks, CA: Sage.

Emerson, R. W. (1836). *Nature*. Boston, MA: James Munroe and Company.

Exploratorium. (2016). *Strandbeest: The dream machines of Theo Jansen*. Retrieved from: https://www.exploratorium.edu/strandbeest.

Face Research Lab. (2018). *Face Research Lab*. Retrieved from: http://facelab.org/.

Fellows, S. (2015, October 5). *Stephen Fellows: Film data and education*. Retrieved from:https://stephenfollows.com/how-many-films-are-made-around-the-world/.

Foo, Y. Z., Simmons, L. W., & Rhodes, G. (2017). Predictors of facial attractiveness and health in humans. *Scientific Reports, 7*, 39731. https://doi.org/10.1038/srep39731.

Friedrich, T. E., & Elias, L. J. (2016). The write bias: The influence of native writing direction on aesthetic preference biases. *Psychology of Aesthetics, Creativity, and the Arts, 10*(2), 128–133. https://doi.org/10.1037/aca0000055.

Fürst, G., Ghisletta, P., & Lubart, T. (2017). An experimental study of the creative process in writing. *Psychology of Aesthetics, Creativity, and the Arts, 11*(2), 202–215. https://doi.org/10.1037/aca0000106.

Girod, M., Rau, C., & Schepige, A. (2003). Appreciating the beauty of science ideas: Teaching for aesthetic understanding. *Science Education, 87*(4), 574–587. https://doi.org/10.1002/sce.1054.

Goffman, E. (1959). *The presentation of everyday self*. New York, NY: Doubleday.

Graham, D., Pallett, P. M., Ming, M., & Leder, H. (2014). Representation and aesthetics of the human face in portraiture. *Art & Perception, 2*, 75–98. https://doi.org/10.1163/22134913-00002026.

Home-Cook, G. (2015). *Theatre and aural attention: Stretching ourselves*. Basingstoke, UK: Palgrave Macmillan.

Hughes, S. M., & Aung, T. (2018). Symmetry in motion: Perception of attractiveness changes with facial movement. *Journal of Nonverbal Behavior*, 1–17. https://doi.org/10.1007/s10919-018-0277-4.

Jacobsen, T. (2017). Aesthetic episodes, domains, and the mind comment on: "Move me…" by Matthew Pelowski et al. *Physics of Life Reviews*, 21, 143–144. https://doi.org/10.1016/j.plrev.2017.02.003.

Jansen, T., & Sheil, B. (2008). Strandbeests. *Architectual Digest*, 78(4), 22–27. https://doi.org/10.1002/ad.701.

Joshi, D., Datta, R., Fedorovskaya, E., Luong, Q.-T., Wang, J. Z., Li, J., & Luo, J. (2011, September). Aesthetics and emotion in images. *IEEE Signal Processing Magazine*, 28(5), 94–115. https://doi.org/10.1109/msp.2011.941851.

Jowett, G. S., & O'Donnell, V. (2015). *Propaganda & persuasion* (6th ed.). Thousand Oaks, CA: Sage.

Kaufman, J. C. (Ed.). (2014). *Creativity and mental illness*. Cambridge: Cambridge University Press.

Kim, Y. E., Schmidt, E. M., Migneco, R., Morton, B. G., Richardson, P., Scott, J., … Turnbull, D. (2010). Music emotion recognition: A state of the art review. *11th International Society for Music Information Retrieval Conference* (ISMIR) (pp. 255–266).

Komter, A. E. (2004). Gratitude and gift exchange. In R. A. Emmons & M. E. McCullough (Eds.), *Psychology of gratitude* (pp. 195–255). New York, NY: Oxford University Press.

Langlois, J. H., Kalakanis, L., Rubenstein, A. J., Larson, A., Hallman, M., & Smoot, M. (2000). Maxims or myths? A meta-analytic and theoretical review. *Psychological Review*, 126(3), 390–423. https://doi.org/10.1037//0033-2909.126.3.390.

Laurentini, A., & Bottino, A. (2014). Computer analysis of face beauty: A survey. *Computer Vision and Image Understanding*, 125, 184–199. https://doi.org/10.1016/j.cviu.2014.04.006.

Liu, S., Erikkinen, M. G., Healey, M. L., Xu, Y., Swett, K. E., Chow, H. M., & Braun, A. R. (2015). Brain activity and connectivity during poetry composition: Toward a multidimensional model of the creative process. *Human Brain Mapping*, 36, 3351–3372. https://doi.org/10.1002/hbm.22849.

Liu, S., Fan, Y.-Y., Guo, Z., Samal, A., & Ali, A. (2017). A landmark-based data-driven approach on 2.5D facial attractiveness computation. *Neurocomputing*, 238, 168–178. https://doi.org/10.1016/j.neucom.2017.01.050.

Livio, M. (2002a). The golden ratio and aesthetics. *Plus Magazine*. Retrieved from: https://plus.maths.org/content/golden-ratio-and-aesthetics.

Livio, M. (2002b). *The golden ratio: The story of Phi the extraordinary number of nature art and beauty*. London, UK: Headline Review.

Lubart, T. I. (2000). Models of the creative process: Past, present and future. *Creativity Research Journal*, 13(3–4), 295–308. https://doi.org/10.1207/S15326934CRJ1334_07.

Lumet, S. (1996). *Making movies.* New York, NY: First Vintage Books.
Minahan, S., & Cox, J. W. (Eds.). (2018). *The aesthetic turn in management.* New York, NY: Routledge.
Moving Art, LLC. (2016). *Gratitude revealed.* Retrieved from: https://gratituderevealed.com/.
Nadal, M., & Skov, M. (2017). Top-down and bottom-up: Front to back comment on "move me, astonish me..." by Matthew Pelowski et al. *Physics of Life Reviews, 21,* 148–149. https://doi.org/10.1016/j.plrev.2017.06.013.
Nichols, B. (2017). *Introduction to documentary* (3rd ed.). Bloomington, IN: Indiana University Press.
Nusbaum, E. C., Beaty, R. E., & Silvia, P. J. (2014). Ruminating about mental illness and creativity. In J. C. Kaufman (Ed.), *Creativity and mental illness* (pp. 395–402). Cambridge, UK: Cambridge University Press.
Okumura, Y., Kanakogi, Y., Kanda, T., Ishiguro, H., & Itakura, S. (2013). The power of human gaze on infant learning. *Cognition, 128,* 127–133. https://doi.org/10.1016/j.cognition.2013.03.011.
Pacioli, L. (1509). *De Divina Proportione.* Venice, IT: Paganini.
Palacios-Sánchez, L., Botero-Meneses, J. S., Pachón, R. P., Hernández, L. B., Triana- Melo, J. D., & Ramírez-Rodríguez, S. (2018). Stendhal syndrome: A clinical and historical overview. *Arquivos de Neuro-Psiquiatria, 76*(2), 120–123. https://doi.org/10.1590/0004-282X20170189.
Pallett, P. M., Link, S., & Lee, K. (2009). New "golden" ratios for facial beauty. *Vision Research, 50,* 149–154. https://doi.org/10.1016/j.visres.2009.11.003.
Pelowski, M., Markey, P., Forster, M., Gerger, G., & Leder, H. (2017). Move me, astonish me...delight my eyes and brain: The Vienna Integrated Model of top-down and bottom-up processes in Art Perception (VIMAP) and corresponding affective, evaluative, and neurophysiological correlates. *Physics of Life Reviews, 21,* 80–125. https://doi.org/10.1016/j.plrev.2017.02.003.
Perrett, D. (2012). *In your face: The new science of human attraction.* New York, NY: Palgrave Macmillan.
Puente, M., & Kelly, C. (2018, February 20). How common is sexual misconduct in Hollywood? *USA Today.* Retrieved from: https://www.usatoday.com/story/life/people/2018/02/20/usa-today-sunshine-project-methodology-explained/310757002/.
Reason, M., Kay, R., Kauppi, J.-P., Tohka, J., Jussi, C., Reynolds, D., ... Pollick, F. (2016). Spectators' aesthetic experience of sound and movement in dance performance: A transdisciplinary investigation. *Psychology of Aesthetics, Creativity, and the Arts, 10*(1), 42–55. https://doi.org/10.1037/a0040032.
Reijnders, S. (2016). Stories that move: Fiction, imagination, tourism. *European Journal of Cultural Studies, 19*(6), 672–689. https://doi.org/10.1177/1367549415597922.

Rota, G.-C. (1997). The phenomenology of mathematical beauty. *Synthese,* *111*(2), 171–182.

Schubert, T. W., Zickfeld, J. H., Seibt, B., & Fiske, A. P. (2018). Moment-to-moment changes in feeling moved match changes in closeness, tears, goose-bumps, and warmth: Time series analyses. *Cognition and Emotion, 32*(1), 174–184. https://doi.org/10.1080/02699931.2016.1268998.

Sheehan, M. J., & Nachman, M. W. (2014). Morphological and population genomic evidence that human faces have evolved to signal individual identity. *Nature Commuinications, 5*(4800), 1–10. https://doi.org/10.1038/ncomms5800.

Shimamura, A. P. (Ed.). (2013). *Psychocinematics: Exploring cognition at the movies.* New York, NY: Oxford University Press.

Simonton, D. K. (2002). Collaborative aesthetics in the feature film: Cinematic components predicting the differential impact of 2,323 Oscar-nominated movies. *Empirical Studies of the Arts, 20*(2), 115–125. https://doi.org/10.2190/RHQ2-9UC3-6T32-HR66.

Skov, M., & Vartanian, O. (Eds.). (2018). *Neuroaesthetics: Foundations and frontiers in aesthetics.* New York, NY: Routledge.

Spry, T. (2011). *Body, paper, stage: Writing and performing autoethnography.* Walnut Creek, CA: Left Coast Press.

Starr, G. G. (2013). *Feeling beauty: The neuroscience of aesthetic experience.* Cambridge, MA: MIT Press.

Tan, Y., Tang, P., Zhou, Y., Luo, W., Kang, Y., & Li, G. (2017). Photograph aesthetical evaluation and classification with deep convolutional neural networks. *Neurocomputing, 228,* 165–175. https://doi.org/10.1016/j.neucom.2016.08.098.

teamLab. (2017). *Moving creates vortices and vortices create movement.* National Gallery of Victoria, Melbourne, Australia.

The University of Texas at Austin. (2018). *Langlois Social Development Lab.* The University of Texas at Austin, College of Liberal Arts, Department of Psychology. Retrieved from: https://labs.la.utexas.edu/langloislab/.

Ureña, L. (2018, March 13). *Celebrating 50 years: Sonic Blossom.* National Portrait Gallery. Retrieved from: http://npg.si.edu/blog/celebrating-50-years-sonic-blossom.

Vazeou-Nieuwenhuis, A., Orehek, E., & Scheier, M. F. (2017). The meaning of action: Do self-regulatory processes contribute to a purposeful life? *Personality and Individual Differences, 116,* 115–122. https://doi.org/10.1016/j.paid.2017.04.040.

Vessel, E. A., Starr, G. G., & Rubin, N. (2013). Art reaches within: Aesthetic experience, the self and the default mode network. *Frontiers in Neuroscience, 7,* 258. https://doi.org/10.3389/fnins.2013.00258..

Wachtel, E. (1993). The first picture show: Cinematic aspects of cave art. *Leonardo*, 26(2), 135–140.

Wypijewski, J. (Ed.). (1999). *Painting by numbers: Komar amd Melamid's scientific guide to art*. Berkeley, CA: University of California Press.

Zaidel, D. W. (2016). *Neuropsychology of art: Neurological, cognitive, and evolutionary persectives* (2nd ed.). New York, NY: Routledge.

CHAPTER 4

Exploring Movement and Direction in Social Sciences

INTRODUCTION

The typical disciplines considered part of the social sciences include anthropology, economics, management, political science, psychology, and sociology. We chose human well-being as the focus for this chapter because it is, and has been, a topic of interest for all societies and it spans all the social science disciplines. Social scientists define, operationalize, and measure human well-being in order to examine what improves or degrades human well-being. Improvements to human well-being or degradations in human well-being can, therefore, be framed as movements that the social sciences investigate. Simplistically speaking, improvements to human well-being can be thought of as movements in one direction while degradations are movements in the opposite direction.

Before we jump into the main explorations of this chapter, there are a few cautions we must address regarding how social science is done. Rigorous social science requires what is considered an improvement to human well-being and what is considered a degradation in human well-being not be left to opinions. The social sciences demand that researchers and practitioners alike, maintain neutrality as they fulfill their social science duties. Lynd (1939) exposed this requirement for neutrality eight decades ago:

© The Author(s) 2018
J. L. S. Chandler and R. E. Kirsch, *Critical Leadership Theory*,
https://doi.org/10.1007/978-3-319-96472-0_4

The social scientist's reason for urging the neutrality of science in such a
world of bias is understandable, but it has unfortunate results that curtail
heavily the capacity of social science to do precisely the thing that it is the
responsibility of social science to do. (Lynd, 1939, p. 182)

Lynd (1939) argued that social scientists are expected to collect and
evaluate data about people in a detached manner, but that detachment
does nothing to ameliorate biases within all the social sciences that dic-
tate what is worthy of study, who are the examiners, and who are the
examined. The social sciences are thus confined to dabbling around,
Lynd (1939) argued, making minor changes within their individual fields
of study while maintaining the inequitable status quo. Alternatively, the
questions worthy of social science study according to Lynd (1939) are:
"What institutions support humankind's needs – and what ones block
them? And what changes in these institutions are indicated?" (Lynd,
1939, p. 201). We aim to explore movement and direction in the social
sciences with these provocative questions in mind, but that does not
mean our objective is to answer them.

The next issue we need to address regarding movement and direction in the social sciences is the concept of causation. Causation sits at
the center of the science half of the social sciences because without it all
we would have are interesting but untestable stories to describe human
behavior. Pearl's (2009) treatment of causation assists this endeavor and
readers are encouraged to inspect his work further because it cogently
presents behavioral analyses and explanations as well as statistical methods and formulations that support social science investigations into
causes. Pearl (2009) argues that the essence of causation that social
scientists are after is the ability to predict the consequences of actions
because the pact that exists between social scientists and policymakers
is that the social scientists generate this knowledge so policymakers can
use the knowledge in crafting policies that improve human well-being.
Equipped with such knowledge, policymakers are supposed to make
decisions that improve well-being. Pearl (2009) argued that discovering causes for effects, while challenging, can be done because causality
"can be understood in terms of simple processes" (p. 357). Paradoxically,
Pearl (2009) also highlighted the common roadblock to uncovering
causation because "scientists rarely consider the entirety of the universe
as an object of investigation. In most cases, the scientist carves out a
piece from the universe and proclaims that piece *in* and...the rest of the
universe is then considered *out*" (p. 350). Pearl's (2009) presentation of

causation is concerned with the inability to adequately reflect truth in such situations because the entirely of the universe is not included in the scope. While Pearl (2009) does not refer to this as bias, it does, however, reflect what Lynd (1939) referred to as bias.

Another caveat is necessary here before stepping into this chapter. Henrich, Heine, and Norenzayan (2010) described the conundrum caused by the fact that the majority of the social psychology data available that has been used for close to a century in determining what is normal for humans comes from what is labeled Western, educated, industrialized, rich, and democratic (WEIRD) societies. In fact, much of the data in the experimental branches of psychology, cognitive science, and economics, as well as other social sciences were collected in studies conducted on undergraduate students in the United States. This skewed body of data has been used to develop all manner of theories about how and why people behave as they do. But Henrich et al. (2010) describe in detail, the many ways in which these data are not representative of humans globally. With that forewarning in mind, we attempted to gather research that provides a global perspective.

HUMAN WELL-BEING

While human flourishing was the phrasing we used in Chapter 1, much of the research on the topic uses the term human well-being. To begin addressing this construct, we must first clarify what is meant by human well-being. While there is no universally accepted definition, organizations concerned about human well-being take great pains to discretely define it and measure it. Consequently, many terms are used by various organizations interested in the issue. For example, "quality of life, welfare, wellliving, living standards, utility, life satisfaction, prosperity, needs fulfilment, development, empowerment, capability expansion, human development, poverty, human poverty, and, more recently, happiness are often used interchangeably with well-being" (McGillivray & Clarke, 2007, p. 3). Many of the current configurations attempting to depict aggregated well-being of individuals in societies still tend to focus on income (McGillivray & Clarke, 2007). In contrast to a focus on national income measures, Krueger, Kahneman, Schkade, Swartz, and Stone (2009) advocated for measuring subjective well-being based on "time use and affective (emotional) experience" (p. 11) and the debates regarding their recommendations continue. Conceptualizing human well-being has shifted over time and King, Renó, and Novo (2014) provided a thorough chronological review of the approaches and indicators used from the late 1960s through the early 2010s to assess human well-being. More recently, Alexandrova (2016) reviewed the range of theories and constructs employed across the social sciences that contribute to the science of human well-being. The focus of this unavoidably brief discussion is on international measures used recently and alongside these human well-being measures are reports that humans' accumulated exploitation of the Earth's resources has put future human well-being at risk (Whitmee et al., 2015).

Emphasizing that human well-being and the well-being of the planet are interdependent, in 2000, the United Nations commissioned a global assessment they titled the "Millennium Ecosystem Assessment" which had the objective of assessing "the consequences of ecosystem change for human well-being and the scientific basis for action needed to enhance the conservation and sustainable use of those systems and their contribution to human well-being" (Hassan, Scholes, & Ash, 2005, p. vii). An ecosystem is a "dynamic complex of plant, animal, and microorganism communities and the nonliving environment interacting as a functional unit" (Hassan et al., 2005, p. vii). and their assessment addressed all types of ecosystems. Human well-being was operationalized to include the following:

> (1) basic material for good life: secure and adequate livelihoods, enough food at all times, shelter, clothing, and access to goods; (2) health: feeling well and having a healthy physical environment, such as clean air and access to clean water; (3) good social relations: social cohesion, mutual respect, and the ability to help others and provide for children; (4) security: secure access to natural and other resources, personal safety, and security from natural and human-made disasters; and (5) freedom of choice and action: the opportunity to achieve what an individual values doing and being. Freedom of choice and action is influenced by other constituents of well-being (as well as by other factors, notably education) and is also a precondition for achieving other components of well-being, particularly with respect to equity and fairness. (Hassan et al., 2005, p. vii)

Their findings concluded that "human activity is putting such strain on the natural functions of Earth that the ability of the planet's ecosystems to sustain future generations can no longer be taken for granted" (Hirsch, 2005, p. 5). Conversely, Raudsepp-Hearne et al. (2010) have argued that while there is evidence that human impact on the Earth has reduced human well-being in some places, "there is only weak evidence that declines in the global biosphere are reducing aggregate human well-being at the global scale" (p. 587). Taking an alternative perspective, with respect to specific scarce minerals used in the production of technologies, Lusty and Gunn (2014) made a case that while demand for those scarce minerals has increased driving the prices up, predictions of calamitous results from exhausting Earth's supply of those minerals are unfounded. They explained that based on the historical marketplace trends, innovations using alternative materials can be expected if nations continue investing in the necessary research (Lusty & Gunn, 2014). However, there are sustainability concerns regarding the continued production of greenhouse gas emissions from the mineral extraction processes. Lastly, they contend that most concerning is "a spectrum of nongeological issues, such as geopolitics, social and cultural issues, competition for land, resource nationalism and environmental challenges, [which] are likely to represent the largest obstacles to secure an adequate mineral supply" (Lusty & Gunn, 2014, p. 269).

Some researchers are interested in zeroing into ecosystem benefits to human well-being arguing that finer levels of analysis are helpful for examining human well-being in specific locations. For example, Coutts and Hahn (2015) reviewed a number of ways in which green infrastructure enhances human well-being. Green infrastructure is "an interconnected network of greenspace that conserves natural ecosystem values and functions and provides associated benefits to human populations" (Coutts & Hahn, 2015, p. 9770). Coutts and Hahn (2015) discussed the following ecosystem services provided by green infrastructure: water quantity and quality, food quantity and quality, air quality, infectious disease modulation, medicine, physical activity, mental health, and spiritual health.

There are other global human well-being assessments besides the Millennium Ecosystem Assessment. Drawing from the Gallup World Poll, Diener and Tay (2015) assessed the following six categories of human well-being in 163 nations:

(1) subjective well-being: life satisfaction, positive feelings and low negative feelings; (2) economic and material well-being; (3) physical health: longevity and lack of illnesses; (4) social and institutional well-being: social support, low corruption, honest elections and respect for others; (5)

quality of the natural environment: clean air, clean water and preserving the environment; and (6) equality: moderate and fair disparities in income and life satisfaction. (p. 136)

The total scores for each category and an average score for each nation were provided and the nations were listed in order from the highest average score to the lowest. The ten highest scoring nations were: Iceland, Norway, Switzerland, Denmark, Luxembourg, Sweden, Singapore, Netherlands, Australia, and New Zealand. The subjective well-being scores for some nations, like Paraguay, Mali, Comoros, Lesotho, and Kyrgyzstan, were quite high compared to their neighbors in the list, while their averages were all about the same (Diener & Tay, 2015). Those variations are worthy of further investigation within nations as they address their national priorities and balance their public policy priorities argued Diener and Tay (2015). Diener has focused on subjective well-being since the mid-1980s and has advocated for including subjective well-being in national human assessments of well-being and now over 40 nations include some measure of subjective well-being (Diener and Tay, 2015).

Another assessment of human well-being is the Sustainable Economic Development Assessment (SEDA) which is a measure applied country by country (Beal, Rueda-Sabater, Yong, & Heng, 2016). It is a diagnostic tool for evaluating human well-being that uses 44 indicators across the dimensions of: income, economic stability, employment, health, education, infrastructure, income equality, civil society, governance, and environment (Beal et al., 2016). The scores obtained in these dimensions are weighted to compute an overall score for a country. Infrastructure, income equality, civil society, and environment score were used as is and scores from the income, health, education, and governance were worth twice as much as those. Then, the economic stability and employment dimensions were worth half as much as those first scores. All of the complex SEDA scores are not explored in detail here. However, there are some key takeaways from their most recent report that apply to this chapter. "To understand how countries stack up in terms of well-being, and to see whether they are gaining ground or falling behind, it is helpful to examine both current level and recent-progress SEDA Scores" (Beal et al., 2016, p. 17). One of the scores they compute compares countries' current scores with the median of their scores from the last five years to provide an indicator of the movement and direction of each country's overall human well-being. Using those indicators, they classified countries into four simple categories: good but losing ground, good and improving, poor and losing ground, and poor but improving (Beal et al., 2016). Note that not all the countries for which they calculated scores were named in this categorization. Included in the "good but losing ground" group were Australia, Belgium, Canada, France, Germany, Greece, Japan, the Netherlands, Norway, Russia, South Korea, Sweden, Switzerland, the UK, and the US. Those in the "good and improving" group included: Bosnia and Herzegovina, Brazil, Malaysia, Poland, Saudi Arabia, and Turkey. Included in the "poor and improving" group were: Bangladesh, Democratic of the Congo, Ethiopia, India, Indonesia, Kenya, Peru, Myanmar, Philippines, Rwanda, Tanzania, Uganda, and Vietnam. Included in the "poor and losing ground" group were: Egypt, Iran, Pakistan, South Africa, and Thailand. Some countries' scores placed them at the crossover point between the categories. For example, Mexico exists halfway between "poor and losing ground" and "good and losing ground" and China exists at the halfway spot of "good and improving" and "good and losing ground" (Beal et al., 2016).

Another set of comparisons that the SEDA analysis included were countries' wealth-to-well-being ratio and their growth-to-well-being ratio. A nation's wealth-to-well-being score is the country's current SEDA score divided by the average worldwide ratio of overall SEDA score by country and per capita GDP (Bealet al., 2016). A nation's growth-to-well-being score is similarly computed using the countries' real GDP growth rates (Beal et al., 2016). Then, these two measures are plotted on a graph revealing how well nations are converting their wealth and growth into well-being for the people. Nations performing below average in converting wealth and growth into well-being for their people were: Democratic Republic of the Congo, Egypt, Greece, Italy, Malaysia, Mexico, Pakistan, Russia, South Africa, Thailand, Uganda, and the US. The last set of SEDA analyses that we want to mention here are the scores that address economic growth and the environment because "countries with faster economic growth tended to have much lower recent-progress scores in the environment" (Beal et al., 2016, p. 20).

The *World Happiness Report 2017* was the fifth year this report was produced (Helliwell, Layard, & Sachs, 2017) and it presents data compiled on 150 countries using data collected from 1000 individuals between the years 2014 and 2016. The survey asks individuals to

Please imagine a ladder, with steps numbered from 0 at the bottom to 10 at the top. The top of the ladder represents the best possible life for you and the bottom of the ladder represents the worst possible life for you. On which step of the ladder would you say you personally feel you stand at this time? (Helliwell et al., 2017, p. 9)

The report lists the 150 countries by the average scores computed from the surveys. The highest average score was 7.537 and the lowest score was 2.693. The top ten countries were: Norway, Denmark, Iceland, Switzerland, Finland, Netherlands, Canada, New Zealand, Australia, and Sweden. These were the same top ten countries in the previous year's report. Seventy countries scores improved from before the global recession to the most recent data collected from 2014 through 2016. The biggest gains were in Nicaragua, Latvia, and Sierra Leone as their scores all increased a little more than one point. Fifty-six nations' scores dropped during that same period with the largest drop in Venezuela, dropping one and a half points.

A similar measure computed globally for human well-being is called the "Happy Planet Index" which is intended to reflect how "well countries across the world are delivering long, happy lives for their populations" (Jeffrey, Wheatley, & Abdallah, 2016, p. 1). To calculate the scores for each nation, first, the average life expectancy scores for a nation are multiplied by the experienced well-being score for the nation. The experienced well-being scores are the same as calculated and used in the World Happiness Report discussed above. The resulting score is then multiplied by the inequality of outcomes measure for the nation. "The inequality of outcomes measure is the difference in the product of mean life satisfaction and mean experienced wellbeing, and the product of inequality-adjusted life satisfaction and inequality-adjusted experienced wellbeing, expressed as a percentage" (The New Economic Foundation, 2016, p. 2). That result is then divided by the "ecological footprint" for the nation, which is the average amount of land needed, per person, to sustain a typical country's consumption patterns" (The New Economic Foundation, 2016, p. 2). The 2016 resulting scores for 140 nations include Costa Rica, Mexico, Columbia, Vanuatu, Vietnam, Panama, Nicaragua, Bangladesh, Thailand, and Ecuador as the top scoring 10 nations. Locating the top nations that appear on the other lists discussed in this section finds Norway at spot number 12, Iceland at 39, Sweden at 61, New Zealand at 38, Denmark at 32, Ireland at 48, Canada at 85, Australia at 105, Finland at 37, and Switzerland at 24. In the 2016 report was the first year the scores were adjusted for the inequality within nations. The 2012 report as the top ten nations in 2012 were: Costa Rica, Vietnam, Colombia, Belize, El Salvador, Jamaica, Panama, Nicaragua, Venezuela, and Guatemala (Abdallah, Michaelson, Shah, Stoll, & Marks, 2012). Costa Rica was also the top listed nation in the 2009 report as well.

Another way to consider human well-being from a different angle can be gleaned from the work by Rutherford et al. (2017) examining the constitutions Rutherford et al. (2017) examining the constitutions of 194 nations. They also analyzed the timelines of amendments to those constitutions specifically looking for 234 provisions addressing specific issues or rights. Those issues or rights included the following social rights and the numbers in parentheses indicate the number of nations that currently address that right in their constitution:

- access to higher education (63),
- compulsory education (120),
- free education (136),
- limits on employment of children (79),
- protection of consumers (49),
- protection of environment (156),
- right to enjoy the benefits of science (25),
- right to equal pay for work (99),
- right to health care (134),
- right to join trade unions (149),
- right to reasonable standard of living (84),
- right to rest and leisure (80),
- right to safe work environment (87),
- right to shelter (74),
- right to strike (96),
- right to work (133),
- state support for children (110),
- state support for the disabled (129),
- state support for the elderly (120), and
- state support for the unemployed (62)

(Comparitive Constituions Project, 2017)

Rutherford et al. (2017) highlighted a process they found influenced constitutional change that they referred to as "hierarchical dependencies between legal provisions, under which the adoption of essential, fundamental provisions precedes more advanced provisions" (p. 2). Thus, it could be argued that as countries increase these rights they are moving to increase the well-being of their citizens.

Another similar, assessment of countries titled the *Democracy Index 2017* (The Economist Intelligence Unit, 2017) recently reported for their tenth year on the state of democracy for 165 independent states and two territories. The Democracy Index uses 60 indicators grouped into five categories: "electoral process and pluralism; civil liberties; the functioning of government; political participation; and political culture" (The Economist Intelligence Unit, 2017, p. 2). In the 2017 report, the scores for 89 countries dropped from their scores in 2016; the scores for 27 countries improved; and the remaining 51 countries' scores remained the same. The countries are also grouped into one of four categories in this report: 19 countries are classified as full democracies, 57 as flawed democracies, 39 as hybrid regimes, and 52 as authoritarian regimes (The Economist Intelligence Unit, 2017). The 10 countries with the highest scores were: Norway, Iceland, Sweden, New Zealand, Denmark, Ireland, Canada, Australia, Finland, and Switzerland. The United States dropped off the full democracy list in 2016 and joined those on the flawed democracy list and it remained in the flawed democracy category in 2017. Countries that changed positions in the listings in 2017 included The Gambia, which moved from the authoritarian regime to a hybrid regime and the one country that moved the most in the other direction was Indonesia which remained a flawed democracy but dropped 20 places in the global rankings (The Economist Intelligence Unit, 2017).

Inglehart's (2018) analysis of human well-being focused on the changing trends in terms of each nation's culture advancing an argument that mirrors the evidence and conclusions in the other studies addressed in this section that as "a society becomes economically more secure, more democratic and more tolerant – increasing its people's freedom of choice in how to live their lives – its people's subjective well-being level should rise" (p. 153). The last way of considering human well-being globally addressed in this section collapses all factors into one measure and is portrayed by the Doomsday Clock. Created in 1947, it "convey[s] threats to humanity and the planet" (Bulletin of the Atomic Scientists, 2017, p. 2). Every year since 1947, the "Bulletin's Science and Security

Board in consultation with its Board of Sponsors, which includes 15 Nobel laureates" decide whether to leave the minute hand where it is or to move it based on their assessment of the danger of "catastrophe from nuclear weapons, climate change, and new technologies emerging in other domains" (p. 2). In 1947, the clock was set to 7 minutes to midnight and since then it has been moved closer to and further away from midnight based on the Board's assessments. In the 2018 statement, the clock was set to 2 minutes to midnight because "world leaders failed to respond effectively to the looming threats of nuclear war and climate change, making the world security situation more dangerous than it was a year ago—and as dangerous as it has been since World War II" (p. 2). Their announcement describes in detail the transnational failures contributing to their decision. They also provided recommended actions for resetting the clock, emphasizing that "this is a dangerous time, but the danger is of our own making. Humankind has invented the implements of apocalypse; so can it invent the methods of controlling and eventually eliminating them" (Bulletin of the Atomic Scientists, 2017, p. 6).

Movement and direction regarding human well-being continues to focus on the interdependencies between human well-being and the well-being of the planet regardless of the measures used or the scope applied. The Rockefeller Foundation–*Lancet* Commission on planetary health argued that "solutions lie within reach and should be based on the redefinition of prosperity to focus on the enhancement of quality of life and delivery of improved health for all, together with respect for the integrity of natural systems" (Whitmee et al., 2015, p. 1974).

HUMAN DECISION-MAKING

Human well-being, individually and collectively, is impacted by human decision-making. Individual people make trillions of individual choices every day to impact their own well-being. Individual choices impact other people's lives as well and some choices have more impact on more peoples' lives than others. Choices made regarding what to purchase, where to live, whom to marry, whom to vote for, how to live, what to do for employment, and on and on collectively determine the well-being assessment results discussed in the previous section. Making decisions is something humans do constantly while they are conscious, and how we do that has been studied in many disciplines. In short, if humans could improve their individual and collective decision-making, they could improve their well-being. But before addressing some theories and research along that vein, we want to dispel the notion that human decision-making is largely unconscious. Newell and Shanks (2014) tackled the claim that human decision-making is largely unconscious, and they concluded that

> inadequate procedures for assessing awareness, failures to consider arti-
> factual explanations of "landmark" results, and a tendency to uncritically
> accept conclusions that fit with our intuitions have all contributed to
> unconscious influences being ascribed inflated and erroneous explanatory
> power in theories of decision making. (Newell & Shanks, 2014, p. 1)

Their review concluded with a recommendation that future research focus on tasks in which participants' attention is diverted away from the experimenter's hypothesis, rather than the highly reflective tasks that were often employed. Now we can explore some of the long-standing theories employed across social sciences to reveal their implications for movement and direction.

Public choice theory comes from economics and has been used in political science to explain how people make choices. Public choice theory has been around since 1948 and it rests on the rational actor theory. The rational actor theory is comprised of the following assumptions about how humans behave:

> (1) humans have sets of well-formed preferences which they can perceive,
> rank, and compare easily; (2) their preference orderings are transitive or
> logically consistent; (3) they always seek the biggest possible benefits and
> the least costs in their decisions; and (4) they are basically egoistic, self-re-
> garding, and instrumental in their behaviour, choosing how to act on the
> basis of the consequences for their personal welfare or that of their imme-
> diate family. (Dunleavy, 2013, p. 3)

The rational actor theory has been criticized for as long as it has been in existence. The theory is useless, argued Hodgson (2012), delineating the reasons that the rational actor theory is unfalsifiable and too general. Because it fits everything, it explains nothing, argued Hodgson (2012) and yet the "response of mainstream economists to these problems has largely to become immersed in the technicalities, rather than to give the economic agents at the core of the theory of human behaviour some real institutional and cultural flesh and blood" (p. 103).

Levine, Chan, and Satterfield (2015) argued that while there is general agreement that the long-standing rational actor theory is "descriptively misleading, and often insufficiently predictive" (p. 22), some of the outmoded assumptions embedded in the rational actor theory continue to persist in the social sciences. They described the "efficient complexity manager" (2015) model as a replacement for the rational actor model for the field of economics. The efficient complexity manager model that Levine et al. (2015) provided posits that humans are fundamentally aimed at efficiency. That means that humans invest the least amount of time possible in deciding on their actions. Humans are, therefore, constantly in what Levine et al. (2015) referred to as triage mode. This means that humans apply summarized analogies from their previous experiences to their current experience to determine if there is a match. In doing this analysis, people can view their situation through various lenses that focus their attention on some features more than others. Those lenses, according to the model are created by our goals (which we may not be conscious of) and our understanding of the options for achieving those goals in the situation. Deciding there is a match allows the person to begin enacting their predetermined behaviors tailored for the immediate situation drawn from their stored analogies (Levine et al., 2015).

Other theorists have criticized the rational choice theory and offered their alternatives. One of those alternatives is called regret theory and it does not replace the rational choice theory, rather it enhances it. Regret theory, as proffered by Loomes and Sugden (2015), has two fundamental assumptions about human decision-making: (1) people experience regret and rejoicing in conjunction with their choices when making decisions; and (2) people try to anticipate their reactions to the choices they are going to make and they use their expectations about their reactions when making choices under uncertainty. Loomes and Sugden (2015) further posited that their theory succeeds where rivals have stumbled because of its ability to adequately attend to accumulated evidence with simplicity. The simplicity of their theory may stem from their refusal to assume anything about the misperceptions by people in their decision-making. Loomes and Sugden (2015) explain that as economists their inclination is to explain as much human behavior as they can in terms of assumptions about rational and undeceived individuals.

Another approach related to public choice theory in studying human decision-making that comes from economics is referred to as game theory. Created in the 1940s (von Neumann & Morganstern, 2007), game theory used mathematical models to portray and predict complex human behavior. The components of game theory include the players of the game which are people who have preferences as they play the game while they are assumed to behave in accordance with the rational actor theory described above. A game has a structure or rules. Players chose strategies, based on the information they gather and analyze about other players, and games have outcomes. In the 1970s, the use of computers advanced game theory models. The game theory framework can be applied to human behavior and decision-making to block out a great deal of detail and foreground specific elements explaining their relationships with clarity. However, game theory, as originally expressed, over-simplified human behavior to the point of not really being very accurate nor useful (Shubik, 2001). Stirling and Felin (2013) addressed the limitations of game theory introducing a revised model that allows for players' preferences to be interdependently connected to the preferences of other individuals in the game. They claim that their model provides a "systematic approach for characterizing a complex society" (p. e56751).

The work by van den Bos, Jolles, and Homberg (2013) also demonstrated a concern for capturing the complexity of decision-making within social contexts. They examined human decision-making by focusing on the fact that the "social environment affects decisions, both via social interactions (e.g., social learning, cooperation, and competition) and social stress effects" (p. 1). They argued, that this aspect of decision-making has been long-neglected in human and animal studies. Additionally, based on the number of humans on the planet and the range of environments where we live, humans "are an exceptionally successful species" (van den Bos et al., 2013, p. 2). Therefore, the dominance of humans on Earth stems from the fact that we are social animals and the social context of human decision-making cannot be overlooked (van den Bos et al., 2013).

Humans are not the only social animals whose decisions are influenced by their social contexts. As readers will notice in Chapter 5, many animals are influenced by their social interactions in deciding where and when to move, where to make a home, where and when to look for food, what to eat, and where to seek out a mate. The social environment influences their decision-making processes and a great deal of learning by social animals is accomplished through observational learning (Zentall & Galef, 1988). Social learning theory argues that in circumstances where social learning produces outcomes increasing survivability for individuals, then individuals tend to conform to the behavior of the majority (van den Bos et al., 2013). The exact behavior does not matter, whatever the majority is doing is what most of the individuals will emulate. In a model that van den Bos and Lind (2013) provided to address this tendency, humans are positioned as trying to decide among many options to respond in their surroundings. Their model begins with an unusual or novel experience for an individual which is something that the person tries to make sense of. This appraisal–inhibition model offered by van den Bos and Lind (2013) contrasts sharply with the rational actor theory view of human behavior discussed previously in this chapter. The appraisal–inhibition model portrays people as "frequently busy appraising what is going on in their social surroundings and how to behave in [their] surroundings" (van den Bos & Lind, 2013, p. 43). The main function of the behavioral inhibition system is to grab a person's attention and trigger them to examine what is happening and make sense of it, assuming that most people prefer to behave in prosocial ways, that is, they want to help other people (van den Bos & Lind, 2013). However, these same people refrain from behaving in prosocial ways in public when no one else does. That is, according to van den Bos and Lind's (2013) model, people only act on their desire to help others when that is the dominant social norm.

Social norms operate in all human groups and humans abide by social norms much of the time without thinking about them consciously (Fehr & Fischbacher, 2004; Ostrom, 2000; Posner & Rasmusen, 1999; Sherif, 1965). Ostrom (2000) succinctly summarized the research that supports the understanding that "modern humans have inherited a propensity to learn social norms" (p. 143). Thus, it was evolutionarily beneficial for humans who had a neural rule for learning and complying with social norms. This depiction is supported by Bicchieri's (2006) work on social norms as well. Moreover, specific kinds of social norms evolved. For example, if most people in a group are cooperating, people tend to cooperate, and they tend to only defect when defecting behavior becomes the norm (Fehr & Fischbacher, 2004). Even though people don't realize it, they are always examining the social norms operating around them (Hechter & Opp, 2001).

Nyborg et al. (2016) discussed how abrupt changes in human social norms have contributed in the past to striking large-scale transformations and suggest that attending to the processes that create and maintain human social norms is a useful strategy for addressing "climate change, biodiversity loss, antibiotic resistance, and other global challenges posing major collective action problems" (p. 42). A recently completed analysis of human decision-making applying a norms perspective was conducted by Beckage et al. (2018) in examining human behavioral impacts on forecasted climate change. They hypothesized the risk that people perceive in extreme climate events influences their behavioral changes and those behaviors can modify greenhouse gas emissions (Beckage et al., 2018). To test their hypothesis, they connected the Climate Rapid Overview and Decision Support (C-ROADS) climate model to a social model to examine how interactions between perceived risks associated with severe weather events projected climate change. The C-ROADS was designed to "build shared understanding of climate dynamics in a way that is solidly grounded in the best available science and rigorously non-partisan, yet understandable by and useful to non-specialists, from policymakers to the public" (Sterman et al., 2012, p. 296). C-ROADS is a simulation tool that supports interactive learning, allowing users to discover on their own how climate change, which is a complex system, behaves (Sterman et al., 2012). Beckage et al. (2018) developed what they referred to as a "Climate Social Model" (p. 80) by coupling the C-ROADS model with the theory of planned behavior from psychology. Put simply, the theory of planned behavior argues that human behavior is influenced by peoples' (1) attitudes about the behavior, (2) the social norms they are aware of about that behavior, and (3) the amount of control they perceive they have over their behavior (Beckage et al., 2018). These researchers focused on the perceptions that people can develop about the risks from extreme weather events and their perceptions of social norms for emission-reducing behaviors.

Using their "Climate Social Model," Beckage et al. (2018) ran 766,656 simulations setting the model to predict the mean temperature rise by the year 2100 and compared their results to running C-ROADS alone. Before addressing the results of their simulations, some details about how social norms operate in their model is essential. According to the climate social model developed by Beckage et al. (2018), when an extreme weather event occurs, like Hurricane Sandy, for example, people take that information in and combine it with their memories of previous extreme weather events and they develop a sense of the amount of risk there is due to climate change. This perceived risk feeds their attitude about themselves doing things that can reduce emissions of greenhouse gases. Their perceptions about the extent to which their behaviors can change greenhouse gas emissions also impact their attitudes. Then, their attitude along with their perceptions of the social norms and their perceived ability to perform the behavior impacts their choices regarding behaviors that can adjust greenhouse gas emissions. Beckage et al. (2018) used their model to examine the impact of human risk perception and associated behavioral changes. The C-ROADS model alone predicted a 4.9 degree (Celsius) temperature increase by the year 2100. The simulation runs using their Climate Social Model, resulted in temperature increases by the year 2100 ranging from 3.4 to 6.2 degrees (Celsius). The 3.4 end of these results seems promising because they indicate that people can change their behavior to reduce greenhouse gas emissions to slow climate change. The lowest temperature increase prediction resulted from moderate-to-high values of both the perceived ability to perform the behavior and the perception that the behavior is commonly performed or approved of by others (Beckage et al., 2018). The highest temperature increase prediction was created by moderate-to-high values of the perceived ability to perform the behavior and low values of the perception that the behavior is commonly performed or approved of by others (Beckage et al., 2018). Thus, their model demonstrated how these two variables associated with social norms were vital to slowing climate change.

Another approach to examining human decision-making taking us in a different direction comes from Argrawal and Sharda's (2013) work. They argued that quantum mechanics are needed in psychology as well as in economics and finance to help analyze, explain, and understand human decision-making. They admitted that they advocated for applying only some aspects quantum mechanics and they did not claim that the human mind is a quantum mechanical object. A quantum mechanical object has characteristics of both particles and waves and subatomic particles are quantum mechanical objects. Quantum mechanics are explained in relation to classical mechanics. Explanations follow a chronology focusing first on the discovery that the human-created classical mechanics did not adequately describe, explain, and predict subatomic phenomena observed in experiments. The explanation of quantum mechanics continues in relation to classical mechanics and Landau and Lifshits (1977) argued four decades ago that "it is in principle impossible, to formulate the basic concepts of quantum mechanics without using classical mechanics" (p. 2). After explaining their caveats, Argrawal and Sharda (2013) applied some quantum mechanics to the math of some game theory equations from some experiments done with undergraduates at Stanford University demonstrating that the game theory mathematical equations can account for some, but not all of the complexity of human decision-making phenomena.

An intriguing proposition from Wolf, Kurvers, Ward, Krause, and Krause (2013) demonstrated mathematically that "a simple quorum decision rule allows decision-makers in groups to increase true positives and decrease false positives simultaneously" (p. 3). Their model works for binary decisions, such as taking action or not taking action because some condition exists or does not exist. Thus, true positives are when people decide to act, and the condition did exist in the situation. False positives, of course, are decisions to act when the condition did not exist. To achieve the improved decision-making results they described, groups need to first obtain the rates of false positives and true positives that each individual in the group generates for just the one kind of decision that they are interested in. Then, the group would need to calculate the average probabilities for the false positives and the true positives for the group. Prepared with these data, the group would then choose a point midway between their average false positive and their average true positive point to improve their group decision-making. Collecting that data would be daunting for any group. Furthermore, a key assumption in Wolf et al. (2013) model is that there is sufficient independence between group members' decisions because if all the group members' perceptions about their situations are alike, there is no value to group decision-making. Additionally, their modeling assumes that the individuals in a group do not vary in their experience dealing with the issue at hand, or their tendency to want to lead a group, or other characteristics (Wolf, et al. 2013). Those assumptions coupled with the near impossible data collection challenge have reduced the likelihood of studies empirically testing this model.

HUMAN MEANING-MAKING

Postman and Weingartner (1969) were professors of education who explained their views on the human mind as an always active organ rather than the way the human mind had often been conceptualized within the field of education as a static noun. They explained:

We prefer the metaphor "meaning making" to most of the metaphors of the mind that are operative in the schools. It is, to begin with, much less static than the others. It stresses a process view of minding, including the fact that "minding" is undergoing constant change. "Meaning making" also forces us to focus on the individuality and the uniqueness of the meaning *maker*. (Postman & Weingartner, 1969, p. 91)

They used the verb "minding" to refer to the process of humans using their minds while conscious. It referred to everything going on in the human mind. Contrastingly, many common descriptions of what the human nervous system is and does read like the following. The nerves in the body gather information from the environment and send that data to the brain, which makes sense of that data, and the brain controls the body's responses to the environment. This simple model exists in introductory psychology courses, in high school biology classes, and on thousands of public-serving websites. Using recent research evidence, Clark (2016) argued for a different understanding of what the human nervous system does, explaining that human perception is not a process of gathering and making sense of sensory inputs. As Clark (2016) explained it, "to perceive the world is to meet the sensory signal with an apt stream of multilevel predictions" (Clark 2016, p. 6). What that means is that the human brain is constantly predicting then comparing its prediction to the incoming data parsing out the expected vs the unexpected and acting on the difference. The gap is what the human brain attends to the most, not the incoming data. The human brain is constantly predicting and refining its predictions explained Clark (2016).

Understanding at a fundamental level that this is how human brains operate has far-reaching implications. Humans are not making meaning by collecting and analyzing data from our surroundings. Instead, we are constantly, at the fundamental and conceptual levels, trying to "get it right" by creating and applying our preconceived understandings onto our experiences (Clark 2016). The model of the human brain as a prediction engine attending only to the gaps identified between its predictions and the analyzed data, is one that values efficiency over accuracy; and efficient processing reduces energy consumption (Clark 2016). If the data input and processing model of the human brain was one wherein the brain is conceived of as a central processor passively receiving and processing data moving to it, Clark's (2016) work shatters that image.

Rather, the human brain is actively imposing its predictions onto the experiences and only attending to the identified gaps. This model also highlights the role that uncertainty plays because the gaps between the predictions and the perceptions are uncertainty. Thus, uncertainty and eliminating it is what the human brain efficiently attends to.

Two varieties of uncertainty, namely, informational uncertainty and personal uncertainty are addressed by van den Bos (2009) who argued that personal uncertainty is more important to "understanding self-regulation and existential sense-making" (p. 198). He defined personal uncertainty as "a subjective sense of doubt or instability in self-views, worldviews, or the interrelation between the two" (p. 198). Informational uncertainty, contrastingly, can be tackled collectively and collaboratively as demonstrated by Wolf et al. (2013) mathematical model addressing collective decision-making which was discussed in the previous section. At the core of personal uncertainty, the understanding that van den Bos (2009) relied on was that it is an unpleasant feeling people work to avoid. Therefore, van den Bos (2009), concluded, people prefer "to live under the illusion of personal certainty" (p. 201). The pressure to maintain their illusions, argued van den Bos (2009), is so strong that an uncertainty management framework would be an apt model for explaining all human sense-making and meaning-making. The implications of such a model would include a shift in how sense-making and meaning-making research experiments are designed and conducted, van den Bos (2009) maintained. One such shift would include measures of participants' personal uncertainty levels in sense-making research experiments.

Whitson and Galinsky's (2008) results align well with the work of van den Bos (2009) who has examined personal uncertainty for decades. Whitson and Galinsky (2008) found that "the need to be and feel in control is so strong that individuals will produce a pattern from noise to return the world to a predictable state" (p. 117). In this case, "noise" refers to meaningless content. Whitson and Galinsky (2008) came to this conclusion after conducting experiments with individuals to determine the likelihood that a feeling of a lack of control is related to personal uncertainty. Whitson and Galinsky (2008) were interested in whether the lack of feeling in control increased participants' descriptions of perceiving something coherent and meaningful in what they were presented in the experiments which consisted only of random stimuli. In the experiments, participants engaged with several types of stimuli.

One used images of very small randomly placed black and white dots. Another experiment provided the participants with stories about companies' financial performance and another set of the experiments asked questions about stories the participants read to determine whether the participants developed superstitious beliefs about the behaviors and outcomes in the stories (Whitson & Galinsky, 2008). The experience of loss of control for the participants in Whitson and Galinsky's (2008) experiments were correlated with their claims that they perceived a pattern where none existed. Interpreting these results within Clark's (2016) explanation of how human brain's functions leaves us with an image demonstrating how powerfully the human brain creates inaccurate perceptions.

FINAL THOUGHTS

The objective of this chapter was to explore some theories and research to uncover some ways in which movement and direction operates in the social sciences. Admittedly, many theories have not been discussed. Rather, we focused on national or global measures of well-being and these have changed over time. Additionally, it discussed the implementation of national and international initiatives that impact human well-being and some ways these can be measured. Unfortunately, even as disparities between individuals or groups within countries becomes more common (Alexandrova 2016), current models do not adequately address economic disparities and vulnerable populations (Rao, van Ruijven, Riahi, & Bosetti, 2017).

One of the large-scale impacts on human well-being is climate change. Because "climate scientists overwhelmingly agree that humans are causing recent global warming" (Cook et al., 2016, p. 1), the movements and directions of the various contributions to climate change as well as efforts to slow or alter those drivers are measured and tracked increase. At the individual level, there are several websites that enable anyone with access to the internet to enter data about their energy use to calculate their contributions. These tools typically also allow individuals to enter speculative entries to see the impact that their individual decisions to change their individual behavior can have on their energy consumption. What is missing from these tools is a comprehensive portrayal of both an individual's contributions to climate change as well as the risks to their well-being from climate change. For example, the kinds of impacts analyzed and presented by Hsiang et al. (2017) at the county level within the United Statesare not integrated with those simple online tools calculating energy expenditures by household. The conclusions presented by Hsiang et al. (2017) project decreases in crop yields as well as increases in mortality rates and violent crime rates county-by-county in the United Statesand their data inform the interactive maps presented on the Climate Impact Lab website (http://www.impactlab.org). However, the interactive functionality to view the detailed projections of impacts beyond temperature is not yet operational on their website. Additionally, there is no capacity for individuals to enter their own data and speculate on changes they could make in their lives. For many individuals, the risks due to climate change on their well-being may seem impossible to calculate and that lack of clarity regarding the risks for individuals. Thus, making sense of the risks of climate change in individual lives and deriving actionable changes from those analyses remains elusive for many.

At the global level, work continues in the area of risk assessment and management. For example, in 2012, the Intergovernmental Panel on Climate Change released their *Managing the Risks of Extreme Events and Disasters to Advance Climate Change Adaptation Special Report* (Field et al., 2012) which was compiled by specialists in disaster recovery, disaster risk management, and disaster risk reduction who worked with experts in climate change. These individuals invested over two years assessing information and writing their report in which they explain that "mitigation of climate change" was not the focus of their report (Field et al., 2012, p. 4). Rather their report accepts disasters and focused on dealing with them. However, their report included the following implications for sustainable development:

- Actions that range from incremental steps to transformational changes are essential for reducing risk from climate extremes.
- Social, economic, and environmental sustainability can be enhanced by disaster risk management and adaptation approaches. A prerequisite for sustainability in the context of climate change is addressing the underlying causes of vulnerability, including the structural inequalities that create and sustain poverty and constrain access to resources.
- The most effective adaptation and disaster risk reduction actions are those that offer development benefits in the relatively near term, as well as reductions in vulnerability over the longer term.
- Progress toward resilient and sustainable development in the context of changing climate extremes can benefit from questioning assumptions

and paradigms and stimulating innovation to encourage new patterns of response.

• The interactions among climate change mitigation, adaptation, and disaster risk management may have a major influence on resilient and sustainable pathways. (Field et al., 2012, p. 20)

Similarly, the World Health Organization held a workshop in Italy in 2013 to share and document experiences in the management and communication of environmental risks. Their resulting key messages were:

• The public is among the key stakeholders that should be involved in risk communication from the outset and can contribute to the assessment and management of risk.
• Information needs to be reframed to be understood by a lay audience.
• Essential elements for effective risk communication are information quality, transparency, simplicity and coherence of messages, receptivity to public concerns, and timing.
• Multisectoral and multi-stakeholder involvement are essential for communicating risk.
• Communication approaches should be based on a clear methodology, be participatory and integrate sociological methods into traditional public health-oriented ones.
• Communication vehicles such as the social media, when used correctly, promote a sharing aspect that creates a sense of active communication.
• A sense of "outrage" can distort risk perception. Outrage plays an important role in the policy debate.
• Uncertainty should be acknowledged as a central component in the management of environmental risks.
• Communication of risk should be embedded within scientific studies from the outset.
• Capacity-building is needed in the area of risk communication. (Theakston, 2013, pp. 50–52)

Complicating the conversation regarding risk assessment and management are the interdisciplinary translations necessary to address risks in an integrated fashion. Referring specifically to the work of the IPCC, Huggel et al. (2013) argued that risks are not conceptualized in a common way by climate scientists and risk management researchers which restricts their ability to amalgamate their results which results less useful data conveyed to the public. They proposed an integrated risk framework in which risk is defined as "as a function of the probability of occurrence of an extreme weather event and the associated consequences, with consequences being a function of the intensity of the physical weather event, the exposed assets and their vulnerabilities" (Huggel et al., 2013, p. 696). But perhaps, the underlying problem stems from applying economic models to human complex behavior. Urry (2015) summarized the challenges of using such models to analyze and quantify the impact of climate change:

> [The] problem in economic models is that most of the time people do not behave as individually rational economic consumers, maximizing their utility from the basket of goods and services they purchase and use. People are creatures of social routine and habit. These routines stem from the many ways that people are locked into social practices and social institutions, including families, households, friendship groups, social classes, genders, work groups, businesses, schools, ethnicities, age cohorts, nations and so on. It is these institutions that organize and structure people's lives. Buying and using goods and services help to constitute these institutions and their typical social practices and itis such practices that are the very stuff of life. (p. 47)

Models for analyzing the complex impacts of climate change on human well-being other than economic models exist. For example, Miller (2009) argued that constructal theory[1] could "become a powerful tool for solving problems of global security and sustainability" and its obscurity among the researchers working on these global problems is one of the major reasons it is not being used there.

It is tempting here to begin discussing leadership since it is highly relevant to the topics in this chapter. However, we will first review movement and directions and the frames for them that are used when studying nonhuman animals and we apply a critical lens as discussed in Chapter 1. That analysis may reveal hegemonic value structures worthy of attention.

---

[1] The Constructal Law or Theory: "for a finite-size system to persist in time (to live), it must evolve in such a way that it provides easier access to the imposed (global) currents that flow through it" (Bejan, 1997, p. 815). This theory has been applied in aesthetics as well and it is explored more fully in Chapter 7.

REFERENCES

Abdallah, S., Michaelson, J., Shah, S., Stoll, L., & Marks, N. (2012). *The happy planet index*. London: The New Economc Foundation.

Agrawal, P. M., & Sharda, R. (2013). OR forum—Quantum mechanics and human decision making. *Operations Research, 61*(1), 1–16. https://doi.org/10.1287/opre.1120.1068.

Alexandrova, A. (2016). Science of well-being. In G. Fletcher (Ed.), *The routledge handbook of philosophy of well-being* (pp. 389–401). New York, NY: Routledge.

Beal, D., Rueda-Sabater, E., Yong, S. E., & Heng, S. L. (2016). *The private-sector opportunity to improve well-being: The 2016 sustainable economic development assessment*. Boston, MA: The Boston Consulting Group.

Beckage, B., Gross, L. J., Lacasse, K., Carr, E., Metcalf, S. S., Winter, J. M., et al. (2018). Linking models of human behaviour and climate alters projected climate change. *Nature Climate Change, 8*, 79–85. https://doi.org/10.1038/s41558-017-0031-7.

Bejan, A. (1997). Constructal-theory network of conducting paths for cooling a heat generating volume. *International Journal of Heat and Mass Transfer, 40*(4), 799–811. https://doi.org/10.1016/0017-9310(96)00175-5.

Bicchieri, C. (2006). *The grammar of society: The nature and dynamics of social norms*. New York, NY: Cambridge University Press.

Bulletin of the Atomic Scientists. (2017, January 25). *2018 Doomsday Clock Statement*. Retrieved from Bulletin of the Atomic Scientists. http://thebulletin.org.

Clark, A. (2016). *Surfing uncertainty: Prediction, action, and the embodied mind*. New York, NY: Oxford University Press.

Comparitive Constituions Project. (2017). Retrieved from the comparitive constituions project. https://www.constituteproject.org/search?lang=en.

Cook, J., Oreskes, N., Doran, P. T., Anderegg, W. R., Verheggen, B., Maibach, E. W., … Rice, K. (2016). Consensus on consensus: A synthesis of consensus estimates on human-caused global warming. *Environmental Research Letters, 11*. https://doi.org/10.1088/1748-9326/11/4/048002.

Coutts, C., & Hahn, M. (2015). Green infrastructure, ecosystem services, and human health. *International Journal of Environmental Research and Public Health, 12*, 9768–9798. https://doi.org/10.3390/ijerph120809768.

Diener, E., & Tay, L. (2015). Subjective well-being and human welfare around the world as reflected in the Gallup World Poll. *International Journal of Psychology, 50*(2), 135–149. https://doi.org/10.1002/ijop.12136.

Dunleavy, P. (2013). *Democracy, bureaucracy and public choice: Economic explanations in political science*. New York, NY: Routledge.

Fehr, E., & Fischbacher, U. (2004). Social norms and human cooperation. *Trends in Cognitive Sciences, 8*(4), 185–190. https://doi.org/10.1016/j.tics.2004.02.007.

Field, C. B., Barros, V., Stocker, T. F., Dahe, Q., Dokken, D. J., Ebi, K. L., et al. (Eds.). (2012). *Managing the risks of extreme events and disasters to advance climate change adaptation.* New York, NY: Cambridge University Press.

Hassan, R., Scholes, R., & Ash, N. (Eds.). (2005). *Ecosystems and human well-being: Current state and trends* (Vol. 1). Washington, DC: Island Press.

Hechter, M., & Opp, K.-D. (Eds.). (2001). *Social norms.* New York, NY: Russell Sage Foundation.

Helliwell, J., Layard, R., & Sachs, J. (Eds.). (2017). *World happiness report.* New York, NY: Sustainable Development Solutions Network.

Henrich, J., Heine, S. J., & Norenzayan, A. (2010). The weirdest people in the world? *Behavioral and Brain Sciences, 33,* 61–135. https://doi.org/10.1017/S0140525X0999152X.

Hirsch, T. (2005). *Living beyond our means: Natural assets and human well-being—Statement from the board.* Washington, DC: Island Press.

Hodgson, G. M. (2012). On the limits of rational choice theory. *Economic Thought, 1*(94), 94–108.

Hsiang, S., Kopp, R., Jina, A., Rising, J., Delgado, M., Mohan, S., et al. (2017). Estimating economic damage from climate change in the United States. *Science, 356*(6345), 1362–1369. https://doi.org/10.1126/science.aal4369.

Huggel, C., Stone, D., Auffhammer, M., & Hansen, G. (2013). Loss and damage attribution. *Nature Climate Change, 3,* 694–696. https://doi.org/10.1038/nclimate1961.

Inglehart, R. F. (2018). *Cultural evolution: People's motivations are changing and reshaping the world.* Cambridge, MA: Cambridge University Press.

Jeffrey, K., Wheatley, H., & Abdallah, S. (2016). *The happy planet index.* London: New Economics Foundation.

King, M. F., Renó, V. F., & Novo, E. M. (2014). The concept, dimensions, and methods of assessment of human well-being within a sociological context: A literature review. *Social Indicators Research, 116,* 681–698. https://doi.org/10.1007/s11205-013-0320-0.

Krueger, A. B., Kahneman, D., Schkade, D., Swartz, N., & Stone, A. A. (2009). National time accounting: The currency of life. *Measuring the subjective well-being of nations: National accounts of time use* (pp. 1–86). Chicago, IL: University of Chicago Press.

Landau, L. D., & Lifshits, E. M. (1977). *Quantum mechanics: Non-relativistic theory* (3rd ed.). New York, NY: Pergamon Press.

Levine, J., Chan, K. M., & Satterfield, T. (2015). From rational actor to efficient complexity manager: Exorcising the ghost of homo economicus with a unified

synthesis of cognition research. *Ecological Economics, 114,* 22–32. https://
doi.org/10.1016/j.ecolecon.2015.03.010.

Loomes, G., & Sugden, R. (2015). Regret theory: An alternative theory of
rational choice under uncertainty. *The Economic Journal, 125,* 513–532.
https://doi.org/10.1111/ecoj.12200.

Lusty, P. A., & Gunn, A. G. (2014, June 23). Challenges to global mineral
resource security and options for future supply. *Special Publications.* London:
Geological Society. https://doi.org/10.1144/sp393.13.

Lynd, R. S. (1939). *Knowledge for what: The place of social science in American
culture.* Princeton, NJ: Princeton University Press.

McGillivray, M., & Clarke, M. (2007). Human well-being: Concepts and measures. In M. McGillivray, M. Clarke, & M. Smyth (Eds.), *Understanding
human well-being: Insights and experiences* (pp. 3–15). Tokyo: United Nations
Press.

Miller, W. O. (2009). Developing constructal theory as a tool for global security
and sustainability. In A. Bejan, S. Lorente, & A. Miguel (Eds.), *Constructal
human dynamics, security and sustainability* (pp. 49–60). Amsterdam: IOS
Press. https://doi.org/10.3233/978-1-58603-959-2-49.

Newell, B. R., & Shanks, D. R. (2014). Unconscious influences on decision
making: A critical review. *Behavioral and Brain Sciences, 34,* 1–61. https://
doi.org/10.1017/S0140525X12003214.

Nyborg, K., Anderies, J. M., Dannenberg, A., Lindahl, T., Schill, C., Schlüter,
M., ..., Carpenter, S. (2016). Social norms as solutions: Policies may influence large-scale behavioral tipping. *Science, 354*(6308), 42–43. https://doi.
org/10.1126/science.aaf8317.

Ostrom, E. (2000). Collective action and the evolution of social norms. *The
Journal of Economic Perspectives, 14*(3), 137–158. https://doi.org/10.1257/
jep.14.3.137.

Pearl, J. (2009). *Causality: Models, reasoning, and inference* (2nd ed.). New York,
NY: Cambridge University Press.

Posner, R. A., & Rasmusen, E. B. (1999). Creating and enforcing norms, with
special reference to sanctions. *International Review of Law and Economics,
19*(3), 369–382. https://doi.org/10.1016/S0144-8188(99)00013-7.

Postman, N., & Weingartner, C. (1969). *Teaching as a subversive activity.* New
York, NY: Dell.

Rao, N. D., van Ruijven, B. J., Riahi, K., & Bosetti, V. (2017). Improving poverty and inequality modelling in climate research. *Nature Climate Change, 7,*
857–862. https://doi.org/10.1038/s41558-017-0004-x.

Raudsepp-Hearne, C., Peterson, G. D., Tengö, M., Bennett, E. M., Holland, T.,
Benessaiah, K., ..., Pfeifer, L. (2010). Untangling the environmentalist's paradox:

Why is human well-being increasing as ecosystem services degrade. *BioScience,* *60*(8), 576–589. https://doi.org/10.1525/bio.2010.60.8.4.

Rutherford, A., Lupu, Y., Cebrian, M., Rahwan, I., LeVeck, B., & Garcia-Herranz, M. (2017). *Inferring mechanisms for global constitutional progress.* Retrieved from Cornell University Library: arXiv:1606.04012v3 [physics. soc-ph].

Sherif, M. (1965). *The psychology of social norms.* New York, NY: Octagon Books.

Shubik, M. S. (2001). Game theory and operations research: Some musings 50 years later (Yale Som Working Paper No. ES-14). Yale School of Management. https://doi.org/10.2139/ssrn.271029.

Sterman, J., Fiddaman, T., Franck, T., Jones, A., McCauley, S., Rice, P., ..., Siegel, L. (2012). Climate interactive: The C-ROADS climate policy model. *System Dynamics Review, 28*(3), 295–305. https://doi.org/10.1002/sdr.1474.

Stirling, W. C., & Felin, T. (2013). Game theory, conditional preferences, and social influence. *PLoS One, 8*(2), e56751. https://doi.org/10.1371/journal. pone.0056751.

The Economist Intelligence Unit. (2017). *Democracy index 2017: Free speech under attack.* New York, NY: The Economist Intelligence Unit.

The New Economic Foundation. (2016). *Happy planet methods paper.* London, UK: The New Economic Foundation.

Theakston, F. (Ed.). (2013). *Health and the environment: Communicating the risks.* Copenhagen: World Health Organization.

Urry, J. (2015). Climate Change and Society. In J. Michie & C. L. Cooper (Eds.), *Why the social sciences matter* (pp. 45–59). New York, NY: Palgrave Macmillan.

van den Bos, K. (2009). Making sense of life: The existential self trying to deal with personal uncertainty. *Psychological Inquiry, 20,* 197–217. https://doi. org/10.1080/10478400903333411.

van den Bos, K., & Lind, E. A. (2013). On sense-making reactions and public inhibition of benign social motives: An appraisal model of prosocial behavior. *Advances in Experimental Social Psychology, 48,* 1–58. https://doi. org/10.1016/B978-0-12-407188-9.00001-6.

van den Bos, R., Jolles, J. W., & Homberg, J. R. (2013). Social modulation of decision-making: A cross-species review. *Frontiers in Human Neuroscience, 7.* https://doi.org/10.3389/fnhum.2013.00301.

von Neumann, J., & Morganstern, O. (2007). *Theory of games and economic behavior: 60th anniversary edition.* Princeton, NJ: Princeton University Press.

Whitmee, S., Haines, A., Beyrer, C., Boltz, F., Capon, A. G., de Souza Dias, B. F., ..., Yach, D. (2015). Safeguarding human health in the Anthropocene epoch: Report of the Rockefeller Foundation-Lancet Commission. *The Lancet, 386,* 1973–2028. https://doi.org/10.1016/S0140-6736(15)60901-1.

Whitson, J. A., & Galinsky, A. D. (2008). Lacking control increases illusory pattern perception. *Science, 322*(5898), 115–117. https://doi.org/10.1126/science.1159845.

Wolf, M., Kurvers, R. H., Ward, A. J., Krause, S., & Krause, J. (2013). Accurate decisions in an uncertain world: Collective cognition increases true positives while decreasing false positives. In *Proceedings of the Royal Society, 280*. https://doi.org/10.1098/rspb.2012.2777.

Zentall, T. R., & Galef, B. G., Jr. (Eds.). (1988). *Social learning: Psychological and biological perspectives*. New York, NY: Psychology Press.

CHAPTER 5

Exploring Movement and Direction in Animal Science

Introduction

We argue that critical leadership must be based on science, not folklore and myths. Concurrent with this argument is our assertion that we must move away from imagery of non-human animals as more savage, less intelligent, less advanced, or contrastingly possessing special powers. The non-human animal behavior addressed in this chapter is not mere imagery. In this chapter we journey through representative animal research to examine how movement and direction is studied.

Leadership is one of the many subject areas that has interlaced and embedded in it many inaccurate layperson misunderstandings, myths, and conflicting notions. In that sense, it is similar to human understanding of the evolution of our own species. Why humans exist and how our species evolved is something studied in universities around the globe, and yet current adult understandings employed are always layered atop nascent beliefs established years prior. One such explanation is that human animals exist to manage and govern all other animals by virtue of our advanced status in the animal kingdom. This notion positions humans as the most advanced animals. However, Gee (2013) dispels the notion that evolution of any species is an "inevitable and inexorable improvement from the past to the future" (p. 42) and provides an explanation for why the evolution of species *seems* to have progressed from less complex to more complex.

© The Author(s) 2018   107
J. L. S. Chandler and R. E. Kirsch, *Critical Leadership Theory*,
https://doi.org/10.1007/978-3-319-96472-0_5

My contention therefore is that the seeming rise in complexity hides a deeper truth—evolution is not just about gain, but about loss. Once one gets away from the idea that evolution does not, in its own nature, demand an increase in complexity, one can see that any apparent increase in overall complexity is driven by a loss of complexity among the individual components that make up the whole. This makes sense once you think of natural selection not as a driver of improvement as a matter of destiny, but the sum of all those circumstances that keep a creature alive only according to its present needs. Natural selection will ensure that organisms will do just enough—and no more—to exploit an advantage, however minuscule, for their progeny ... There is a selective advantage, therefore, in being as simple as possible. (Gee, 2013, p. 46)

Gee (2013) continues his argument that through evolution individual species lost complexity (i.e., became simpler) and organisms live symbiotically or parasitically intertwined to result in seemingly more complex organisms on the surface. One example of the symbiotic and parasitic symbiosis that human lives rely on are the trillions of microbes living in every human gut of up to 1000 species of bacteria, many of which it is theorized, we cannot thrive without. Peering into the current research aims among the human gut biome research community, reveals that

Over the last decade, the perception of the gut has experienced a substantial paradigm shift. The gut acquired physiological roles that go well beyond classical characteristics of a bioreactor. The ensemble of the gut microbes were lifted to the status of a 'new organ' of the human body which plays crucial roles for human physiology. (Brüssow, 2016, p. 554)

Let's think through this. The DNA of the "new organ" referred to consists of the DNA of the represented bacteria, not the DNA of the host, and yet the suggestion is for the purposes of furthering research, that the bacteria be collectively considered an organ of the host's. The language used in the human microbiome project mirrors the understanding that, "we are supraorganisms composed of human and microbial components" (Turnbaugh et al., 2007, p. 804).

A few more myths deserve to be shattered here as well. There is a misconception that organisms have a desire, need, or are compelled to become more complex. But natural selection does not have foresight. The phrase "survival of the fittest" is used synonymously with natural selection and that phrase is incomplete and misleading (Smith & Sullivan, 2007). Survival is only one component of selection and fitness does not simply refer to the biggest, fastest, or strongest. Fitness is an organism's likelihood of reproducing and it is in constant flux because it represents the confluence of complex interdependencies between the organism in its environment (Smith & Sullivan, 2007). In addition, the myth that humans evolved from monkeys, chimpanzees, or apes must be dispelled because humans and other primates share a common ancestor over five million years ago, but they have always been distinct lineages (Smith & Sullivan, 2007). Therefore, we continue our understanding that humans are not superordinate beings nor is it enough in leadership research to give a simple nod acknowledging that humans are animals too. Our purpose in this chapter is not to chastise leadership theorists and researchers for relying on inaccurate images and beliefs about evolution or about any of the animals discussed in this chapter. However, because many of the animals discussed in this chapter have long been imbued with mythological and spiritual meanings around the globe, we argue that those enduring and inaccurate understandings must be thoroughly, emphatically, and repeatedly swept away to begin to illuminate constructs of movement and direction that can contribute to our conceptualization of critical leadership among humans.

Stepping into the research realm of animal science requires that we shift the vocabulary used previously for this chapter. Adopting the terminology of the applicable research realm supports this shift in perspective. Introductory biology classes inform us that both plants and animals are capable of movement in response to external stimuli, and that movement in animals is more frequently referred to as locomotion. Examples of types of locomotion include: walking, crawling, swimming, slithering, flying, diving, running, creeping, hopping, gliding, burrowing, and brachiating. Locomotion is often studied within a context of examining evolutionary fitness as framed by the production of offspring that survive and breed. Within that context, the qualities that natural selection favors are: speed, acceleration and maneuverability, endurance, economy of energy, and stability (Alexander, 2003). Mathematics, engineering, and physics are used in addition to physiology and biology to model and study animal locomotion (Alexander, 2003; Biewener, 2003). Therefore, in this chapter, the word "movement" appears less frequently and the word "locomotion" is more often used to refer to the purposeful movement of animals.

Many research programs collect and analyze data on various species' locomotion, applying theories and models and this chapter will summarize selected research threads. Some researchers, like Bejan and Marden (2006), have approached the problem from the other side devising a theory to explain the evolution of species' locomotion first and then collecting data to test it. Drawing from the engineering principle of optimization, which aims to generate the most output for the least energy, they considered animal locomotion as the "flow of mass from one location to another" (Bejan and Marden, 2006, p. 342). Thus treating animal locomotion in the same manner that rivers, winds, and ocean currents are represented and studied as flows allowed Bejan and Marden (2006) to theorize that because "effective use of energy is important over a lifetime, the basic design of most animals should evolve toward locomotion systems that optimize distance per cost" and called their theory "constructal theory" (p. 342). They tested their theory with data from insects, birds, lizards, fish, and mammals and found that within an order of magnitude it fit the data. Their model is not a predictive one like many others addressed in this chapter. "It does not maintain that animals must act or be designed in a predictable fashion, only that over large size ranges and diverse species, predictable central tendencies should emerge" (p. 344).

Chapman et al. (2011) were also interested in flow; however, it was species' strategies for maneuvering through air and water flows to get to their destinations that interested them. Animals can passively use flows to propel them from one place to another, but most animals must maneuver through those forces to get to where they want to go. Chapman et al. (2011) reviewed recent research and developed eight categories to describe the ways that animal species tend to maneuver through flows. The categories they created include two that allow the animals to drift with the flow and one in which the animals actively move directly into the flow like salmon do when swimming up rivers and streams. The other five categories they devised encompass the ranges of directional aims employed by species to account for the strength and direction of the flow they are experiencing (Chapman et al., 2011). The categories that Chapman et al. (2011) devised range from passive downstream drifting to upstream fighting the current.

A limitation in this research is that the goal location must be assumed. Flocks or schools may adjust their target mid-journey due to anthropogenic threats, severe weather, or in cases where they are only trying to reach a general area rather than a specific spot. However, most of the data Chapman et al. (2011) examined imply that the animals studied can determine the flow direction impacting them. Furthermore, many species use more than one orientation on a given journey to deal with changes in flows or to adjust their path as they get close to their goals and a wide variety of species use the same strategies (Chapman et al., 2011). Chapman et al. (2011) concluded that evolutionary forces produced the capabilities they analyzed across species. They also cautioned that several species may increasingly be challenged by anthropogenic threats to their capacity to migrate. For example, research on the causes of night-migrating bird fatalities due to crashes into communications towers suggests that the non-flashing red lights interfere with the birds' ability to navigate safely around the towers (Gehring, Kerlinger, & Manville, 2009). However, Gehring et al.'s (2009) suggestions fly in the face of conflicting research that concluded that while there is a greater risk of mortality from bird crashes into man-made towers and buildings, that mortality "has had no discernible effect on long-term population dynamics among North American landbirds" (Arnold & Zink, 2011, p. 2).

The research discussed in this chapter addresses animal movement in the context of living with others of their same species. Many species of animals either live in groups either all their lives or during significant times in their lives. Group living incurs some benefits and some costs. Living in groups is beneficial. In some situations it can decrease threats from predators. Animals also live in groups for ecological reasons such as food and space defense, being able to find resources by following knowledgeable members of the group; temperature control such as keeping each other warm in cold environments; and social reasons such as alloparental care, grooming, and learning. There are also some costs to group living such as increased competition for food and space, which may mean greater energy expenditure if the group needs to travel farther, and increased chances of disease transmission. Many animal species have dominance hierarchies or other forms of social behaviors (such as displays) that keep aggression at a minimum. The benefits must outweigh the costs given the number of animals that live in groups. Therefore, groups have provided, on balance, an evolutionary advantage.

Northern Bald Ibis Pairs Swap Positions Reciprocally in V-Formation Flying

When addressing animal locomotion, bird migrations offer a unique phenomenon to study because flying expends a greater proportion of energy and also gets the animal farther than equivalent investments in walking, running, or swimming resulting in birds' collective travel routes spanning almost the entire globe (Newton, 2008). Because flight requires proportionally more energy than other means of locomotion, much research focuses on the ways that birds economize energy as that was one of the qualities that natural selection favors listed above. Individual birds can alter the shape of their bodies, their wings, and their tails in flight to economize; and some species make use of an undulating flight that saves energy (Newton, 2008). Flying in flocks reduces the energy output collectively for the flock. For example, red knots (*Calidris canutus*), who migrate in flocks along the eastern coast of the United States and stop to fuel up on horseshoe crab eggs while migrating, on average, flew about five kph faster in flocks than alone (Newton, 2008). By far, the most recognizable way, for lay people, that flocking birds reduce their energy output is by flying in V-formations and those images also adorn the covers of leadership books.

Flying in V-formations means that the birds flying at the point of each V expend more energy in that position. When flying behind another bird, one can minimize its energy output by adjusting its position relative to the bird ahead and by synchronizing its wingbeat patterns. While this is not surprising, research conducted by Portugal et al. (2014) has provided a few surprises regarding V-formation flying. Using the latest technologies and working with free-flying birds that had been reared and trained to follow a small ultralight plane to learn their migration route, the researchers collected the relevant variables while the small flock of young Northern bald ibises (*Geronticus eremita*) harnessed with GPS logging devices flew (Portugal et al., 2014). Portugal et al.'s (2014) research confirmed many of the aerodynamic assumptions that had been speculated and added specific details regarding the birds' abilities and choices in avoiding the downwash and maximizing their use of the upwash.

One of the variables they examined was the position of each bird during a 43-minute flight. Examining just a seven minute segment of the 43-minute flight, their conclusions depicting the overall shape of the flock and the relative position of each bird were that "certain individuals showed general preferences for a particular area in the V-formation, but the variability in positioning in the flock resulted in no clear leader" (Portugal et al., 2014, p. 400). Specifically, two of the birds' histograms seemed to reveal two preferred regions, one bird seemed to have three preferred regions, and two birds seemed to be all over the place. More importantly, this group of researchers discovered that the young birds took turns, in pairs, flying in the position requiring more energy and in the position requiring less energy (Voelkl et al., 2015). In other words, the birds, dyadically, took turns leading and following. An important discovery was that the swapping of positions was *not* due to the lead bird becoming exhausted and dropping back. As the 14 young birds had been reared by humans, the researchers checked if the position swapping behavior they observed demonstrated a preference for swapping flying positions with nestmates or with siblings and there was no such preference. They also sought out correlations for the birds' social preference when on the ground and their dyadic pairings while flying and found no correlations, from which they concluded that "overall spatial proximity at the time of swapping seems to be a better predictor for direct turn-taking than social preference for specific birds" (Voelkl et al., 2015).

ALL FISH IN A SCHOOL ACCRUE ENERGY BENEFITS

Birds flying in flocks are not the only animals that benefit in energy savings by migrating collectively. Marras et al. (2015) demonstrated that regardless of their position in the school, all fish reap some energy savings from swimming in a school rather than swimming alone at the same speed. Similar to the young Northern bald ibises flying in their V-formations, the fish accrue a little larger energy savings when swimming in a following position, but unlike the ibis, even the fish swimming at the front of a school accrue some energy savings when swimming with a school. Researchers create, use, and modify multiple models in their study of flocking birds and schooling fish. In their review of such models, Hemelrijk and Hildenbrandt (2012) concluded that the existing models focus on the animals general locomotion and sensory capacities to produce "patterns at the level of the group that resemble empirical data emerge by self-organization from local, behavioural interactions among individuals" (p. 734); however, the models do not yet adequately address all the variables that impact and influence individual behavior.

FASTING, EGG-CARRYING, MALE EMPEROR PENGUINS HUDDLE TO CONSERVE ENERGY

Obviously, the amount of movement allowing individuals to save energy among fasting male emperor penguins (*Aptenodytes forsteri*) during the winters in Antarctica is drastically less than that of the ibises while flying in their V formations and of any species of fish swimming, and yet the purpose of their collective movements is the same. Zitterbart, Wienecke, Butler, and Fabry (2011) filmed a group of such males, most who were carrying eggs, for a four-hour period when the air temperature varied between −33°C and −43°C revealing that all the penguins in groups were making small steps every 30–60s. Their collective movements can be thought of as a wave through the group and multiple smaller groups existed and moved and merged during the four-hour period filmed (Zitterbart et al., 2011). Additionally, Zitterbart et al. (2011) discovered that while in their densely packed groups "individual penguins do not change their positions relative to their neighbors, and they do not force their way in or out of a huddle" (p. 2). Furthermore, the penguins in a huddle all tend to face the same direction and individuals joining the huddle tend to join by waddling up behind another individual and moving closer, whereas those individuals moving away from a huddle tend to have no one on front of them. Zitterbart et al. (2011) also concluded that it is "unclear whether the traveling wave in a huddle is triggered by a single or few leading penguins and follows a well-defined hierarchy among group members" (p. 3) but they speculated that simple rule-following behavior similar to that documented with flocking birds and schooling fish was occurring.

WHERE ARE WE GOING? MIGRATION NAVIGATION

Tackling the question from an evolutionary perspective of how many individuals in a migrating group are involved in navigating, Guttal and Coiuzin (2010) worked on a model like the ones that Zitterbart et al. (2011) referred to above to incorporate "the costs and benefits of obtaining directional cues from the environment and evolvable social interactions among migrating individuals" (Guttall & Couzin, 2010, p. 16172). What this means is, they made two adjustments to the model, one was to account for the variation among animals' abilities to acquire accurate navigation-related information. Each species, of course, has their own abilities and the capacity of each animal with these talents varies and Guttall and Couzin (2010) factored for that variability by allocating a cost to the individual animals who use their navigational skills. Their inclusion of it as a cost in the model was not that the more an animal used their skills the higher their costs would be; it was factored in that the more skill an animal had, the higher costs they'd pay. The second adjustment to the model Guttal and Coiuzin (2010) made was to assume that migrating animals each possess traits that impact who they prefer to be close to and the amount and timing and type of closeness with others in their group they prefer and that those preferences collectively positively impact the togetherness of their migratory behavior. They lumped all these traits together and created one variable for it so that individuals with the more of this togetherness trait incur more cost.

Running their model, Guttal and Coiuzin (2010) found that for groups whose population density in an area was very low, all the individuals evolved to possess and use their own navigation skills and they all had extremely low levels or none of the togetherness trait. They labeled these animals "leaders" and this evolution results in solitary migrations for species. At the other extreme, their model resulted in non-migratory populations where the population density is very high and no individuals evolve to use their navigation skills and the togetherness trait is high for all the animals (Guttall & Couzin, 2010). Between these two extremes, populations exist that contain some individuals who demonstrate high levels of navigation ability and some individuals who demonstrate high levels of togetherness traits and these populations migrate collectively.

Guttal and Coiuzin (2010) then ran their model by allowing individuals in populations to adjust their acting upon their level of togetherness trait and on their navigation abilities as the previous iterations left those constant for each evolution. When allowing for individual expression of possessed traits to vary, they found that "migratory individuals in our model do not evolve context-dependent interactions even when given the possibility to do" (Guttall & Couzin, 2010, p. 16174). Put very simply, their model posits that within migrating species, there are animals that know where to go and are acting solely on their private knowledge and the rest of the group do not possess that knowledge and are simply much more social animals that because they like to be close to others, they follow.

Cao, Olshevsky, and Xia (2014) also tweaked one of the models that Zitterbart et al. (2011) referred to above. Their examination of the challenges of migration focused on how animals reach consensus and they considered the fact that one individual is following another as consensus. Then Cao et al. (2014) posited that some individuals exist that can be considered "first followers" (p. 10042) and they claimed that such individuals can "sense or acquire, directly, the leader's information" (p. 10042). These first followers are individuals who more quickly align themselves with an individual, thus, creating the position of leader through their act of following. Thus, their abrupt break from the others signals who they have chosen to follow. To clarify, it is their act of swift following that creates a leader and triggers the following responses in all the other followers. Cao et al. (2014) provide several mathematical proofs using their model.

Locomotion and direction are not only important for migration, they are also important in foraging behaviors. For example, research has demonstrated how bees share information about where they found pollen with other bees in their hive through a waggle dance that communicates direction and distance (Seeley, 1985). Animals demonstrate a variety of information-sharing and decision-making behaviors.

Couzin, Krause, Franks, and Levin (2005) produced a model to depict group decision-making that could apply as well to swarms of insects who do not possess the capacity to recognize individuals as it does to family groups of migrating geese or a school of fish. Their model assumes that only some individuals in the group have a desired direction to travel in while all are attempting to maintain a minimum distance between themselves and others by turning away from those they are near when they are too close. This avoidance behavior is the highest priority. If no individuals are too close, then the individual is attracted to and aligns itself with the others it is close to. The individuals who have a preference of a direction to travel in balance that with the influence of the social interactions. Their model resulted in a very small proportion of individuals who need to know where they are going for the entire group to still arrive there successfully. When they allowed for equal numbers of individuals with a direction preference to possess different preferences in running the model, the group randomly selects one of the preferences when the difference between the two directions is sufficiently large enough.

Flack, Biro, Guilford, and Freeman (2015) extended the model that Couzin et al. (2005) produced by incorporating a preference factor to account for variation in which individual another individual prefers to be near. They set these preferences to be either strong or weak. Their results revealed that groups with no underlying social structures (i.e., no preferences for other individuals) missed their target location by an average of just over 500 meters. The groups in which each individual possessed one strong preference had an accuracy slightly better than this. The groups with random social structures showed no change in accuracy. However, groups who were programmed to possess more than one strong preference per individual demonstrated a decrease in navigational accuracy.

For the remainder of their examinations they adjusted the weighting for the individuals' preferences to adhere to their own target destination. That meant the degree to which they would forgo their own preferences and stick close to another individual in the group who was either adhering to its own preferences or likewise forgoing its preferences to follow someone else was flexible. They referred to this trait as assertiveness. Their results revealed that

> navigation was most accurate in groups in which the individuals with the most social-followers were also highly assertive. Interestingly, hierarchical organization became less effective when highly followed individuals paid less attention to their target information (unassertive social-leaders). As described before such social-leader[s] tend to be located at the centre of the group, but, because they disregard the navigational choices of their surroundings, they do not benefit from averaging information from the other group members. As a consequence, the mismatch between assertiveness and network position results in less-efficient navigation. (Flack et al., 2015, p. 6)

STICKLEBACK FISH FOLLOW A QUORUM WHEN FORAGING

Above, the energy benefits all fish traveling in schools reap and how few individuals in a migrating group must possess the navigational details about where the group is going to achieve group success was discussed. Animals that live in groups have their own experiences to draw from and they can also observe others in their group and draw conclusions from their behavior. Doing so while migrating, foraging, and when predators are threatening can help an individual survive. Foraging is not an entirely solitary endeavor even for animals who are considered solitary. For example, research on rodents and several bird species who cache food reveals the complex ways that they also observe each other and steal from each other's hiding places (Hopewell, Leaver, & Lea, 2008).

What movement and direction decisions are made within groups during foraging? Ward, Krause, and Sumpter (2012) have been studying this question with three-spined stickleback fish (*Gasterosteus aculeatus*) testing the quorum-based decision model that they created from their previous experiments with this species. For this experiment, Ward et al. (2012) caught 400 wild, juvenile three-spined sticklebacks which are only 30 mm in length. A Y-shaped aquatic maze where replica fish could be mechanically moved to serve as potential leaders was used in which the replicas were moved toward an area where the real fish could see, but not eat, their favored food. After a set amount of time, the replica fish were moved away from the food toward an area of safety (i.e., a shady area). The experiments were done with either just one replica fish, or with two replica fish, or with no replica leaders. Each trial was conducted with either one real fish, two real fish, four real fish, or eight real fish. Each real fish was provided only one try in the experimental maze, so none of them had been in it before.

Ward et al.'s (2012) results revealed that when one fake fish was mechanically trolled through the water toward the food, the real fish followed more often, regardless of the size of their group, than if no fake leader fish were present. When two fake leader fish moved toward the food, it was only the frequency of the groups of eight real fish following that increased. However, that frequency did not hold for the groups of eight then following the two fake leaders away from the food. By contrast, there was a similar frequency of following two fake leaders initially and then later away from the food with real fish groups of two and four and the solitary ones. Ward et al. (2012), thus, concluded that there are additional aspects contributing to the decision-making process that emerges from the fishes' interactions in their specific environments. Pike and Laland (2010) had previously conducted similar research with nine-spine sticklebacks (*Pungitius pungitius*) and reported what they believed to be clear evidence that the fish more frequently followed the larger groups of fake fish demonstrating what they referred to as conformist behavior.

Nakayama, Stumpe, Manica, and Johnstone (2013) examined stickleback foraging pairs' behaviors to determine their adaptability. They experimentally manipulated the environments of the pairs to compare the behavior of the fish. In their previous work, they had already discovered that these fish enact consistent individual differences in behaviors that they labeled shy and bold. Applying those criteria, they observed their fish and gave them ratings of shy or bold based on their observations. Then, they employed tests of fish pairs in which each pair contained one bold fish and one shy fish. One test rewarded the behavior of the shyer fish for following and rewarded the bolder fish for leading. The other test rewarded the bolder fish for following and the shyer fish for leading. In both tests, based on the configuration of the testing tank, the fish relative to each other in the spaces provided to them could be in one of four unique states arrived at by eight individual actions of each individual in a pair. Analyzing the results, Nakayama et al. (2013) concluded that both the bold fish and the shy fish were influenced by being rewarded for adopting behaviors contrary to their temperaments. However, the impact of rewarding the bold fish for following was more impactful than rewarding the shy fish for leading. Similarly, rewarding the shy fish for following and the bold fish for leading also resulted in more impact among the followers than leaders.

Do Cattle Call Quorums When Foraging?

Reinhardt and Reinhardt's (1981) research over three decades ago detailed the social cohesion in a herd of domesticated zebu cattle (*B. t. indicus*) in Kenya who were kept separate from others using three years of visual observations and concluded that cattle are similar to primates in that they invest more time with certain individuals in their group than others. Some of the individuals that they cattle invested more time with are related to them and some of them are not. They also noted the movement of the herd and kept track of who followed whom, but they offered no speculations to explain why one female was the most followed (Reinhardt & Reinhardt, 1981). They had named the cattle and the name they assigned her name was Alma. They described her as

> an average cow in terms of age, reproduction, weight and social rank status. However, she obviously was a most attractive individual whose movements were attentively observed by the other members of the herd. This social attractiveness may well account for the fact that an exceptionally large number of animals grazed more frequently close to Alma than to other partners. (Reinhardt & Reinhardt, 1981, p. 147)

They attempted to explain, circularly, that Alma was the most attractive because she was the most followed and she was followed because she was the most attractive.

Seoane's (2015) research relying on data from four female free-ranging semi-feral cows (*Bos taurus*) who were fitted with GPS tracking devices in the Andean forests of Argentina. Seoane (2015) collected the position of each cow every hour for one month in order to test "multi-state random walk models" (p. S44) and while "multi-state random walk models have been developed and used mostly in migratory animals such as elk, or marine mammals that travel long distances to feed ... cattle have similar behaviors in terms of travelled distances" (p. S51). The goal was to determine the extent to which those models were useful in predicting the movement of all the semi-feral cattle in the area. Seoane (2015) concluded that the models only partially matched the real behavior of the cattle studied and that a timescale for studying the animals' movements of smaller than six hours was necessary.

Šárová, Špinka, Panamá, and Šimeček (2010) collected data from a herd of 15 Gasconne cows (*Bos taurus*) wearing GPS tracking devices for a 3-week period in a pasture of the Institute of Animal Science in Prague, Czech Republic. They tracked the cows' positions at one minute intervals. The general purpose of their study was to test their hypothesis that cows who demonstrated more aggressive behaviors toward herd members (i.e., threats and head butting) exert more influence on the herd's movement. They counted the number of times that the cows exhibited aggressive behaviors and developed an index to use in their correlations. Their detailed hypotheses were that the more aggressive cows would:

1. be found closer to the front of the herd.
2. be found closer to the centre of the herd whereas submissive animals are found at the periphery.
3. change direction less when moving.
4. cover shorter distances during their movements.
5. be aligned with their neighbours than more subordinate cows.
6. be aligned with the direction of movement of the herd (Šárová et al., 2010, p. 1039).

To test their hypotheses under the varying situations that the cow herd exhibited, Šárová et al. (2010) classified the activity of the entire herd as either resting, foraging, or traveling when at least one third of the herd was engaged in that activity. The herd was thus categorized at times as engaging with more than one activity. Šárová et al. (2010) calculated the correlations between the aggression index of individuals and their positions relative to the others in the herd to test each hypotheses above resulting in support for numbers 1, 3, 5, and 6 while the herd was traveling; number 1 and 4 while the herd was foraging; and none of the specific hypotheses were supported while the herd was resting.

VERVET MONKEYS AND HUMPBACK WHALES OBSERVE AND ADHERE TO SOCIAL NORMS REGARDING NOVEL FOOD

A great deal of our explorations thus far into the realm of the scientific study of nonhuman animal locomotion and direction has included the use of mathematical models. The level of precision they provide is high but the level of behavioral complexity they can convey is much lower. Additionally, the thought of reducing human behavior to mathematical models is objectionable to some people. An example that demonstrates behavioral flexibility is found in van de Waal, Borgeaud, and Whiten's (2013) research on foraging behaviors of wild vervet monkeys (*Chlorocebus pygerythrus*) in the Mawana Game Reserve in South Africa. Their research demonstrated that the animals were willing and able to "abandon personal foraging preferences in favor of group norms new to them" (van de Waal et al., 2013, p. 483). The way in which they accomplished their research involved a novel methodology. They habituated four different groups of monkeys with two trays of dyed corn. One of the trays of corn dyed one color had been also treated with a substance that was distasteful to the monkeys. Thus, over three monthly sessions with those trays of food, the monkeys learned to avoid the corn dyed the color that designated it as the distasteful corn. Then, van de Waal et al. (2013) again set out the trays of the two colors of corn four to six months later but this time none of the corn had the distasteful substance added. Some monkeys tried the corn dyed the color that had originally been distasteful, but most of the monkeys continued their preference for the color of corn that had originally been the only palatable one. Moreover, all the infants mimicked their mothers and ate only the corn that she ate. Their preferences continued for five trials. During the research, 15 young males immigrated into the study group. Ten of them had been in one of the other groups that had been provided two colors of dyed corn as well and in their original group, the palatable corn was dyed the color of the distasteful corn for the group they were joining. Seven of those ten males immediately chose the corn that the locals were eating rather than the one they had learned was the palatable one in their group originally. Eventually, all but one of those ten males ate the preferred color of corn of the local group. The five unknown males who came from areas that were not part of the study also chose the preferred color of corn when no higher-ranking animals were dominating that tray of corn.

Allen, Weinrich, Hoppitt, and Rendell (2013) also studied the cultural transmission of norms regarding novel foods among wild animals in their study of humpback whale (*Megaptera novaeangliae*) behavior in the Gulf of Maine. They used network-based diffusion analysis because it uses an association matrix "which estimates the proportion of time that individuals are associated, to quantify the extent to which social network structure explains the spread of a behavior" (Allen et al., 2013, p. 486). The behavior they were studying was the whales' smacking the surface of the water with their tail flukes one to four times and then creating a wall of bubbles to entrap their prey. The whales then swooped up from below the prey with their mouths wide open to eat as many of the tiny prey as possible. In 1980, only one humpback in the Gulf of Maine was observed to use this foraging technique and between 1981 and 1989 a dramatic increase in the number of whales using that technique was observed. To test the hypothesis that this lobtail feeding behavior was culturally transmitted, Allen et al. (2013) analyzed data maintained by the Whale Center of New England (WCNE) spanning 27 years (1980–2007) that included 73,790 sightings of 653 humpbacks who were sighted 20 or more times in a particular area. Allen et al.'s (2013) analysis revealed that the social transmission hypothesis was overwhelmingly supported and they further argued that using the network-based diffusion analysis was a powerful advantage because

> it allows the simultaneous consideration of ecological, social, and genetic factors as predictors of individual learning rates, thus moving away from sterile arguments about excluding such factors in the development of behavior and instead reflecting the reality that all behavior develops as an interaction of multiple factors. (p. 488)

THERE'S NO SUCH THING AS AN ALPHA WOLF

Hutchinson, Vickers, Jackson, and Wilkes (2006) and subsequently Meglich and Gumbus (2015) employed the notion of an alpha wolf to frame their research results on workplace bullying. They referred to aggressive bullying "alpha wolves" to weave narratives about human behavior in the workplace. However, the wolf behavior they used as an analogy deserves more attention than they provided to understand real wolf behavior. Mech (1999) has dispelled the notion that competition among wolves (*Canis lupus*) to attain dominance is natural behavior within wild wolf packs. Mech (1999) further dispelled notions regarding breeding and the inheritance of dominance, reporting that whether in captivity or in the wild, all wolves bred when they had the opportunity. It is important to note that Mech (1966), himself fostered the idea of the alpha wolf and intragroup aggression starting in his doctoral research in the late 1960s, that he later dispelled. His original idea that natural wolf packs are formed by unrelated wolves coming together at the start of winter fighting amongst themselves to establish a "pecking order" was not supported. These mistaken concepts were created by Mech (1966) and others observing wolves that were captured, moved, and confined. The confined wolves were with no other individuals from their own packs, rather they were with individuals they did not know and their interactions were chaotic. Mech's (1999) subsequent research observing wolves in their own habitat revealed that wolves live in extended family units that include adult-sized offspring. Mech (1999) explained that in large multi-litter packs the term "alpha" may serve to differentiate older breeders from younger ones, however, he also emphasized that "the point here is not so much the terminology but what the terminology falsely implies: a rigid, force-based dominance hierarchy" (p. 1198).

Muro, Escobedo, Spector, and Coppinger's (2011) research also supports the dissolution of the alpha wolf notion which portrays one wolf in the pack as the one making the decisions and forcing the others to conform. They created a computational model and compared empirical data of the hunting behavior of wolves to their model and concluded that their model adequately depicts and predicts complex wolf-pack hunting behavior. Their model includes two simple rules that they posit the wolves are enacting. Those rules were: (1) move toward the prey until a minimum safe distance to the prey is reached; and (2) when at the safe distance, move away from the other wolves that are within the safe area. "We show that two simple decentralized rules controlling the movement of each wolf are enough to reproduce the main features of the wolf-pack hunting behavior: tracking the prey, carrying out the pursuit, and encircling the prey until it stops moving" (Muro et al., 2011, p. 192). These researchers reduced the seemingly complex behavior to two simple rules that individuals perform that required no communication between the individuals during the hunt. Thus, no communication mechanisms nor skills are necessary, neither is a specific hierarchical social structure within the wolf pack.

We offer an alternative explanation for wolf-pack hunting behaviors that is simpler than explanations based on assumptions of high levels of wolf intelligence. It is not our intention to argue that wolves lack significant communicative and cognitive skills, but rather to suggest a model that can explain their behaviors without assuming that they have special abilities or hierarchical social skills. (Muro et al., 2011, p. 196)

The simple rules that Muro et al. (2011) detailed resulted in the complex emergent behaviors of relay running, prey circling, and ambushing that have been described by other researchers as resulting from wolves' ability to anticipate likely future events and from communicating and coordinating their hunts.

Bailey et al. (2013) conducted a review of research on carnivores' group hunting behaviors concluding that across the species studied, there was "no evidence that [the] behaviour would require advanced cognitive abilities" (p. 1) providing additional support to the dissolution of the alpha wolf myth. From the available research, they only found 18 of 270 species (7%) of carnivorans whose cooperative hunting had been studied, see the list below. They speculate that the number of carnivoran species that hunt cooperatively is much higher but understudied.

two of 13 otter species (15%)
nine of 38 canid species (23%),
one of four hyena species (25%),
five of 41 felid species (12%), and
one of 36 viverrid species (3%). (Bailey et al., 2013, p. 6)

Cooperative hunting has long been used as evidence that a species who demonstrate the behavior are evolutionarily more advanced so Bailey et al. (2013) began their review with a detailed breakdown of exactly what cooperative hunting is. Their breakdown provided a refinement to the existing understanding and using that, they then went on to exhaustively examine all the studies. They concluded that for over half the species that are reported to employ cooperative hunting,

There is no obvious reason to suppose that this level of hunt organisation requires any unusually advanced cognitive ability compared to other species or other activities (such as foraging or food storing), as it could be achieved by following simple rules in combination with some degree of associative learning. (Bailey et al., 2013, p. 13)

Explanations that the carnivores are employing simple behavior rules that do not require any coordination nor communication fit the data. Their conclusions cast doubts on many researcher speculations that the behavior must be coordinated and synchronized through communication and is mediated by social relationships among the group.

STALLION AGGRESSION VARIES

Sigurjonsdottir, Thorhallsdottir, Hafthorsdottir, and Granquist (2012) observed 93 adult and subadult and 42 foals semiferal horses (*Equus caballus*) who lived in a 215-hectare pasture for a total of 316 h in May of 2007 on a farm in East-Landeyjar in the south of Iceland. Laws in Iceland prevent the importation of horses and free-roaming stallions are prohibited, so multiple stallions living within a shared enclosed location is rare. For that reason, the selected group of four stallions and their respective bands who all lived within one pasture provided a novel research opportunity for documenting their behavior.

Sigurjonsdottir et al. (2012) plotted each of the bands home ranges discovering that there was a 20% overlap among them, although the bands did not occupy those overlapping areas while another band was there. In other words, they kept their distance. The band of the stallion who herded his band a total of 84 times during the observation period occupied the largest home range and the stallion who herded his band only 5 times during that same period occupied a much smaller home range that was also bounded on three sides by the pasture fencing. The other two stallions herded their bands 50 and 56 times. The stallions invested significantly less time grazing than the other horses and significantly more time standing alert. During the observation period, a total of 112 encounters were documented between bands and a small percentage of those interactions were between the stallion of one band and the mares or subadults of another band and another small percentage of those interactions was between the subadult mares from different bands. During the time of the study one new stallion and nine new mares were introduced into the pasture to observe the reactions of the resident stallions. Over 80% of the interactions were between the stallions, including interactions between the new stallion and the existing four. Sigurjonsdottir et al. (2012) were not surprised that the number of encounters between the new stallion and one of the residents was double the number of encounters among the long-standing resident stallions. They categorized the interactions as either "assessment without touching or violent acts" (p.

4) and there were at least twice as many assessments without touching as the number of violent acts in each comparison of resident-to-resident or resident-to-newcomer interactions. Additionally, there were significantly more violent act type interactions between the newcomer stallion and one of the residents than the interactions between the residents.

Some feral horse groups include more than one stallion. These are called multi-stallion bands and some researchers have speculated that the stallions form cooperative coalitions as a strategy for dealing with the resources available. The reasoning is that the primary stallion tolerates some loss of mating opportunities to the subordinate stallion because that stallion also assists in defending the band. Linklater, Cameron, Stafford, and Minot (2013) observed six multi-stallion bands of feral horses (*Equus caballus*) in the Kaimanawa ranges east of Waiouru, New Zealand, before and after removing the subordinate stallion from two bands for two months to test the assumption that such subordinate stallions assist the primary stallion of the band by protecting the band. Their results were contrary to the expectations. If subordinate stallions assist by defending mares, then upon their removal, Linklater et al. (2013) expected the primary stallions to increase their proximity to the mares in their bands and that did not occur. Furthermore, after removal of the subordinate stallions, reductions in aggression from the primary stallion toward the mares in his band were observed. After the subordinate stallions were released, they returned to the same bands from which they had been removed, and the frequency of aggression from the primary stallion toward the mares in his band returned to pre-removal levels. Lastly, the frequency of aggressive challenges from neighboring band stallions toward the two stallions whose subordinates had been removed did not change during the period when the subordinate stallions were absent. While Linklater et al. (2013) acknowledged the limitations of their study that spanned only two months and only included two bands, they also suggested that the underlying question that they and their colleagues should be seeking to answer regarding multi-stallion bands is not why they exist, but why so few such bands exist.

Relocated Elk Work to Regain Their Equilibrium

Until now, we have been discussing animal movement and direction associated primarily with migrating, obtaining food, mating, and caring for young. Some of the movements have been experimentally manipulated in the lab; and some have been observed in the wild and some in captivity, while some have been mathematically modeled. This section addresses the movement and direction of millions of animals across an entire continent spanning a century. It is estimated that at least 10 million elk populated North America before the 1600s. Those numbers included six subspecies, of which two are now extinct and the current estimates are that there are only about 1 million elk living in scattered populations across North America (Popp, Toman, Mallory, & Hamr, 2014). For over a hundred years, periodic efforts have been made to capture and relocate elk in attempts to restore their numbers in specific locations. The earliest such project included in their review was conducted from 1893 through 1906 soon after the last remaining individuals of a now extinct subspecies were killed (Popp et al., 2014). Popp et al. (2014) concluded that the early relocation efforts were largely unsuccessful, but that some recent efforts have demonstrated some success.

Elk movement data from one of the relocation projects included in Popp et al.'s (2014) review that was deemed successful was used by Haydon et al. (2008) to "develop a model of population spread that includes group dynamics to examine the interactions of movement and group cohesion on long-term population growth rate" (p. 1102). Between 1998 and 2001, 120 Manitoban elk (*Cervus canadensis*) were relocated from Elk Island National Park, Alberta, to 30 km southeast of Bancroft Ontario. There were two separate captures and releases completed a little over a year apart with varying strategies employed. The first group of 36 adult females, 14 adult males, 10 juvenile females, and 10 juvenile males were fitted with radio collars and were tracked usually from the ground and sometimes from the air. All the data from their movement was used to create the model. The second group included 20 adult females, 13 adult males, 11 juvenile females, and 6 juvenile males and only ten of the adult females in this group were fitted with GPS collars and only the first location identified from these tracking devices was used in the model. Haydon et al. (2008) categorized the animals' movements as either "encamped" or as "ranging" based on previous research done with elk. Using those two categories, their data indicated that the released elk who were in groups, invested almost no time ranging as they invested 99.1% of their time in the encamped state. Solitary elk, in contrast, invested 18.8% of their time ranging (Haydon et al., 2008). Additionally, they noted that elk in larger groups left the large group less frequently than individuals leaving smaller groups and that solitary elk more frequently joined groups close by than groups further away (Haydon et al., 2008). To be sure, there are many more models to be employed in the analysis for predicting the movements of relocated elk and Popp et al. (2014) recommend that more research is necessary to improve on successes.

The reason that the 120 elk were relocated was not explicitly provided by Haydon et al. (2008), but the Rocky Mountain Elk Foundation, the Ontario Federation of Anglers and Hunters, and the Safari Club International provided financial support for the project (Rosatte, Hamr, Young, Filion, & Smith, 2007) and across North America, these types of organizations with hunting interests have long been financial supporters of this type of relocation project while other organizations have voiced their concerns about elk relocation efforts. For example, the North American Elk Breeders Association

> opposes any wild elk relocation/restoration project that does not adhere to the minimum interstate movement requirements for farmed elk set forth by the United States Department of Agriculture or the Canadian Food Inspection Agency relating to Tuberculosis, Brucellosis and Chronic Wasting Disease. Any such projects not complying with these minimum requirements may put both farmed and free-ranging elk and deer at risk. (Lowe, 2015)

Relocating to supplement native game species was the predominant thrust behind relocation efforts in Australia, Canada, New Zealand, and the United States in the 1970s and 1980s (Griffith, Scott, Carpenter, & Reed, 1989). A subsequent review of relocations, assessing 180 cases of animal relocations conducted over a 20-year period, Fischer and Lindemayer (2000) concluded that primary purposes for animal relocations were to "solve human–animal conflicts, to supplement game populations, or for conservation" (p. 7). However, they noted that the reasons for relocations are rarely reported explicitly and that is unfortunate, since the reason for the relocation is often related to the challenges encountered in the relocation project (Fischer & Lindenmayer, 2000). They also discussed several projects which moved animals to new locations to solve human–animal conflicts in which all the relocated animals soon died or moved back to their original ranges. Thus, the failures were largely attributed to the inappropriateness of the locations chosen. The majority of Fischer and Lindenmayer's review (2000) focused on

relocations for conservation purposes and they identified five major suggestions for improving relocations as a conservation tool: (1) use more
rigor in analyzing the options for achieving the aims for which relocation
is but one option; (2) explicitly define success; (3) monitor the results
adequately and appropriately to determine the outcome; (4) account for
the resources required; and (5) document and publish the results.

To be sure, as human encroachment into what had been safe areas for
wild animals continues, the likelihood of animal–human conflict increases
as does the mortality rates for wildlife whose habitats are fragmented by
roads and railways. Beckmann, Clevenger, Huijser, and Hilty (2012)
reviewed several efforts regarding roads and railways to minimize their
impact on wildlife and their habitats. Some of the innovative projects
included a citizen science approach that relies on long-term partnerships
in communities in which citizen observations generate large datasets for
many research projects. These challenges may pale in comparison with the
challenges posed by climate change. Recently, an independent group of
30 scientists, scholars, and policymakers titling themselves the "Managed
Relocation Working Group" (Schwartz et al., 2012) noted that the
"magnitude of projected climate change, suggests that humans may be
forced to choose between the unfortunate alternatives of witnessing
extinctions and intentionally manipulating species' distributions in efforts
to prevent extinction and maintain biodiversity" (p. 732). This group
made it clear that the terminology "managed relocation" referred to

the intentional act of moving species, populations, or genotypes to a
location outside [their] known historical distribution for the purpose of
maintaining biological diversity or ecosystem functioning as an adaptation strategy for climate change …. Managed relocation is distinct from
other types of conservation-motivated translocations, including biological
control of invasions, restoration of populations within a native range, and
rewilding, because it entails moving a target outside its historical distribution in response to climate change for the benefit of natural resources management. (Schwartz et al., 2012, p. 733)

Final Thoughts

This chapter addressed research revealing some examples of how movement and direction is conceptualized and studied among nonhuman animals. We reviewed several ways in which nonhuman animals' movement
in relation to others of their species with whom they interact is analyzed

to uncover fragments useful to our discussion growing across Chapters 3 through 6. Many of the examinations of animal movement, or loco-motion, and direction discussed in this chapter addressed animal move-ment at what Nathan et al. (2008) referred to as a coarse level rather than a fine one. Nathan et al. (2008) proposed a unifying paradigm termed "movement ecology" for studying movements of all organisms. They argued that such a framework is necessary because the current use of idiosyncratic terminologies and classifications created and used for different animal groups or within varying geographic regions produces results that cannot be integrated (Nathan et al., 2008). Their framework consists of (1) the external factors that impact the organism's state, it's motion capacity, and it's navigation capacity; (2) the internal state of the organism which addresses why it moves; (3) the navigation capac-ity of the organism which addresses to where it moves; (4) the motion capacity of the organism which addresses how it moves; and (5) the resulting motion path (Nathan et al., 2008). They mapped four current approaches used in the study of animal movement to their framework (biomechanical, cognitive, random, and optimality) to demonstrate how their proposed framework could "provide a theoretical scaffold to syn-ergize research" (Nathan et al., 2008, p. 19058) across those existing approaches. Building on Nathan et al.'s (2008) framework, Jachowski and Singh (2015) reviewed recent technical advances that allow research-ers to collect a variety of physiological measures that provide some details regarding the internal states of animals and offered revisions to Nathan et al.'s (2008) framework to expand the role of animal physiol-ogy. Jachowski and Singh (2015) also cautioned against making assump-tions about the physiologies of animals and they argued they "must first be evaluated through rigorous direct sampling of physiological state to obtain corroborative evidence" (p. 8).

In contrast with Nathan et al.'s (2008) framework, Pellis et al. (2014) argued that regularities of movements to accomplish species-specific objectives can be maintained by what they refer to as simple neural rules. Furthermore, they argued that animal movements demonstrate a vari-ety of biases. Most individuals of a species will perform a sequence of actions is a specific way. They referred to that as a neural bias and they argued that such biases developed because they were evolutionarily ben-eficial. Individuals with the built-in bias acted faster than animals without it. They argued that evolutionary selection resulted in many neural rules shared across species as we inherited them from our long ago common ancestors. Pellis et al. (2014) provided several examples of the neural rules but discovering and delineating all of them was not their aim. Their central argument was that a set of nested neural rules exist across species within which reside species-specific rules. At the highest level, the neural rules do not govern movements themselves, they simply govern the execution of the next level of nested neural rules. This nesting continues to the point of the neural rules that govern specific actual movements. Thus, there are levels of neural rules that impact the selection and combinations of rules selected at the level of action.

Pellis et al. (2014) also emphasized that the environment is "not simply the passive substrate in which behavior occurs, but rather it actively interacts with an animal to make behavior possible" (p. 133). It is not as if the brain and the body are trying to accomplish something in the abstract and once it is analyzed and a decision is made, then it is applied to the specific context. Rather, the interaction of the body in its environment as sensed by all the sensing functions of the organism are an ongoing part of what Nathan et al. (2008) might refer to as the internal state. On that point, both Nathan et al. (2008) and Pellis et al. (2014) seem to agree. The brain, the body, and the environment are equally important in bringing about the animal's movement. In other words, animal movement is an emergent property of the unique interaction of the animal and its environment. This is a view quite different from one that frames animals as acting *upon* their environments.

Unsurprisingly, there are competing theoretical frameworks for the study of animal movement, yet the lack of a mutual understanding does not deter research. In fact, the lack of agreement may spur development along innovative avenues. Innovation was the primary goal of Xing and Gao (2014) who offered their compilation of 134 computational intelligence algorithms with the hope that they will be used by multidisciplinary researchers who will in turn modify them, contributing to the ongoing refinement process. Interestingly, some of the models included in this chapter are related to some of the algorithms included in their book. Such algorithms are used both to predict and explain animal behavior. Animal models can be usefully employed in research precluding the need for costly and interfering observing and documenting real animals. Furthermore, the resulting algorithms are also used in the design of various artificial intelligence applications and in understanding human behavior. Consequently, the focus in generating such models and algorithms is but one thread in the research that involves animals.

We are not arguing for a view of any animal behavior, including human, that is simply mechanistic and predictable, but we must acknowledge that there are aspects of animal behavior that are predictable. Switching gears for a moment, we need to address specifically human behavior. Kenrick and Griskevicius (2013) produced an entertaining exposition of the human animal. Drawing from evolutionary psychology, they presented and discussed what they called the seven human "subselves" that interact and influence our behavior. The subselves they discussed were: self-protector, disease avoider, affiliate, status attainer, mate-acquirer, mate-retainer, and kin caretaker (Kenrick & Griskevicius, 2013) and they arranged these hierarchically in the order listed as that is the order in which the human behaviors demonstrating evidence for this theory typically appear developmentally. They provided amusing examples of research and lived experiences that they re-explain considering the details about these various subselves.

There is one all-encompassing question that has implications for human behavior viewed through the lens of these proposed subselves. There is no assumption that a need or desire drives humans to be accurate in their analysis or their thought processes. The discussion of the subselves reiterates the same point repeatedly. Humans, like all living things, evolved by capitalizing on characteristics and behaviors that were *adaptive*, not based on what was *accurate*. They provide a simple example of an error that humans make all the time called auditory looming. Pursuing this phenomenon further, Neuhoff (2001) discovered that "sounds that approached listeners were perceived as stopping closer than sounds that departed, despite identical stopping points" (p. 100). Researchers of this phenomena argue that the human brain has a built-in bias to perceive the sensory data incorrectly and that this bias arose because it was evolutionarily advantageous. "If the source is perceived as closer than it actually is, then the listener will have longer than expected to prepare for the source's arrival" (Neuhoff, 2001, p. 100). This is but one example of a neural rule that the human brain biases.

Central to applying Kenrick and Griskevicius's (2013) notions of subselves, is an appreciation for both the proximate and the distal causes for human behavior, as the unique balancing of them results in understandable, yet, unpredictable behavior in individuals. The balancing of what they referred to as the proximate and distal causes may be the same things as the nested neural rules from Pellis et al. (2014) work. If humans also operate using neural rules that reside within a nested hierarchy as presented above, then it is reasonable to suggest that the lowest level of those neural rules might reside a neural rule that directs the individual to abide by what are referred to as the social norms of the groups one belongs to. Such an understanding aligns with the research presented in this chapter even though the behaviors studied were only referred to as social norms in the studies of the whales and monkeys. Yet, the similarities between the ways in which social norms operate among non-human animals and how they operate among humans cannot be escaped.

Consider a mosquito annoyingly buzzing around you, a bird delicately alighting on a branch near you, or a loved pet enthusiastically greeting you when you return home. Each of these imagined movements is imbued with human physiological impositions and understandings. The bird delicately alights on the branch to reflect our envious fascination with bird flight. The mosquito annoyingly buzzes because we dislike the itchy welts we know can result from encounters with mosquitoes. Our pets greet us enthusiastically because we ascribe motives and emotions to our pets every day. The language we choose to label nonhuman animal movement and direction is, of course, chosen by humans rather than by those performing the movements we anthropomorphize. The fact that humans are animals is a tired truism, and yet it bears repeating while also searching for true parallels that can be gleaned from the research done with nonhuman animals. Care must be taken to attend to recent research while also avoiding over-extending the similarities.

REFERENCES

Alexander, R. M. (2003). *Principles of locomotion*. Princeton, NJ: Princeton University Press.
Allen, J., Weinrich, M., Hoppitt, W., & Rendell, L. (2013). Network-based diffusion analysis reveals cultural transmission of lobtail feeding in Humpback Whales. *Science, 340*, 485–488. https://doi.org/10.1126/science.1232769.
Arnold, T. W., & Zink, R. M. (2011). Collision mortality has no discernible effect on population trends of North American birds. *PLoS One, 6*(9). https://doi.org/10.1371/journal.pone.0024708.
Bailey, I., Myatt, J. P., & Wilson, A. M. (2013). Group hunting within the Carnivora: Physiological, cognitive and environmental influences on strategy and cooperation. *Behavioral Ecology and Sociobiology, 67*(1), 1–17. https://doi.org/10.1007/s00265-012-1423-3.
Beckmann, J. P., Clevenger, A. P., Huijser, M. P., & Hilty, J. A. (Eds.). (2012). *Safe passages: Highways, wildlife, and habitat connectivity*. Washington, DC: Island Press.

Bejan, A., & Marden, J. H. (2006). Constructing animal locomotion from new thermodynamics theory. *American Scientist, 94*(861), 342–349.

Biewener, A. A. (2003). *Animal locomotion.* New York, NY: Oxford University Press.

Brüssow, H. (2016). Biome engineering—2020. *Microbial Biotechnology, 9*(5), 553–563. https://doi.org/10.1111/1751-7915.12391.

Cao, M., Olshevsky, A., & Xia, W. (2014). Focused first followers accelerate aligning followers with the leader in reaching network consensus. *Proceedings of the 19th world congress the international federation of automatic control* (pp. 10042–10047). Cape Town, South Africa. https://doi.org/10.3182/20140824-6-za-1003.01839.

Chapman, J. W., Klaassen, R. H., Drake, V. A., Fossette, S., Hays, G. C., Metcalfe, J. D., …, Alerstam, T. (2011). Animal orientation strategies for movement in flows. *Current Biology, 21*(20), R861–R870. https://doi.org/10.1016/j.cub.2011.08.014.

Couzin, I. D., Krause, J., Franks, N. R., & Levin, S. A. (2005). Effective leadership and decision-making in animals on the move. *Nature, 433,* 513–516. https://doi.org/10.1038/nature03236.

Fischer, J., & Lindenmayer, D. B. (2000). An assessment of the published results of animal relocations. *Biological Conservation, 96,* 1–11. https://doi.org/10.1016/S0006-3207(00)00048-3.

Flack, A., Biro, D., Guilford, T., & Freeman, R. (2015). Modelling group navigation: Transitive social structures improve navigational performance. *Journal of the Royal Society Interface, 12*(108). https://doi.org/10.1098/rsif.2015.0213.

Gee, H. (2013). *The accidental species: Misunderstandings of human evolution.* Chicago: University of Chicago Press.

Gehring, J., Kerlinger, P., & Manville, A. M. (2009). Communication towers, lights, and birds: Successful methods for reducing the frequency of avian collisions. *Ecological Applications, 19*(2), 505–514. https://doi.org/10.1890/07-1708.1.

Griffith, B., Scott, J. M., Carpenter, J. W., & Reed, C. (1989). Translocation as a species conservation tool: Status and strategy. *Science, 245*(4917), 477–480. https://doi.org/10.1126/science.245.4917.477.

Guttall, V., & Couzin, I. D. (2010). Social interactions, information use, and the evolution of collective migration. *Proceedings of the National Academy of Sciences, 107*(37), 16172–16177. https://doi.org/10.1073/pnas.1006874107.

Haydon, D. T., Morales, J. M., Yott, A., Jenkins, D. A., Rosatte, R., & Fryxell, J. M. (2008). Socially informed random walks: Incorporating group dynamics into models of population spread and growth. *Proceedings of the Royal Society, 275,* 1101–1109. https://doi.org/10.1098/rspb.2007.1688.

Hemelrijk, C. K., & Hildenbrandt, H. (2012). Schools of fish and flocks of birds: Their shape and internal structure by self-organization. *Interface Focus, 2*, 726–737. https://doi.org/10.1098/rsfs.2012.0025.

Hopewell, L. J., Leaver, L. A., & Lea, S. E. (2008). Effects of competition and food availability on travel time in scatter-hoarding gray squirrels (Sciurus carolinensis). *Behavioral Ecology, 19*, 1143–1149. https://doi.org/10.1093/beheco/arn095.

Hutchinson, M., Vickers, M. H., Jackson, D., & Wilkes, L. (2006). Like wolves in a pack: Predatory alliances of bullies in nursing. *Journal of Management and Organization, 12*(3), 235–250. https://doi.org/10.1017/S1833367200003989.

Jachowski, D. S., & Singh, N. J. (2015). Toward a mechanistic understanding of animal migration: Incorporating physiological measurements in the study of animal movement. *Conservation Physiology, 3*, 1–12. https://doi.org/10.1093/conphys/cov035.

Kenrick, D. T., & Griskevicius, V. (2013). *The rational animal*. New York, NY: Basic Books.

Levitis, D. A., Lidicker, W. Z., & Freund, G. (2009). Behavioural biologists do not agree on what constitutes behaviour. *Animal Behavior, 78*, 103–110. https://doi.org/10.1016/j.anbehav.2009.03.018.

Linklater, W. L., Cameron, E. Z., Stafford, K. J., & Minot, E. O. (2013). Removal experiments indicate that subordinate stallions are not helpers. *Behavioural Processes, 94*, 1–4. https://doi.org/10.1016/j.beproc.2013.02.005.

Lowe, T. (2015, May). NAEBA's position on wild elk relocation projects. *North American Elk*, pp. 1–2.

Marras, S., Killen, S. S., Lindström, J., McKenzie, D. J., Steffensen, J. F., & Domenici, P. (2015). Fish swimming in schools save energy regardless of their spatial position. *Behavioral Ecology and Sociobiology, 69*(2), 219–226. https://doi.org/10.1007/s00265-014-1834-4.

Mech, L. D. (1966). The wolves of Isle Royale. *Fauna of the national parks of the United States*. Washington, DC: U.S. Government Printing Office. Retrieved from: https://www.nps.gov/parkhistory/online_books/fauna7/fauna.htm.

Mech, L. D. (1999). Alpha status, dominance, and division of labor in wolf packs. *Canadian Journal of Zoology, 77*(8), 1196–1203. https://doi.org/10.1139/cjz-77-8-1196.

Meglich, P. A., & Gumbus, A. (2015). Alpha and omega: When bullies run in packs. *Journal of Leadership and Organizational Studies, 22*(4), 377–386. https://doi.org/10.1177/1548051815594008.

Muro, C., Escobedo, R., Spector, L., & Coppinger, R. P. (2011). Wolf-pack (Canis lupus) hunting strategies emerge from simple rules in computational simulations. *Behavioural Processes, 88*, 192–197. https://doi.org/10.1016/j.beproc.2011.09.006.

Nakayama, S., Stumpe, M. C., Manica, A., & Johnstone, R. A. (2013). Experience overrides personality differences in the tendency to follow but not in the tendency to lead. *Proceedings of the Royal Society, 280.* https://doi.org/10.1098/rspb.2013.1724.

Nathan, R., Getz, W. M., Revilla, E., Holyoak, M., Kadmon, R., Saltz, D., & Smouse, P. E. (2008). A movement ecology paradigm for unifying organismal movement research. *Proceedings of the National Academy of Sciences of the United States of America, 105*(49), 19052–19059. https://doi.org/10.1073/pnas.0800375105.

Neuhoff, J. G. (2001). An adaptive bias in the perception of looming auditory motion. *Ecological Biology,* 87–110. https://doi.org/10.1207/s15326969eco1302_2.

Newton, I. (2008). *The migration ecology of birds.* London: Elsevier.

Pellis, S. M., Pellis, V. C., & Iwaniuk, A. N. (2014). Pattern in behavior: The characterization, origins, and evolution of behavior patterns. In M. Naguib, L. Barrett, H. J. Brockmann, S. Healy, J. C. Mitani, T. J. Roper, & L. W. Simmons (Eds.), *Advances in the study of behavior* (Vol. 46, pp. 127–189). Oxford: Elsevier.

Pike, T. W., & Laland, K. N. (2010). Conformist learning in nine-spined sticklebacks' foraging decisions. *Biology Letters,* 466–468. https://doi.org/10.1098/rsbl.2009.1014.

Popp, J. N., Toman, T., Mallory, F. F., & Hamr, J. (2014). A century of elk restoration in Eastern North America. *Restoration Ecology, 22*(6), 723–730. https://doi.org/10.1111/rec.12150.

Portugal, S. J., Hubel, T. Y., Fritz, J., Heese, S., Trobe, D., Voekl, B., …, Usherwood, J. R. (2014). Upwash exploitation and downwash avoidance by flap phasing in ibis formation flight. *Nature, 505,* 399–402. https://doi.org/10.1038/nature12939.

Reinhardt, V., & Reinhardt, A. (1981). Cohesive relationships in a cattle herd (Bos indicus). *Behaviour, 77*(3), 121–151. https://doi.org/10.1163/156853981X00194.

Rosatte, R., Hamr, J., Young, J., Filion, I., & Smith, H. (2007). The restoration of Elk (Cervus elaphus) in Ontariao, Canada: 1998–2005. *Restoration Ecology, 15*(1). https://doi.org/10.1111/j.1526-100x.2006.00187.x.

Šárová, R., Špinka, M., Panamá, J. L., & Šimeček, P. (2010). Graded leadership by dominant animals in a herd of female beef cattle on pasture. *Animal Behaviour, 79,* 1037–1045. https://doi.org/10.1016/j.anbehav.2010.01.019.

Schwartz, M. W., Hellmann, J. J., McLachlan, J. M., Sax, D. F., Borevitz, J. O., Brennan, J., …, Early, R. (2012). Managed relocation: Integrating the scientific, regulatory, and ethical challenges. *BioScience, 62*(8), 732–743. https://doi.org/10.1525/bio.2012.62.8.6.

Seeley, T. D. (1985). *Honeybee ecology: A study of adaptation in social life*. Princeton, NJ: Princeton University Press.

Seoane, N. (2015). Modelling free-range cattle movements in forests using multistate random walks. *Journal of Biological Systems, 23*(1), S43–S54. https://doi.org/10.1142/S0218339015400045.

Sigurjonsdottir, H., Thorhallsdottir, A. G., Hafthorsdottir, H. M., & Granquist, S. M. (2012). The behaviour of stallions in a semiferal herd in Iceland: Time budgets, home ranges, and interactions. *International Journal of Zoology*. https://doi.org/10.1155/2012/162982.

Smith, C. M., & Sullivan, C. (2007). *The top 10 myths about evolution*. Amherst, NY: Prometheus Books.

Turnbaugh, P. J., Ley, R. E., Hamady, M., Fraser-Liggett, C., Knight, R., & Gordon, J. I. (2007). The human microbiome project: Exploring the microbial part of ourselves in a changing world. *Nature, 449*(7164), 804–810. https://doi.org/10.1038/nature06244.

van de Waal, E., Borgeaud, C., & Whiten, A. (2013). Potent social learning and conformity shape a wild primate's foraging decisions. *Science, 340*, 483–485. https://doi.org/10.1126/science.1232769.

Voelkl, B., Portugal, S. J., Unsöld, M., Usherwood, J. R., Wilson, A. M., & Fritz, J. (2015). Matching times of leading and following suggest cooperation through direct reciprocity during V-formation flight in ibis. *Proceedings of the National Academies of Sciences, 112*(7), 2115–2120. https://doi.org/10.1073/pnas.1413589112.

Ward, A. J., Krause, J., & Sumpter, D. J. (2012). Quorum decision-making in forging fish shoals. *PLoS One, 7*(3). https://doi.org/10.1371/journal.pone.0032411.

Xing, B., & Gao, W.-J. (2014). Biology-based CI algorithms. In J. Kacprzyk & L. C. Jain (Eds.), *Innovative computational intelligence: A rough guide to 134 clever algorithms*. Cham: Springer.

Zitterbart, D. P., Wienecke, B., Butler, J. P., & Fabry, B. (2011). Coordinated movements prevent jamming in an Emperor Penguin huddle. *PLoS One, 6*(6). https://doi.org/10.1371/journal.pone.0020260.

CHAPTER 6

Exploring Movement and Direction in Engineering

Introduction

The specific field of engineering that this chapter explores is geotechnical engineering which is concerned with the top few hundred meters of the Earth's surface for the purposes of civil engineering structures (Briaud, 2013). According to the American Society of Civil Engineers (2017) "geotechnical engineering utilizes the disciplines of rock and soil mechanics to investigate subsurface conditions" (p. 1). Geotechnical engineering was chosen for this chapter because the ground is fundamental to human life. *Homo sapiens* have walked on the ground and ate plants growing in the ground for over 300,000 years (Hublin et al., 2017). Thus, it is not surprising that the word "ground" appears in many meaning-packed metaphorical expressions used in leadership contexts; such as, keeping one's feet solidly on the ground, breaking ground, gaining ground, ground rules, an ear to the ground, middle ground, on shaky ground, and covering a lot of ground. The ground is important for human life not just for these reasons. The biodiversity of the life in the ground directly affects aboveground ecosystem processes in fundamental ways that affect human life (Bardgett & van der Putten, 2014). So, it is fitting that we address the field of engineering that works with the ground.

Understanding how movement matters to geotechnical engineers and how movement is studied starts with acknowledging that the ground is not inert nor is it stationary. The ground is like a sponge; it is a living

© The Author(s) 2018
J. L. S. Chandler and R. E. Kirsch, *Critical Leadership Theory*,
https://doi.org/10.1007/978-3-319-96472-0_6

system that moves and changes (Briaud, 2013). For millennia, strategies for creating structures for human use have focused on building them to resist nature's forces. In other words, to resist movement that can damage the structure. Geotechnical engineers play a pivotal role in evaluating and measuring features of the ground and predicting the movement of the earth that is likely to impact the proposed structure. Counterbalancing forces are designed based on the calculations that geotechnical engineers make. Geotechnical engineers apply physics and geometrical knowledge with knowledge about soils to predict ways in which the specific soil in specific locations are likely to respond to the human forces and natural forces exerted on structures.

Modern human-made structures are not simply sitting on top of the ground, rather they are embedded in the ground to increase their stability. The way in which foundations bear the weight of a structure helps it remain level and stable for human use. Buildings are not the only human-built structures that require a foundation to support them. Roads require foundations too and geotechnical engineers are the ones who compute the requirements for those foundations based on the specific geological attributes of each site. Geotechnical engineers also design retaining structures like levees, dikes, dams, reservoirs, channels, embankments, tunnels as well as the foundations for marinas, wharves, and ocean anchors for things like oil platforms. Geotechnical engineering is part of civil engineering and like all parts of civil engineering, the goal is to plan, design, build, and maintain human infrastructure systems such that their capacity exceeds the demands upon them (Frost, Roozbahani, Peralta, Mallett, & Hanumasagar, 2017).

Some disciplines can point to one individual as being instrumental to its creation and Karl Terzaghi is that person in geotechnical engineering (Das & Sobhan, 2014, p. 8). However, before he came along, structures were created that relied on geotechnical principles, even if those principles were not documented nor well-understood. For example, geotechnical engineering work transformed England's mucky dirt roads that were impassable much of the year into forty-foot wide level gravel highways in the mid-1800s (Guldi, 2012) and currently, there at least 36 million km of roads on Earth across 223 countries (U.S. Central Intelligence Agency, 2017).

Cement is the key ingredient for concrete and concrete is the most common civil engineering material used for building the civil infrastructure that is key to human development. For close to a century the cement produced for structures and infrastructure contributes at least 4% of the global annual CO_2 emissions that are contributed to climate change (Canadell et al., 2007). While global efforts are underway to mitigate CO_2 emissions (European Cement Research Academy, 2017), based on recent predictions, CO_2 emissions from producing cement are projected to peak in the coming decades before they drop after 2050 (van Ruijven et al., 2016). Analyzing past practices and considering future predictions about the impacts of human infrastructure is bringing changes to every discipline, including geotechnical engineering.

In the United States, a federally funded research center is investigating biological and bio-inspired processes that can "create a paradigm shift in the practice of geotechnical engineering from one that depends on energy and materials intensive solutions to one that minimizes the impact of its engineering solutions" (National Science Foundation, 2017). This research center is called the Center for Bio-mediated and Bio-inspired Geotechnics (CBBG) and it is not alone; the Geotechnical and Environmental Research Group Innovation and Knowledge Centre (IKC) located at the University of Cambridge which was established in 2011 (University of Cambridge, Geotechnical and Environmental Research Group, 2017) is also tackling similar challenges. For both these research centers, looking to nature makes sense because nature has efficient biological processes effectively overcoming some of the challenges that vex geotechnical engineers today. Examples include:

> ant excavation processes that are 1,000 times more energy efficient than human tunneling machines; carbonate-cemented sand that is exceptionally resistant to erosion and earthquakes; and self-sensing and self-healing tree root structures that are 10 times more efficient than any mechanical soil reinforcing system developed by humans. (CBBG Fact Sheet, 2015)

The *Climate Science Special Report: A Sustained Assessment Activity of the US Global Change* (Wuebbles, Fahey, & Hibbard, 2017) also explains why developing more sustainable geotechnical engineering materials, methods, models, and approaches is necessary.

While our ancestors have only walked on the ground over the last 300 millennia, Earth has been evolving for over four and a half billion years. The Earth's movement includes not just earthquakes and major events such as plate tectonics. Earth's movement also includes landslides, sinkholes, sediment transportation, and dust storms. In addition to the earth

moving itself, water moves the earth too. Water is "a fundamental component of the dynamic Earth system; water participates in nearly every
geological process" (Hancock & Skinner, 2000, p. 1095). Water's freezing and thawing action have split large boulders into smaller rocks and
split those into ever smaller pieces for a long time. Water, in its various
forms, has moved and continues to move boulders, rocks, sand, silt, and
clay. For example, over three decades ago, estimates were that globally at
least 12.2 billion metric tons of sediment were deposited annually in the
oceans from rivers (Milliman & Meade, 1983). While many major rivers
around the globe have drastically reduced the volume of sediment they
are depositing into the ocean, more recently, the estimate is still between
15 and 20 billion metric tons (Walling, 2006). Not only does water
move earth at this macro-scale, water in soil must always be considered
when dealing with geotechnics because the layer of Earth that geotechnical engineers work with is continually participating in the hydrologic
cycle.

Wind also moves earth. While airborne dust can easily been cast as a
culprit by focusing on its contribution to human health problems, road
and aviation accidents, and the loss of topsoil for human food production; dust also participates in fertilization process and can enhance precipitation (UNEP, WMO, UNCCD, 2016). Recognizing that only
about 25% of the sand and dust storms can be attributed to human
activity, the United Nations recently commissioned an analysis of these
storms worldwide to determine whether dust storms have gotten worse
in recent decades and what can be done to prevent them and protect
humans from their impact (UNEP, WMO, UNCCD, 2016). Their com-
mittee concluded that "global annual dust emissions have increased by
25% to 50% over the last century due to a combination of land use and
climate changes" (UNEP, WMO, UNCCD, 2016, p. xi). This prompts
an acknowledgment that humans are part of nature; therefore, our collective impact on the Earth's movement must be considered as well. For
example, "human-caused earthquakes have been studied as an environmental hazard since the twentieth century. The data specifically show
that human-made mass changes can advance the clock of natural seismic
cycles and induce or trigger new earthquakes" (Klose, 2013, pp. 129–
130). Demands on human infrastructure also include wear and tear due
to nature. Measuring and predicting demands from nature and from
human usage requires making assumptions about the future. Predicting
the future is inexact and yet it must be done, so prediction models are

used. Looking to and learning from the past has been done in geotechnical engineering for its young life of only about a century.

Some geotechnical engineering basics will be helpful here to ground the reader's understanding. Soil laboratories measure properties and behavior of soil so those measurements can be used in formulas and models to predict how the soil is likely to respond to forces exerted on it or in it. Soil is composed of solid particles and voids and the voids can contain gas or liquid. Soil is composed of many things. The largest percentage of soil is tiny pieces of minerals which are classified by their size, largest to smallest they are labeled sand, silt, and clay. The next most prominent component of soil is water. Following water is dead organic material. After organic material are gases and they can occupy the same spaces in soil as water does. There are also microorganisms that comprise soil and that includes fungi, bacteria, and larger organisms like insects and worms. All the components interact with each other impacting soil's capacity to move or resist movement.

Reviewing the basics regarding what movement and direction is in geotechnical engineering before diving into the details of the specific recent geotechnical research are necessary now. Fundamentally, geotechnical engineers are focused on reducing, eliminating, dampening, or tempering movement that can adversely impact human-made structures or the ground itself. The goal is to stabilize human-made structures so that those structures can provide the value they were designed for. Geotechnical challenges focus on the force on a structure from one direction and calculating the balancing forces to achieve stability. Therefore, geotechnical engineers are focused on movement and directions and they have hundreds of formulas they use every day. To use a very simple example, let's consider a small building. Its weight will create a measurable force on the ground from gravity. The requirement is for the building to provide a stable and level space for humans to use. Because the ground is a living system, it is not uniform, so simply setting a building on the ground would likely result in the soil beneath the building settling unevenly. The uneven settling would likely result in cracks in the walls of the building or other damage to the building that makes it unusable or reduces its lifespan. The larger and more complex the human-made structures are, the more complex the measurements of movement and direction are in geotechnical engineering.

Calculating the amount of friction naturally occurring in soil is a core geotechnical engineering skill and the friction is computed as an angle.

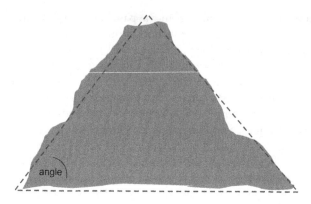

Fig. 6.1   The friction angle of a soil pile

When soil moves, the particles do not slide effortlessly past each other. They catch against each other slowing, and eventually, stopping movement. Friction is the collective resistance of the snags and catches that occur between soil particles where they contact each another. Imagine digging a hole and piling up the soil you dug. Piles of soil are created by the collective friction among the individual particles.

When a pile of soil is dumped onto a flat surface with normal gravity in an unrestricted space, the shape of the resulting pile can be thought of as resembling a triangle (Fig. 6.1). Measuring the angle at the foot of the triangle is referred to as the soil friction angle and is part of the soil's shear strength. This number allows for comparing the naturally occurring friction between soils. Soils with more friction provide more resistance to movement and soils with less friction will provide less resistance to movement. The more friction among the particles of soil, the larger the friction angle is. If the friction in the soil can be increased, the soil will be more resistant to movement and that benefits building foundations because more movement can be counterbalanced. All soil has some natural friction. If it did not, it would form a pool, like water.

Accurately predicting the possible movement of soil is necessary for all geotechnical endeavors. One of the uses for those predictions is to calculate the parameters necessary for foundations to provide stability for the above-ground structures they support. Therefore, this chapter focuses on bio-inspired geotechnical engineering research to increase the shear strength of soil and also on research into mimicking organisms' capacity to move through soil.

ROOTS IMPACT SOIL

Plant roots have been altering soil for millennia. One example of their impact was to shape rivers into the winding banked structures they are today argued Davies and Gibling (2012). The roots of tree-like plants during the Carboniferous period, about 300 million years ago, were instrumental in shaping rivers into the recognizable structures as we know them today. As was mentioned above, the earth is movable and is always moving. A mound or a hill or a mountain has the same properties as the pile described with Fig. 6.1. Its stability is dependent on its shear strength which is the capacity for the soil and rock components to resist forces, such as gravity, wind, and water. This is a natural property of soil and rock and is also something that geotechnical engineers have devised ways to increase.

While roots are not considered components of soil according to the definition provided above, they certainly are prevalent in soil. Early work by geotechnical engineers includes Grigson et al.'s (1947) recognition of the impact of plant roots and they hoped that research "dealing entirely with some of the biological aspects of engineering might be presented to The Institution [of Civil Engineers]" (p. 36). Much more recently, Ola, Dodd, and Quinton (2015) argued that while the use of vegetation for erosion control has been a customary practice around the world, most of this research has focused on the above-ground properties of plants, and little investment has been made in researching plant roots. This focus is evidenced in the commonly used model to predict erosion control referred to as the "Morgan–Morgan–Finney erosion prediction model" (Morgan & Duzant, 2008, p. 90). This model addresses "vegetation effects described in relation to percentage canopy cover, percentage ground cover, plant height, effective hydrological depth, density of plant stems and stem diameter" (Morgan & Duzant, 2008, p. 90). However, plant roots impact soil in many ways, namely by impacting water absorption, physically moving soil, relationships with bacteria and with fungi, and physically binding soil. Additionally, where roots are growing, the type of roots, and the degree to which roots resist breaking, all contribute to the ability of the soil to stick together (Khalilnejad, Hj.Ali, & Osman, 2011). Plant roots, in general, have a high resistance to breaking when pressure is applied and thus they add to the shear strength of the soil in which they live (Ola et al., 2015). Plant roots grow in response to the conditions of the soil and the capacities of the plant. Whether the plant is a cultivated crop or is wild, its roots are rarely alone in the soil. Roots of multiple plants can be thought to be competing for the same resources, which includes space. Addressing how the potential root-space gets occupied, O'Brien and Brown (2008) modified a model they helped develop (Gersani, Brown, O'Brien, & Maina, 2001) that addresses how plants compete for nutrients with their roots. They extended the model to consider the distance roots grow from the base of the plant as a cost so that the model "predicts where a plant will (1) have exclusive, uncontested rooting space; (2) have space ceded to it by a competitor; (3) cede space to a competitor; and (4) have space in which both competitors grow roots" (O'Brien & Brown, 2008, p. 444). How plant competition impacts their root development and subsequently impacts soil shear strength appears to not yet have been studied. However, the impact that roots have on soil stability has been studied.

Milleret, Le Bayon, Lamy, Gobat, and Boivin (2009) sought to quantify changes in soil properties caused by roots. They used leek roots (*Allium porrum*), a common fungus that penetrates the cells of plant roots (*Glomus intraradices*), and earthworms (*Allolobophora chlorotica*). Fungi is neither plant nor animal. A life form of its own, fungi feeds on the energy created by and stored in plants and animals. The largest living known organism on earth is a honey fungus (*Armillaria bulbosa*) living in Oregon (Smith, Bruhn, & Anderson, 1992) weighing in at over 100 tons and over 1500 years old is it also the oldest living known organism. Besides occupying this noteworthy position as the largest and oldest known organism, fungi perform essential ecosystem processes such as decomposing organic material driving the Earth's carbon cycle (Dighton, 2016). The fungi examined in this study help plants capture phosphorus, sulfur, nitrogen, and other micronutrients (Brundrett, 2002). Milleret et al. (2009) sterilized and sieved soil and packed it in pots so that the soil across all the experimental pots was identical. They combined their three variables such that all were examined alone and in all combinations possible with the other variables. Their study spanned 35 weeks as they examined the impact of the leek roots, fungal mycelium (mycelia are the part of the fungi that find the resources it needs and feeds on them), and earthworms. They measured the water content of the soil and the ratio of voids to solids in the soil and concluded that the earthworms destabilized the soil whereas the leek roots and fungal mycelium together without earthworms produced a synergistic effect stabilizing the soil.

Varying results have been reported in related studies. For example, Hallet et al. (2009) conducted similar experiments, concluding that plant roots had the greatest impact on soil stability and the presence of fungi did not matter. Conducting slightly different experiments, Hudek, Sterk, van Beek, and de Jong (2014) evaluated the efficiency of an evergreen shrub with the misleading common name of Oregon grape (*Mahonia aquifolium*), for controlling soil erosion control under various conditions using the Revised Morgan–Morgan–Finney model. This shrub is a native of western North America and is not related to grape vines. The shrubs they studied from June 2007 through May 2008 were growing in the Visegrád Hills in the north of Hungary. There were four plots of these shrubs that were 4, 12, 20, and 25-years-old of various sizes. Additionally, a bare soil plot was used as a control (Hudek et al., 2014). Unfortunately, their study did not demonstrate that the *Mahonia aquifolium* roots had an appreciable effect in reducing surface soil erosion caused by runoff rainwater as measured using the Revised Morgan–Morgan–Finney model. However, Hudek et al. (2014) explained that the effect of the roots, while not evident using the Revised Morgan–Morgan–Finney model, still mattered.

Also interested in the soil stabilizing impacts that shrub roots have on slopes, Veylon, Ghenstem, Stokes, and Bernard (2015) examined the impact of roots on soil stability focusing on the water extraction accomplished by the roots and the roots' physical contribution to the shear strength of the soil. They grew small shrubs from seeds they sprouted allowing the shrubs to grow for 10 months, *Jatropha curcas*, *Rhus chinensis*, and *Ricinus communis*. They chose these shrubs because they are commonly used on slopes to increase stability and they each grow distinctive types of roots. They planted the shrubs in special two-tiered plant boxes they designed that would facilitate their shear testing by applying pressure to the side of the upper section of the box while the lower section remained stationary. These tests allowed them to measure the pressure necessary to slide the top section of the box off the bottom section, tearing through the roots that had grown through that soil. From their tests, they concluded that taproot systems tended to increase the shear strength of the surrounding soil, while distributed fibrous roots only increased the soil cohesion (Veylon et al., 2015).

Swarz et al. (2015) were also interested in slope stability not erosion, and they developed a new empirical-analytical model that they named the compressed rooted soil model (CoRos) that captures one of the impacts that roots have on soil. Swarz et al. (2015) conducted laboratory experiments on roots they collected from spruce trees (*Picea abies*) cutting root sections between 4 inches and 15 inches below the surface of the soil. They protected the roots they collected from drying out and carefully incorporated them in soil in their lab to simulate a natural state in their test unit devised to compress the soil in a controlled and measured manner. They conducted the experiment multiple times varying the placement of the roots to produce a large dataset of results. They also tested root-free soil and then they created a model from the results that quantifies the behavior of a rooted soil under compression. Their work demonstrates that "root reinforcement for realistic root distributions has a major effect on the stiffness and strength of rooted soils under compression" (Swarz et al., 2015, p. 2119). Their model can easily be used for slope stability calculations.

The meta-analysis conducted by García-Ruiz et al. (2015) provides some useful suppositions about soil erosion research. They analyzed the variability among published erosion rates to assess the validity of the methods used in the estimation of erosion rates in soil erosion studies. They found that "no general rule, normalized approach, or universal criteria have been applied to the study of erosion processes and to determining erosion rates" (García-Ruiz et al., 2015, p. 167). Nevertheless, they produced a multivariate model that includes several basic environmental factors that accounts for 50% of the variance in reported erosion rates (García-Ruiz et al., 2015). However, they also underscored the remaining disconnects among the research that prevents a more complete integrated picture.

Living Organisms Are Components of Soil

"Soils would not exist without the complex and heterogeneous activities of microorganisms" (Buscot, 2005). Up to a trillion bacteria can live in a typical gram of top soil and while water is the component that has the largest impact on soil properties, the bacteria that live in the soil also impacts its strength and permeability (DeJong, Proto, Kuo, & Gomez, 2014). Additionally, soil includes enzymes and nucleic acids that can survive and maintain their activity outside of the microorganisms that created them after being absorbed by clay particles (Nannipieri, Pietramellara, & Renella, 2014). Finally, there are viruses and other proteins similar to viruses that cause infections, called prions, that exist in soil (Nannipieri et al., 2014). Very little research on how these smallest of microbiota impact soil from a geotechnical engineering perspective has been completed, but a substantial amount has been conducted on the bacteria that comprise soil.

One of the ways that bacteria impact the soil is through their biological processes. *Sporosarcina pasteurii*, is common soil bacteria suitable for use in experiments because they produce enzymes that facilitate desired chemical reactions. Enzymes are proteins that accelerate chemical reactions. In this case, enzymes are proteins created by the bacteria that occur in soil and can also exist alone in the soil. The enzyme produced by *Sporosarcina pasteurii* triggers a chemical chain reaction through which calcium carbonate (from calcium ions already present in the water in the soil) precipitates out of the water onto the surface of the mineral particles of soil (DeJong, Fritzges, & Nüsslein, 2006). The calcium carbonate can adhere to the surface soil particles which increases the friction between soil particles. The calcium carbonate can also form between mineral particles cementing them together. All that microscopic roughness and cementing can change the resistance capacity of soil.

A quicker and closer view of this same calcification process can be seen in household plumbing. Kitchen faucets often have a fine mesh screen on the aerator which mixes air with the water to reduce water usage. Common homeowner maintenance advice suggests cleaning aerators periodically to remove buildup. Part of the buildup includes calcium carbonate which precipitates out of the water onto the mesh by a similar chemical reaction that operates in soil. Calcium carbonate precipitation is a naturally occurring phenomena and is responsible for creating travertine limestone. Montoya and DeJong (2013) are researching similar cementation processes to determine the utility of the bonds that can be created among soil particles.

Researchers are also focusing on enzyme-induced carbonate precipitation (EICP) which is the same process of precipitating calcium carbonate out of the water as crystals that stick to the mineral particles except that this approach uses an enzyme derived from plants to trigger the process rather than relying on the bacteria to produce the enzyme (Hamdan, 2015). Challenges currently exist as the enzyme can only be purchased in a medical quality form and it is very expensive. Additionally, the enzyme can be very effective, meaning it triggers the chemical reaction to happen too rapidly, preventing the solution from penetrating into the soil.

Tackling this second challenge, Hamdam, Zhao, Mujica, Kavazanjian, and He (2016) conducted experiments to assess the use of three hydrogels to assist in the enzyme-induced carbonate precipitation for soil stabilization. Their hypothesis was that hydrogels would slow down the chemical reaction while also holding the enzyme in contact with the soil, extending reaction time, increasing precipitation efficiency, and enhancing the formation of a soil crust. Guar and xanthan gums were found to have the greatest water retention ability and to significantly reduce water evaporation (Hamdam et al., 2016).

Termite mounds have been of interest because they are bioengineered structures that provide stable living environments for generations of termites for decades. Udoeyo, Cassidy, and Jajere (2000) investigated the possibility of using termite mound soils for construction concluding that the soil could be used as an additive to enhance the strength of both mortar and concrete. Their tests adding mound soil in mortar resulted in an increase of up to 20.35% in compressive strength. Pereira (2008) described the use of synthetic termite saliva or *saliva de cupim* in the production of earthen building restoration projects for seventeenth-century building in Brazil. Using a similar approach, Sujatha et al. (2014) experimented with bacteria extracted from freshly created termite mounds as an ingredient in making concrete to increase its durability. Sujatha et al. (2014) found the strength of their experimental cement mortar was 18% stronger than untreated mortar. Relatedly, Faria, Battistelle, and Neves (2016) reported that using *saliva de cupim* resulted in a 25.28% reduction in the amount of cement required to achieve the same compression strength of blocks. Furthermore, Sahoo, Sathyan, Kumari, Sarkar, and Davis (2016) subsequently produced similar increases in concrete strength using *Bacillus sphaericus* to precipitate calcium carbonate in the curing of concrete achieving a strength increase of 23%. Kandasami, Borges, and Murthy (2016) compared the soil in a mound of fungus-growing termites (*Odontotermes obesus*) to the surrounding soil identifying significant differences between them. The termite mound soil, cemented by the termites using their secretions and excretions, was found to be ten times stronger than the surrounding soil; whereas the mineral composition of the surrounding soil and the soil of the termite mounds did not significantly differ.

Insects are not the only living organisms actively altering the spoil in which they live. In sandy or fine particle soils, thick biofilms can grow around mineral particles (Pastorella, Gazzola, Guardarrama, & Marsili,

2012). A biofilm is any group of microorganisms in which cells stick to each other and often also to a surface (López, Vlamakis, & Kolter, 2010). A common biofilm that we all experience is dental plaque. Li et al. (2015) devised a method for in situ, real-time imaging of biofilms creating minerals. They used their technique to reveal that a biofilm of bacterium, *Pseudomonas aeruginosa*, created carbonate deposits starting at the base of the biofilm rather than at the surface as had been expected. Li et al. (2015) argued that their observations support an acceptance that biofilms demonstrate a high degree of variety in their biomineralization capacities and generalized assumptions about biofilms are best avoided.

Chung, Krajmalnik-Brown, and Rittmann (2008) would not likely be accused of underestimating the power of biofilms. They devised an application allowing naturally occurring bacteria (*Dehalococcoides ethenogenes*) to transform carcinogens in the soil into harmless components (Chung et al., 2008). They deployed a device that enhances local bacteria populations that complete the transformation by providing hydrogen in a way that encourages the development of a biofilm. They have identified the precise genes within the exact bacterial strains that make the enzymes that are responsible for converting trichloroethene into harmless ethene (Chung et al., 2008). Their research on bioremediation of soils includes biostimulation and bioaugmentation which are just two of the nine bioremediation approaches discussed in Boopathy's (2000) review of the advantages and disadvantages of bioremediation. Since their review, Juwarkar, Misra, and Sharma (2014) have conducted a more recent review highlighting the advantages and challenges of bioremediation.

BIOLOGICAL EARTH-MOVERS AND MOVERS THROUGH EARTH

While there are many animals that burrow in the ground including foxes, badgers, prairie dogs, mongooses, bandicoots, burrowing owls, ferrets, tortoises, aardvarks, toads, chipmunks, rabbits, pikas, mice, moles, and voles; some geotechnical engineers are interested in the efficient ways that much smaller animals move through soil. Their interest stems from a desire to reduce the cost of human tunneling. Most of the cost of building tunnels, whether they are for transportation, utilities, or mining, is spent on extracting the soil. Furthermore, the most significant cost factors of tunnel projects arise from the geological characteristics of the site (Efron & Reed, 2012). The methods for soil excavation that humans employ is extremely inefficient when compared to what some animals can accomplish, for example, ant colonies. The capacity of ant colonies to efficiently excavate intricate underground spaces has drawn attention within the geotechnical engineering discipline because their efficiency in moving soil compared to their size and their energy expenditures far surpasses that of humans. Espinoza and Santamarina (2010), studied the excavation strategies used by harvester ants (*Pogonomyrmex barbatus*) in multiple types of soil under varying conditions of wetness. They sought to determine correlations between ant behavior and conditions of the tunnel surface. The ant behavior they were interested in was particle removal and rates of digging. They concluded that "geometric and force-balance relations define ants' digging behavior in soils" (Espinoza & Santamarina, 2010, p. 614). What that means is the ants' digging behaviors were responsive to their environments, but their behaviors also revealed some commonalities under all soil conditions. Specifically, the consistent tunneling behavior was that the minimum diameter of their tunnels was at least twice the height of the ants. This allowed at least two ants to maneuver past each other in a tunnel. Additionally, a single ant's grabbing capacity was always restricted to less than or equal to their mandible size. Furthermore, stable tunnel diameters were less than or equal to four times the size of the large particles in the soil. Espinoza and Santamarina (2010) concluded ants' resulting tunnels are "mechanically-convenient and energy-efficient" (p. 615) and where the tunnels go is more about going where the earth *allowed* the ants to easily tunnel rather than going to specific predetermined locations.

Monaenkova et al. (2015) were similarly interested in ants in their study, but they focused on nests created by fire ants (*Solenopsis invicta*) to determine "principles at the macroscale (nest level) and microscale (individual level) by which superorganisms collectively excavate" (p. 1296). They also examined the ants' behaviors in a variety of wetness conditions, but instead of using natural soil of various types, they created their own substance by mixing quantities of tiny glass beads of specific diameters with water in which the ants were placed and observed. They did this to control the size particles since that was one of their variables under study. Their results surprised them. The size of the particles did not impact the nest size as long as the water content was sufficient (Monaenkova et al., 2015). Another surprise was that although these ants could create larger pellet sizes than they did, these ants created a

consistently smaller pellet size in all conditions. The researchers speculated that such a strategy allowed the ants to adapt to their conditions
readily because regardless of the water percentage in the soil, their tunnel
diameters are consistent and passing each other in tunnels while carrying
a load limits the size loads they could carry.

In related research, Cao and Dornhaus (2008) examined the issue
of crowding for ants. They examined the impact of restricted nest space
on ants (*Temnothorax rugatulus*) and found that the metabolic rates in
crowded colonies were 14.2% greater than colonies in large uncrowded
nests. The researcher did not provide a reason for the increase in metabolic rate, but the issues of crowding could impact other research results.
Additionally, since ant size relates to width of the tunnels they create,
it may be helpful to review the research done on the consistency of
ant body sizes within species. The research conducted by Gravish et al.
(2017) with red fire ants (*Solenopsis invicta*) was positioned as supporting the investigations necessary for the design, development, and testing of subsurface autonomous robot teams that could be deployed at an
earthquake or other disaster sites. They conducted an experiment in artificial environments consisting of identically sized glass particles and they
compared the tunnels of groups of small worker ants, large worker ants,
with those constructed by a naturally occurring group of fire ants that
includes large and small workers. The large ant group created wider and
shorter tunnels than the small ant group. However, in both conditions,
the ants excavated an amount of material that correlated to the number
of ants working below the surface.

Analyzing a transportation strategy of ants, Cook, Franks, and
Robinson (2014) sought to analyze the network structures of the trails
used by ants (*Formica lugubris*) in the wild who belong to colonies that
live in multiple nests that are not connected by underground tunnels.
Their findings diverged from previous lab studies revealing that ants in
a natural setting created and used trail networks that contained multiple connections and they did not result in minimized trail length. Cook,
Franks, and Robinson speculated that "robustness may be an important factor in network construction" (p. 509) for ants. Another tangen-
tial study by Gravish, Monaenkova, Goodisman, and Goldman (2013)
with fire ants (*Solenopsis invicta*) examined what these ants do when they
slip and fall in tunnels. They speculated that the ants' ability to recover
depended on tunnel diameter. For their experiments, they constructed
artificial tunnels with precise diameters in their lab and a method for

inducing the ants to fall. The method they used to induce falls involved experiences for the ants that were much more severe than the normal bumping into each other that ants normally encounter in their tunnels and yet, in 52% of the trials, the ants did not fall. Analyzing the 48% of the trials when ants fell, revealed first that the diameter of the tunnel plays a significant role in whether the ant falls at all and also in its recovery. The fire ants they studied used antennae in additional to their limbs in their attempts to prevents falls and to recover from them. In fact, surprising the researchers, these ants used their antennae regularly for locomotion (Gravish et al., 2013). The researchers argued that ant locomotion and the tunnels they construct are an intricately connected system in which the space has been constructed by the very organism using it. Additional support for the viability of semi-autonomous underground tunneling devices is provided by the research by Aguilar et al. (2017) and these are envisioned for use in exploratory geotechnical applications.

Billington, Walton, Whitbread, and Mangan (2017) explain that "the gold-standard test of [biomimetic] solutions is their verification in the same natural environments in which animal data was recorded allowing direct comparison between animal and robot behavior" (p. 515). Additionally, verification usually involves two different examinations. The first focuses on implementing a model and testing it in simulated environments. The second step demands evaluating a robot in the environment it was designed for (Billington et al., 2017). Some earthworm experimental models have been developed and tested recently because earthworm locomotion is promising for the creation of self-propelled subterranean investigators that could replace the current process of expensive and time-consuming drilling to obtain soil samples. Daltorio et al. (2013) were interested in locomotion efficiency limitations due to lost energy focusing on the assumption that an earthworm's weight is equally distributed among its segments and that the worm is dragging its body causing friction for the entire distance traveled. Tackling the design challenges that previous robot worms faced by having only half their segments in motion at any given time, they designed their robot worms to use their other segments to grip the surface for friction. Unlike many of the other models being tested, most of the segments of the robot Daltorio et al. (2013) created are not in contact with the surface it interacts with at any given time, yet the robot can still move with little slippage. Zarrouk, Sharf, and Shoham's (2016) subsequent efforts also focused on the points at which their worm robot contacts its surroundings. They experimented with their earthworm robot fitted with flexible contact points that are capable of transferring and displacing external forces against them to other parts of its body similar to real earthworms. Using such a design, the energy required to move their robot was ¼ of the requirements that worm robots using rigid contact points require (Zarrouk et al., 2016). Building on Daltorio et al.'s (2013) work, Fang, Li, Wang, and Xu (2015) proposed a new approach to controlling the segmented locomotion of worm-like robots using what they referred to as "phase coordination" (p. 2) rather than the wave-like rules that other researchers used to control their worm-like robots. Fang et al. (2015) tested their phase coordination method with the eight-segment worm robot they created demonstrating that no significant loss in performance occurs and it reduces the number of independent phase variables to one making the programming simpler. Interestingly, their phase-difference approach can also generate peristalsis waves in the robot's locomotion without the existence of wave-like rules. Then there is the work of Horchler et al. (2015) on a new modular soft robotic worm similar to the one created by Fang et al. (2015). They used a mesh created from 3-D printing using commercially available materials to support widespread testing of their approach. Their six-segment robotic worm was able to move along level ground in a peristaltic motion.

These research results are promising, but these robotic worms discussed thus far were not designed to "eat" soil and move beneath the surface of the soil. Neither was the robot created by Omori, Nakamura, and Yada (2009), however, they did test their peristaltic crawling robot by covering it with film to conduct experiments in the dirt. Unfortunately, their tests in dirt only involved creating a tubular hole through dirt that allowed the robot to move through the hole. They did not include any excavating capacity with their robot, so it was unable to travel underground. Subsequent work adding excavating capacities resulted in a robot designed to excavate lunar soil and complete scientific investigations (Omori, Murakami, Nagai, Nakamura, & Kubota, 2013). This robot consisted of a propulsion unit and an excavation unit. The excavation unit deployed an auger that rotated inside the robotic worm moving the soil from the front, through the unit depositing the soil at the midpoint of the entire unit. The robot mimics earthworm movements extending axially and then expanding radially while contracting axially creating a high degree of friction with its body and its environment. Aydin, Molnar, Goldman, and Hammond (2018) have recently made some advances with another design that they recently presented but a great deal more work is required before a usable wormlike robot can be deployed for underground exploration.

FINAL THOUGHTS

Geotechnical engineers have devised ways to counter, resist, temper, dampen, reduce, mitigate, control, and guide movement of soil for human purposes for at least a century. To accomplish those goals, geotechnical engineers have focused on understanding and quantifying soil movement generated by nature; that is gravity, wind, rain, and temperature changes as well as more severe movements like earthquakes. Researching soil as a living system and interdisciplinarily addressing issues of soil quality as defined by human usage has been an evolving challenge more recently tackled (Karlen et al., 1997) expanding the scope of the movements and directions of geotechnical interest. More recently, that scope of interest has necessarily been expanded to include anthropogenic climate impacts from the things that the engineering profession has created. Consider the CO_2 emissions from the production of concrete discussed at the start of this chapter while reviewing the National Research Council's (2003) list of top 20 achievements in engineering that shape the current world.

1. Electrification
2. Automobile
3. Airplane
4. Water Supply and Distribution
5. Electronics
6. Radio and Television
7. Agricultural Mechanization
8. Computers
9. Telephone
10. Air Conditioning and Refrigeration
11. Highways
12. Spacecraft
13. Internet
14. Imaging
15. Household Appliances
16. Health Technologies
17. Petroleum and Petrochemical Technologies
18. Laser and Fiber Optics
19. Nuclear Technologies
20. High-performance Materials. (National Research Council, 2003, p. 1)

Highways are not the only item on this list contributing to climate change, certainly the burning of petroleum has contributed as well. One way of viewing the problems caused by the very technologies that have been designed and created to improve the lives of humans is to refer to the dual nature of technology (Vaesen, 2011), and remember that forecasting consequences are a responsibility of engineers regardless of the goals of their individual projects. Indeed, the National Academy for Engineering's (2017) list of grand challenges for engineering reveals some challenges that have been brought about by human activity, most noticeably the need for carbon sequestration methods:

1. Make Solar Energy Economical
2. Provide Energy from Fusion
3. Develop Carbon Sequestration Methods
4. Manage the Nitrogen Cycle
5. Provide Access to Clean Water
6. Restore and Improve Urban Infrastructure
7. Advance Health Informatics
8. Engineer Better Medicines
9. Reverse-Engineer the Brain
10. Prevent Nuclear Terror
11. Secure Cyberspace
12. Enhance Virtual Reality
13. Engineer the Tools of Scientific Discovery. (National Academy of Engineering, 2017, p. 1)

Carbon has always moved naturally between the atmosphere and plants, soils, and the ocean, but human activities of clearing forests and burning fossil fuels has caused an increase of carbon in the atmosphere as CO_2 that has contributed to climate change (Sundquist et al., 2008). Geologic carbon sequestration is one strategy for capturing CO_2 and storing it underground to reduce the impact it has on the Earth's climate. Debates among professionals about the feasibility of this approach including the likelihood of inducing earthquakes continues.

In pondering such unintended consequences, we can revisit Katz's (2011) examination of the engineering ethical conundrum by considering the engineering achievements of the Nazis to ground us. Katz's (2011) argument concluded that there are no neutral technologies; therefore, the sustainability and ethicality of the applications of the technologies created by engineers must be considered by every engineer. Katz (2011) argued that since "all technological artifacts have values embedded within them, then whatever engineers create will embody a particular set of political, ethical, social, and cultural norms and ideologies" (p. 580). He further argued that refusing to acknowledge this reality and "remain[ing] in the thrall of the traditional view that the design and creation of technology are ethically neutral, then we will be repeating the mistakes of the Nazi engineers" (2011, p. 581).

Keeping Katz's (2011) cautions in mind, we return to the Engineers' Creed adopted in 1954 in the US by the National Society of Professional Engineers which tells us:

> I dedicate my professional knowledge and skill to the advancement and betterment of human welfare. I pledge: To give the utmost of performance; To participate in none but honest enterprise; To live and work according to the laws of man and the highest standards of professional conduct; To place service before profit, the honor and standing of the profession before personal advantage, and the public welfare above all other considerations. In humility and with need for Divine Guidance, I make this pledge. (National Society of Professional Engineers, 2018)

This prompts us to ask, how do geotechnical engineers assess their projects, be those research, educational, or commercial projects, to ensure their work contributes to the betterment of human welfare? This question addresses the movement and direction of entire societies caused by engineers' creations and urges us to recall the various scores of human well-being provided in Chapter 4. While engineers' creations have contributed to the increases in human well-being scores, they have also contributed to decreases in those scores.

Within the CBBG research environment, a life cycle sustainability cost measure approach is used (National Science Foundation, 2017) to assess the full lifecycle feasibility and impact of the investigated geotechnical technologies as part of the Center's mandate to "create a paradigm shift in the practice of geotechnical engineering from one that depends on energy and materials intensive solutions to one that minimizes the impact of its engineering solutions" (National Science Foundation, 2017). However, Guinée's (2016) recent analysis revealed from a review of over 20 life cycle-based approaches that while their contributions are increasingly important to enable adequate assessments of technologies and strategies available around the world for humans to meet their needs, substantial challenges remain because no agreed-upon methodology exists. Additional work by Grubert (2018) argues that while recent advances in building effective life cycle measures have been fruitful, there is still a great deal more work to be done. Namely, (1) ensuring that social scientists are involved, and (2) that values and diverse cultural contexts are considered (Grubert, 2018).

REFERENCES

Aguilar, J., Monaenkova, D., Linevich, V., Savoie, W., Dutta, B., Kuan, H., ... Goldman, D. I. (2017). Active matter with intent: Clog control in excavating collectives. *Bulletin of the American Physical Society*. Los Angeles, CA: American Physical Society.

American Society of Civil Engineers. (2017). *Geotechnical engineering*. Retrieved from American Society of Civil Engineers (ASCE): http://www.asce.org/geotechnical-engineering/geotechnical-engineering/.

Aydin, Y. O., Molnar, J. L., Goldman, D. I., & Hammond, F. L. (2018, April). *Design of a soft robophysical earthworm model*. Livorno: IEEE Robotics & Automation Society.

Bardgett, R. D., & van der Putten, W. H. (2014). Belowground biodiversity and ecosystem functioning. *Nature, 515*, 505–511. https://doi.org/10.1038/nature13855.

Billington, A., Walton, G., Whitbread, J., & Mangan, M. (2017). Using the robot operating system for biomimetic research. In *Living Machines 2017* (pp. 515–521). Stanford, CA. https://doi.org/10.1007/978-3-319-63537-8_44.

Boopathy, R. (2000). Factors limiting bioremediation technologies. *Bioresource Technology, 74*, 63–67. https://doi.org/10.1016/S0960-8524(99)00144-3.

Briaud, J.-L. (2013). *Introduction to geotechnical engineering: Unsaturated and saturated soils*. Hoboken, NJ: Wiley.

Brundrett, M. C. (2002). Coevolution of roots and mycorrhizas of land plants. *New Phytologist, 154*, 275–304.

Buscot, F. (2005). What are soils? In A. Varma & F. Buscot (Eds.), *Microorganisms in soils: Roles in genesis and functions*. Berlin: Springer. https://doi.org/10.1007/b137872.

Canadell, J. G., Le Quéré, C., Raupach, M. R., Field, C. B., Buitenhuis, E. T., Ciais, P., ... Marland, G. (2007). Contributions to accelerating atmospheric CO_2 growth from economic activity, carbon intensity, and efficiency of natural sinks. *Proceedings of the National Academy of Sciences, 104*(47), 18866–18870. https://doi.org/10.1073/pnas.0702737104.

Cao, T. T., & Dornhaus, A. (2008). Ants under crowded conditions consume more energy. *Biological Letters,* *4,* 613–615. https://doi.org/10.1098/rsbl.2008.0381.

CBBG Fact Sheet. (2015). Retrieved from CBBG: https://cbbg.engineering.asu.edu/wp-content/uploads/2017/02/CBBG-Fact-Sheet.pdf.

Chung, J., Krajmalnik-Brown, R., & Rittmann, B. E. (2008). Bioreduction of Trichloroethene using a Hydrogen-based membrane biofilm reactor. *Environmental Science and Technology,* *42*(2), 477–483. https://doi.org/10.1021/es702422d.

Cook, Z., Franks, D. W., & Robinson, E. J. (2014). Efficiency and robustness of ant colony transportation networks. *Journal of Behavioral Ecological Sociobiology,* *68,* 509–517. https://doi.org/10.1007/s00265-013-1665-8.

Daltorio, K. A., Boxerbaum, A. S., Horchler, A. D., Shaw, K. M., Chiel, H. J., & Quinn, R. (2013). Efficient worm-like locomotion: Slip and control of soft-bodied peristaltic robots. *Bioinspiration & Biomimetics,* *8*(3). https://doi.org/10.1088/1748-3182/8/3/035003.

Das, B. M., & Sobhan, K. (2014). *Principles of geotechnical engineering* (9th ed.). Boston, MA: Cengage Learning.

Davies, N. S., & Gibling, M. R. (2012). Evolution of fixed-channel alluvial plains in response to Carboniferous vegetation. *Nature Geoscience,* *4,* 629–633. https://doi.org/10.1038/NGEO1237.

DeJong, J. T., Fritzges, M. B., & Nüsslein, K. (2006). Microbially induced cementation to control sand response to undrained shear. *Journal of Geotechnical and Geoenvironmental Engineering,* *132*(11), 1381–1392. https://doi.org/10.1061/(asce)1090-0241(2006)132:11(1381).

DeJong, J., Proto, C., Kuo, M., & Gomez, M. (2014). Bacteria, bio-films, and invertebrates…the next generation of geotechnical engineers? In *Geo-Congress 2014 Technical Papers* (pp. 3959–3968). Atlanta, GA: ACSE.

Dighton, J. (2016). *Fungi in ecosystem processes* (2nd ed.). Boca Raton, FL: CRC Press.

Efron, N., & Reed, M. (2012). *Analysing international tunnel costs: An interactive qualifying project.* Worcester, MA: Worcester Polytechnic Institute.

Espinoza, D. N., & Santamarina, J. C. (2010). Ant tunneling: A granular media perspective. *Granular Matter,* *12,* 607–616. https://doi.org/10.1007/s10035-010-0202-y.

European Cement Research Academy. (2017). *Development of state of the art-techniques in cement manufacturing: Trying to look ahead, revision.* Geneva: World Business Council for Sustainable Development.

Fang, H., Li, S., Wang, K. W., & Xu, J. (2015). Phase coordination and phase–velocity relationship in metameric robot locomotion. *Bioinspiration & Biomimetics,* *10*(6). https://doi.org/10.1088/1748-3190/10/6/066006.

Faria, O. B., Battistelle, R. A., & Neves, C. (2016). Influence of the addition of "synthetic termite saliva" in the compressive strength and water absorption of compacted soil-cement. *Ambiente Construído, 16*(3), 127–136. https://doi. org/10.1590/s1678-86212016000300096.

Frost, J. D., Roozbahani, M. M., Peralta, A. F., Mallett, S. D., & Hanumasagar, S. S. (2017). The evolving role of materials in geotechnical infrastructure systems. *Journal of Structural Integrity and Maintenance, 2*(2), 89–99. https:// doi.org/10.1080/24705314.2017.1318044.

García-Ruiz, J. M., Beguería, S., Nadal-Romero, E., González-Hidalgo, J. C., Lana-Renault, N., & Sanjuán, Y. (2015). A meta-analysis of soil erosion rates across the world. *Geomorphology, 239*, 160–173. https://doi.org/10.1016/j. geomorph.2015.03.008.

Gersani, M., Brown, J. S., O'Brien, E. E., & Maina, G. (2001). Tragedy of the commons as a result of root competition. *Journal of Ecology, 89*, 660–669.

Gravish, N., Garcia, M., Mazouchova, N., Levy, L., Umbanhowar, P. B., Goodisman, M. A., & Goldman, D. I. (2017). Effects of worker size on the dynamics of fire ant tunnel construction. *Journal of the Royal Society Interface.* https://doi.org/10.1098/rsif.2012.0423.

Gravish, N., Monaenkova, D., Goodisman, M. A., & Goldman, D. I. (2013). Climbing, falling, and jamming during ant locomotion in confined environments. *Proceedings of the National Academy of Sciences, 110*(24), 9746–9751. https://doi.org/10.1073/pnas.1302428110.

Grigson, R. R., Lee, J. M., McFetters, J. H., MacLean, D. J., Reynolds, R. H., Ward, W. H., ... Brown, C. B. (1947). Discussion: Soil drainage with particular reference to road engineering—Road engineering division. *The Institution of Civil Engineers Engineering Division Papers, 5*, 35–56. https://doi. org/10.1680/idivp.1947.13012.

Grubert, E. (2018). Rigor in social life cycle assessment: improving the scientific grounding of SLCA. *The International Journal of Life Cycle Assessment, 23*(3), 481–491. https://doi.org/10.1007/s11367-016-1117-6.

Guinée, J. (2016). Life cycle sustainability assessment: What is it and what are its challenges? In R. Clift & A. Druckman (Eds.), *Taking stock of industrial ecology* (pp. 45–68). Cham: Springer.

Guldi, J. (2012). *Roads to power.* Cambridge, MA: Harvard University Press.

Hallett, P. D., Feeney, D. S., Bengough, A. G., Rillig, M. C., Scrimgeour, C. M., & Young, I. M. (2009). Disentangling the impact of AM fungi versus roots on soil structure and water transport. *Plant and Soil, 214*, 183–196. https:// doi.org/10.1007/s11104-008-9717-y.

Hamdam, N., Zhao, Z., Mujica, M., Kavazanjian, E., & He, X. (2016). Hydrogel-assisted enzyme-induced carbonate mineral precipitation. *Journal of Materials in Civil Engineering, 28*(10). https://doi.org/10.1061/(asce) mt.1943-5533.

Hamdan, N. (2015). *Applications of enzyme induced carbonate precipitation (EICP) for soil improvement* (Doctoral dissertation, Arizona State University). Available through the online database ASU Electronic Theses and Dissertations.

Hancock, P. L., & Skinner, B. J. (Eds.). (2000). *The Oxford companion to the Earth*. Oxford: Oxford University Press. https://doi.org/10.1093/acref/9780198540397.001.0001.

Horchler, A. D., Kandhari, A., Daltorio, K. A., Moses, K. C., Anderson, K. B., Bunnelle, H., ... Quinn, R. D. (2015). Worm-like robotic locomotion with a compliant modular mesh. In *Biomimetic and Biohybrid Systems—4th International Conference, Living Machines 2015* (pp. 26–37). Barcelona, Spain.

Hublin, J.-J., Ben-Ncer, A., Bailey, S. E., Freidline, S. E., Neubaur, S., Skinner, M. M., ... Gunz, P. (2017). New fossils from Jebel Irhoud, Morocco and the pan-African origin of Homo sapiens. *Nature, 546*, 289–292. https://doi.org/10.1038/nature22336.

Hudek, C., Sterk, G., van Beek, R. L., & de Jong, S. M. (2014). Modelling soil erosion reduction by Mahonia aquifolium on hillslopes in Hungary: The impact of soil stabilization by roots. *CATENA, 122*, 159–169. https://doi.org/10.1016/j.catena.2014.06.017.

Juwarkar, A. A., Misra, R. R., & Sharma, J. K. (2014). Recent trends in bioremediation. In N. Parmar & A. Singh (Eds.), *Geomicrobiology and biogeochemistry* (pp. 81–100). Berlin, Heidelberg: Springer.

Kandasami, R. K., Borges, R. M., & Murthy, T. G. (2016). Effect of biocementation on the strength and stability of termite mounds. *Environmental Geotechnics, 3*(EG2), 99–113. https://doi.org/10.1680/jenge.15.00036.

Karlen, D. L., Mausbach, M. J., Doran, J. W., Cline, R. G., Harris, R. F., & Schuman, G. E. (1997). Spoil quality: A concept, definition, and framework for evaluation (A guest editorial). *Soil Science Society of America Journal, 61*(1), 4–10. https://doi.org/10.2136/sssaj1997.03615995006100010001x.

Katz, E. (2011). The Nazi engineers: Reflections on technological ethics in hell. *Science and Engineering Ethics, 17*, 571–582. https://doi.org/10.1007/s11948-010-9229-z.

Khalilnejad, A., Hj.Ali, F., & Osman, N. (2011). Contribution of the root to slope stability. *Geotechnical and Geological Engineering, 30*(2), 277–288. https://doi.org/10.1007/s10706-011-9446-5.

Klose, C. D. (2013). Mechanical and statistical evidence of the causality of human-made mass shifts on the Earth's upper crust and the occurrence of earthquakes. *Journal of Seismology, 17*, 109–135. https://doi.org/10.1007/s10950-012-9321-8.

Li, X., Chopp, D. L., Russin, W. A., Brannon, P. T., Parsek, M. R., & Packman, A. I. (2015). Spatial patterns of carbonate biomineralization in biofilms. *Applied and Environmental Microbiology, 81*(21), 7403–7410. https://doi.org/10.1128/AEM.01585-15.

López, D., Vlamakis, H., & Kolter, R. (2010). Biofilms. *Cold Springs Harbor Perspectives in Biology.* https://doi.org/10.1101/cshperspect.a000398.

Milleret, R., Le Bayon, R. C., Lamy, L., Gobat, J. M., & Boivin, P. (2009). Impact of roots, mycorrhizas and earthworms on soil physical properties as assessed by shrinkage analysis. *Journal of Hydrology, 373*(3–4), 499–507. https://doi.org/10.1016/j.jhydrol.2009.05.013.

Milliman, J. D., & Meade, R. H. (1983). World-wide delivery of river sediment to the oceans. *The Journal of Geology, 91*(1), 1–21.

Monaenkova, D., Gravish, N., Rodriguez, G., Kutner, R., Goodisman, M. A., & Goldman, D. I. (2015). Behavioral and mechanical determinants of collective subsurface nest excavation. *The Journal of Experimental Biology, 218,* 1295–1305. https://doi.org/10.1242/jeb.113795.

Montoya, B. M., & DeJong, J. T. (2013). Healing of biologically induced cemented sands. *Géotechnique Letters, 3,* 147–151. https://doi.org/10.1680/geolett.13.00044.

Morgan, R. P., & Duzant, J. H. (2008). Modified MMF (Morgan–Morgan–Finney) model for evaluating effects of crops and vegetation cover on soil erosion. *Earth Surface Processes and Landforms, 32,* 90–106. https://doi.org/10.1002/esp.1530.

Nannipieri, P., Pietramellara, G., & Renella, G. (2014). Soil as a biological system. *Omics in soil science* (pp. 1–7). Norfolk: Caister Academic Press.

National Academy of Engineering. (2017). *14 grand challenges for engineering in the 21st century.* Retrieved from National Academy of Engineering: http://www.engineeringchallenges.org/challenges/16091.aspx.

National Research Council. (2003). *A century of innovation: Twenty engineering achievements that transformed our lives.* Washington, DC: The National Academies Press. https://doi.org/10.17226/10726.

National Science Foundation. (2017). *Engineering research Center for Bio-mediated and Bio-inspired Geotechnics (CBBG).* Washington, DC.

National Society of Professional Engineers. (2018). *Engineers' Creed.* Retrieved June 25, 2018, from National Society of Professional Engineers. https://www.nspe.org/resources/ethics/code-ethics/engineers-creed.

O'Brien, E. E., & Brown, J. S. (2008). Games roots play: Effects of soil volume and nutrients. *Journal of Ecology, 96,* 438–446. https://doi.org/10.1111/j.1365-2745.2008.01354.x.

Ola, A., Dodd, C., & Quinton, J. N. (2015). Can we manipulate root system architecture to control soil erosion? *SOIL, 1,* 603–612. https://doi.org/10.5194/soil-1-603-2015.

Omori, H., Murakami, T., Nagai, H., Nakamura, T., & Kubota, T. (2013). Development of a novel bio-inspired planetary subsurface explorer: Initial experimental study by prototype excavator with propulsion and excavaction usnits. *ASME Transactions on Mechatronics, 18*(2), 459–470.

Omori, H., Nakamura, T., & Yada, T. (2009). An underground explorer robot based on peristaltic crawling of earthworms. *Industrial Robot, 36*(4), 358–364. https://doi.org/10.1108/01439910910957129.

Pastorella, G., Gazzola, G., Guardarrama, S., & Marsili, E. (2012). Biofilms: Applications in bioremediation. In G. Lear & G. D. Lewis (Eds.), *Microbial biofilms: Current research and applications* (pp. 73–98). Norfolk: Caister Academic Press.

Pereira, H. N. (2008). Saliva de cupim: Recent experiments with termite mound soil and termite saliva as stabilizers for earthen structures. In *Terra 2008: The 10th International Conference on the Study and Conservation of Earthen Architectural Heritage* (pp. 247–252). Bamako, Mali.

Sahoo, K. K., Sathyan, A. K., Kumari, C., Sarkar, P., & Davis, R. (2016). Investigation of cement mortar incorporating Bacillus sphaericus. *International Journal of Smart and Nano Materials, 7*(2), 91–105. https://doi.org/10.1080/19475411.2016.1205157.

Smith, M. L., Bruhn, J. N., & Anderson, J. B. (1992). The fungus Armillaria bulbosa is among the largest and oldest living organisms. *Nature, 356,* 428–431.

Sujatha, S., Sarayu, K., Annaselvi, M., Ramachandra, M. A., Ramesh, K. V., & Nagesh, R. I. (2014). Soil bacteria for the strength enhancement of cement mortar. *Journal of Civil Engineering Research, 4*(2A), 51–54. https://doi.org/10.5923/c.jce.201401.10.

Sundquist, E., Burruss, R., Faulkner, S., Gleason, R., Harden, J., Kharaka, Y., ... Waldrop, M. (2008). *Carbon sequestration to mitigate climate change.* Washington, DC: U.S. Geological Survey.

Swarz, M., Rist, A., Cohen, D., Giadrossich, F., Egorov, P., Büttner, D., ... Thormann, J. J. (2015). Root reinforcement of soils under compression. *Journal of Geophysical Research: Earth Surface, 120*(10), 2103–2120. https://doi.org/10.1002/2015jf003632.

Udoeyo, F. F., Cassidy, A. O., & Jajere, S. (2000). Mound soil as construction material. *Journal of Materials in Civil Engineering, 12*(3), 205–211. https://doi.org/10.1061/(asce)0899-1561(2000)12:3(205).

UNEP, WMO, UNCCD. (2016). *Global assessment of sand and dust storms.* Nairobi: United Nations Environment Programme. Retrieved from: https://uneplive.unep.org/media/docs/assessments/global_assessment_of_sand_and_dust_storms.pdf.

University of Cambridge, Geotechnical and Environmental Research Group. (2017). Retrieved from University of Cambridge: http://www-geo.eng.cam.ac.uk/about-us.

U.S. Central Intelligence Agency. (2017). *The world fact book*. Retrieved from U.S. Central Intelligence Agency: https://www.cia.gov/library/publications/the-world-factbook/rankorder/2085rank.html.

Vaesen, K. (2011). The functional bias of the dual nature of technical artefacts program. *Studies in History and Philosophy of Science, 42*(1), 190–197. https://doi.org/10.1016/j.shpsa.2010.11.001.

van Ruijven, B. J., van Vuuren, D. P., Boskaljon, W., Neelis, M. L., Saygin, D., & Patel, M. K. (2016). Long-term model-based projections of energy use and CO_2 emissions. *Resources, Conservation and Recycling, 112*, 15–36. https://doi.org/10.1016/j.resconrec.2016.04.016.

Veylon, G., Ghenstem, M., Stokes, A., & Bernard, A. (2015). Quantification of mechanical and hydric components of soil reinforcement by plant roots. *Canadian Geotechnical Journal, 52*(11), 839–1849. https://doi.org/10.1139/cgj-2014-0090.

Walling, D. E. (2006). Human impact on land–ocean sediment transfer by the world's rivers. *Geomorphology, 79*, 192–216. https://doi.org/10.1016/j.geomorph.2006.06.019.

Wuebbles, D., Fahey, D., & Hibbard, K. (2017). *Climate science special report: A sustained assessment activity of the U.S. Global Change*. Washington, DC: U.S. Global Change Research Program.

Zarrouk, D., Sharf, I., & Shoham, M. (2016). Energetic analysis and experiments of earthworm-like locomotion with compliant surfaces. *Bioinspiration & Biomimetics, 11*(1). https://doi.org/10.1088/1748-3190/11/1/014001.

CHAPTER 7

Tenets of Critical Leadership Theory and Their Implications

FINDINGS FROM THE TRANSDISCIPLINARY EXPLORATIONS

We used the constituent elements of leadership, that is, movement and direction, to guide our exploration within the broad disciplinary fields in the previous four chapters. In so doing, we did not narrowly define movement and direction and that allowed for an expansive exploration. Consequently, our exploration included movement and direction of non-human animals in their interactions with each other, the movement and direction of national measures of human well-being, how humans are moved to investigate and create beauty, and movement of and through the relatively thin layer of the earth's surface that is responsible for sustaining life. We explored the movements and directions of some tangible things like whales and soil. We also explored the movement and direction of abstract concepts like happiness, democracy, and freedom of choice. The context of our explorations varied widely as well. Some of our explorations were on an intimate scale such as our exploration of the emotion of being moved which occurs within an individual human and is uniquely reflective of an individual's core values. And some of our explorations were at the global scale like our exploration of the contribution to the rising levels of CO_2 that come from the production of concrete. In addition to the individual research projects we briefly explored and the insights you can glean from those, we also encountered three recurring components that each deserve some discussion before proceeding further.

© The Author(s) 2018   167
J. L. S. Chandler and R. E. Kirsch, *Critical Leadership Theory*,
https://doi.org/10.1007/978-3-319-96472-0_7

The Anthropocene Epoch

One of the recurring components we encountered can be presented within the context of what has been proposed as the name of the current Epoch in which we are living, that is the Anthropocene Epoch, described as:

> Human activity has been a geologically recent, yet profound, influence on the global environment. The magnitude, variety and longevity of human-induced changes, including land surface transformation and chang- ing the composition of the atmosphere, has led to the suggestion that we should refer to the present, not as within the Holocene Epoch (as it is currently formally referred to), but instead as within the Anthropocene Epoch. (Lewis & Maslin, 2015, p. 171)

The body responsible for defining "the units (periods, epochs, and age) of the International Geologic Time Scale; thus setting global standards for the fundamental scale for expressing the history of the Earth" (2017, p. 1) is the International Commission on Stratigraphy and it has not yet added the Anthropocene Epoch. However, the name is already being used by many who are addressing complex global issues such as Bates and Saint-Pierre's (2018) work using mathematical viability theory and considering the Earth as a "Social-Ecological System built around Money" (p. 244) to model stochastic uncertainty that can produce conclusions for making public policy decisions that can increase human sustainability on the planet.

The exact date of the start of the Anthropocene Epoch has not been settled and humans have walked the Earth for at least 300,000 years (Hublin et al., 2017). So, some of the human existence has existed within the Anthropocene Epoch. What is it about giving a new name to the Epoch in which we live that impacts the field of leadership? There isn't a direct connection, but referring to the Anthropocene Epoch stim- ulates a focus on humans' ever-present and ever-increasing impact on the Earth that reduces sustainability. Human impact, of course, includes climate change and several specific projects addressing climate change appeared in our explorations in the preceding chapters. To announce that those with an interest in leadership will need to be mindful of human sustainability issues is an understatement. The concerns go far beyond a general hand-wringing or a scolding exercise castigating *lead- ership* as a set of individuals who got us into this predicament and there- fore the current individuals referred to as *leaders* are now the only ones that must get us out of it. Nor is the constant restating that the current situation has been of our own making going to solve anything. But our predicament also calls us to envision alternatives. Thompson and Bendik-Keymer (2012) invited us to do just that:

> suppose we thought about how we might flourish in a new global climate? Suppose, too, that we understood flourishing as the ancients did. Suppose it were thoroughly ethical, moving beyond conceptions of subjective well-being to involve a broad conception of human excellence, beginning with the capabilities needed to live a life with dignity and moving onto virtues and vices of a new world, even well-worked-out relationships between our lives, our institutions, and the extrahuman world. Flourishing would involve a just and attentive relationship to our environment, rather than an unintentionally destructive one, and would involve restoring aspects of the environment we had unintentionally destroyed or accepting the novel ecosystems we have unintentionally created (Hobbs 2000). To flourish in a new global climate would then include more than adapting to radically new environmental conditions in order to carry on much as we had before. It would eschew desperate and paralyzed resignation to impending catastrophe (Hamilton 2010). It would mean changing our sense of ourselves, especially our virtues and vices, and finding what kinds of social conditions best clarify and support our dignity and decency. (pp. 1–2)

Thompson and Bendik-Keymer's (2012) invitation is not without its embedded challenges. It is not enough just to imagine all the possible ways for all humans to flourish in a new world; we must also consider how to create and engage with social structures that avoid totalitarian rules emanating from just one definition of what is flourishing. For it does not take much imagination to see doomsday forecasts being used to incite fear that then flows efficiently through social networks allowing people to be effectively controlled. Such flows of energy through social networks are discussed next.

The Constructal Law

Another recurring component we encountered in our explorations was a new law of nature that its proponents claim explains all movement and direction of flows of energy within and through all things, living, or non-living, and thus impacts all disciplines. The Constructal Law or Theory initially proposed by Bejan (1997) from within the field of mechanical engineering and materials science was summarized as follows: "for a finite-size system to persist in time (to live), it must evolve in such a way that it provides easier access to the imposed (global) currents that flow through it" (p. 815). Subsequently, Merkx (2007) explained how the constructal law applies to social dynamics and revealed that it relies upon the assumption that people adhere to the rational actor theory. Additionally, Merkx (2007) argued that

> any sustained series of human interactions becomes by its very nature a network, and that all networks, other things being equal, evolve toward efficiency. If they do not, they are replaced by other networks. The more that such a network evolves in the direction of efficiency, the more it will tend to look like other efficient networks, i.e., the more it will resemble the tree systems found in nature.... In any case, the individual motivations in social contexts, or the differences among constituent parts in systems of nature, are simply not relevant to understanding the evolution of networks, which is driven by emergent properties common to tree networks in both nature and social life. (p. 37)

This explanation seems to argue for a sort of relentless progression of human social networks that are not based on enacting collective human values for the sustainability of humans. Rather, it seems to argue for deterministic changes over time such that the network itself becomes more efficient. Such an image evokes a force similar to Hal in *2001: A Space Odyssey* (Kubrick, 1968), making human social networks seem like they are easy to manipulate. Furthermore, if the changes in the networks are responding and shifting and changing only to make the flow of energy through it more efficient, then it seems like leadership processes to move specific things and beings in specific directions play no role whatsoever. Let's take a closer look. The caveat, other things being equal, in this explanation deserves some attention because we argue that critical leadership activities could be those other things and according to the tenets we offer for critical leadership, it would not be equal. This explanation also highlights some of the systemic social organizational processes that we refer to later in this chapter that critical leadership's purpose is to disrupt.

The Human Brain

The third recurring component that we encountered in our explorations presented in the preceding four chapters involves an overall understanding of how the human brain operates. The influences that one's assumptions and understandings about how humans' brains operate are

[handwritten margin note: Like a accounting Pool & human system in US]

extensive. Clark's (2016) work that we cited in Chapter 4 explained that human brains are prediction machines, constantly creating predictions and then comparing perceptions from the senses to those predictions and only attending to the gaps. This was described as the most efficient processing model because from the synaptic level all the way up, this approach uses the fewest resources. Miller and Clark's (2018) latest work updated the model to provide a refined explanation of what the human brain does. Their latest explanation describes a tight coordination of "processes of continuous reciprocal causation that weave together bodily information and 'top-down' predictions, generating a unified sense of what's out there and why it matters" (2018, p. 2559). This updated explanation is described as:

> one in which perception and action are complementary manifestations of a single adaptive regime, whose core operating principle is the reduction of precision-weighted prediction error. Adaptive predictions cannot, however, take shape in an organismic vacuum. What my brain predicts, moment-by-moment, needs to be delicately geared to what I need, and to what I need to be doing. And what I need, and what I need to be doing, are both matters that depend heavily upon both my current physiological states and the shape and progress of current world-engaging activity. (Miller & Clark, 2018, p. 2561)

What does this refined understanding of how the human brain operates (which is still not complete) mean for leadership? It's complicated. First, we must keep in mind that scientific progress is not linear and that it takes time for researchers and theorists in one field to absorb and integrate relevant findings from other fields. While this is happening, we are wise to use caution because "we are at the very beginning of applying brain science to human behavior, including manager and leader behavior, and that there is a lot of junk science to contend with" (Eichinger, 2018, p. 89). And "although proponents of neuroleadership are optimistic, if we know anything about the functions of the human brain and our interpersonal behaviours, it is that they are exquisitely complex and context dependent" (Kuhlmann & Kadgien, 2018, p. 103). Indeed, Wall (2014) mentioned the NeuroLeadership Institute which is a for-profit organization advertised as "a leading global research organization and the pioneer of bringing neuroscience to leadership" (NeuroLeadership Institute, 2018) in his critique of such junk science. Yet, we need not wait to root out and discard outmoded representations of how the human brain functions that are embedded in leadership imagery, models, and language. Even if we don't refer to the human brain explicitly, our personal and inaccurate assumptions about how it functions are embedded in the metaphors and analogies we rely on to convey meaning. Recall the images for the covers of leadership books discussed in Chapter 2 and the movements and directions embedded in those images. Understanding the human brain as a central processor of incoming messages and creating outgoing commands is a persistent oversimplification of the kinds of movements and directions that function in the human brain. Those assumptions and obsolete metaphors are often ingrained in the field of leadership. For example, for over two decades Morgan (2006) relied upon these images as well as a reference to how holograms are produced to discuss the human brain as a metaphor for organizations rather than survey and draw from the ever-growing and current findings from human brain research.

CRITICAL LEADERSHIP TENETS

By exploring various fields of inquiry and how they understand and use notions of movement and direction, we have identified the recurring components elucidated above. These components contribute to the bedrock for the tenets that follow, but the tenets themselves still require some foregrounding to explain how they can be of service to building a study of leadership that is critical. We do not offer these tenets to be a final, exhaustive list of boxes to be checked in order to qualify leadership scholarship as critical. Neither do we assume that these are the only possible tenets for guiding critical leadership scholarship. Rather, the components above and the resultant tenets are non-exhaustive possibilities for ways of challenging the orthodox patterns of thought in leadership studies that result from our immanent critique. We recommend reading these tenets as potential ways of making critical leadership studies manifest.

We also think it is important to reiterate our insights from Chapter 1 about what it means to do critical analysis and to maintain that narrow frame. By emphasizing its etymological origins of diagnosing crisis and offering restorative action, we emphasize the embeddedness of leadership in broader social contexts and how it interrelates with myriad other fields of study. In so doing, we hope to avoid an understanding of the term *critical* that defaults either to an evidence-weighing processes of critical thinking, or an understanding of *critical* that simply means important.

א Wilson perspective

Additionally, we work to adhere to our own tenets in this discussion. Just like labeling some individuals *leaders* can too easily result in labeling everything they do as leadership which confounds one's ability to study leadership critically, we do not advocate for labeling some leadership scholars as critical leadership scholars as if all their analysis is done critically. Critical examinations of leadership are concerned with all manner of topics and constructs; they are not limited to what we address in discussing these tenets. We, therefore, offer these tenets in the spirit of operationalizing a critical perspective. That is, with the understanding of critical analysis and our analysis of movement and direction in various fields of study, we think these tenets can serve as good conceptual prompts for doing leadership studies critically. In the subsections that follow, we state each tenet and provide our theoretical justification for it and highlight some of the transdisciplinary linkages.

Tenet 1

Those who engage in critical leadership studies act on the recognition that systemic oppression exists in all societies. Critical leadership researchers and theorists examine processes that perpetuate social inequities that exist in all social organizations, and also acknowledge their own enmeshment in these systems and act to disrupt those systems.

Our first tenet acknowledges that oppression is a structural feature of societies. While at first blush this may seem like a claim of resignation or cynicism, looking at the structures of society for oppression opens new opportunities by moving the level of analysis from individual behavior to social structures. Doing so places the emphasis for oppression not solely on the ethical content of individual behaviors or individual interactions, but rather on the ways in which the individual participates within social structures, institutions, and organizations. In other words, changing the level of analysis from the individual to the institutional, organizational, or social precludes the "bad apples" defense. Much in the way that the rules of the game direct the actions of players, so too do the norms and incentives of organizations and institutions direct, reward, or limit the behaviors of individuals within those organizations. Cycles can be observed whereby the basic structure of the game is left in place because only the surface rules are slightly shifted to allow for labeling some individuals as transgressors, which gives the appearance of change, but the basic game continues. Shifting patterns of collusion have been examined and detailed, for example, Chandler's (2016) work with Whiteness norms.

Nevertheless, a leadership scholar adopting a critical perspective might point out the structural complexity of institutional arrangements that produce oppressive social relations and suggest that they change. While this may seem Sisyphean, changing institutions must be possible, since they are historically determined. Further, when the researcher has a critical attitude as established in Chapter 1, the researcher should not accept the inevitability of oppression. As a result, we suggest that part of this tenet is an invocation for the researcher to not only analyze oppressive social structures, but also to work toward changing them. Agitating for change is integral, otherwise, researchers would only devote their time to describing these social arrangements, perhaps noting their oppressive relations, but not suggesting that they be changed. Understanding that oppressive relations are not necessary, but rather contingent on historically determined systems, researchers may find that it becomes easier to suggest that while institutions may produce oppression, this need not be so.

The overview of how the human brain operates provided above shows an immediate shortcoming of much of what exists currently in leadership studies for critiquing social structures. The ability for humans to predict or internalize data is less the result of being an efficient calculator of inputs, data, and stimuli, but rather establishes a continuity that is contingent on experiences being predictable. As a result, humans tend to, subconsciously, reinforce structures that allow them to make their understanding of the world coherent. One way of doing this is taxonomizing phenomena. To use the example of leadership, which can be a difficult and ambiguous turn, there are a series of organizational, institutional, and social structures that make the term coherent, and thus a taxonomy of leadership emerges wherein there is movement and direction. Even given that within those assumptions, there are possibilities to flesh out different kinds of organizations, leadership is still too easily reduced to a list of expressions, all that fit in the broader parameter of the organizational, institutional, and social assumptions embedded in that taxonomy. At that point, questions about what leadership means in the context of how it understands its own movement and direction as a force among other fields of study becomes precluded. Instead, leadership scholars refine the taxonomy, and practitioners of leadership select which patterns best suit their personalities or situations and do not investigate the phenomenon of leadership itself, or how it is more broadly situated.

Reducing a field of study to a taxonomy can lead to some rather banal applications in the practice of leadership. Where matters of leadership might otherwise prompt a critical investigation of how people might reflect on the modes of oppression that exist, how they perpetuate them, and how they can change, there is instead a toolkit of a certain number of styles of leadership to fix problems that frustrates potentially critical insight. In this case, manifestations of oppression are reduced to procedural technical problems and a search for the right kind of leader or the right kind of leadership strategy, tool, or methdology to solve them commences.

To end our discussion of this tenet, we return to the notion of the individualistic bad apples defense, because it deserves some additional elaboration. We established above that the bad apples defense precludes the social-level analysis that a critical leadership studies should strive for, but it is just as important to point out which dominant norms are being reinforced. We will especially emphasize how an individualistic assumption of actors within structures rely on notions of merit and responsibility. Not only are these assumed norms a diversion from the broader level analysis that is required of critical leadership studies, but they also erase any insight into systemic oppression. We will rely on a critical theorist we discussed in Chapter 2, Herbert Marcuse, and his theory of one-dimensionality to make our case.

Marcuse (1968a) argues that it is difficult for individuals within advanced industrial societies to envision or strive for alternative social arrangements, because the logic of the established order is so totalizing (Chandler & Kirsch, 2018). The practical implication here is a flattening out of rationality, where the only rational paths of action or ways of life are ones that reinforce the existing order, as we describe above. This also comports with our thematic finding that human brains are always predicting, and they have a capacity to find patterns where none exist. The result is a society where the structural forces are taken as at least a given, if not an ideal good, and since the structures are not perceived as changeable, the unequal or unfair outcome is squarely placed on either ranking by merit or individual responsibility. Claiming that a society or an organization operates using meritocratic processes ignores the reality that the tenet forces us to acknowledge. Claims of meritocracy also reinforces the perceived unchangeability of the given order. Merit and personal responsibility are thus two sides of the same coin in one-dimensional thought that reinforce existing structures of oppression, by assuming that any hierarchical or oppressive relations are the result of individual actions or ethical worth, all sorted within a fundamentally fair, good, or at least unalterable social structure (Marcuse, 1968a). Looking at these factors as purely individual explanations or modes of analysis fails to take into account the broader social structures that produce oppressive social relations in the first place.

Tenet 2

Critical leadership research acknowledges that power is the performance of hegemonic behaviors that reinforce hierarchies. It also acknowledges that hegemonic behavior exists everywhere thus it is centered in the research.

We do not seek in this tenet to give the final word on what power is, but rather to situate it as a phenomenon vis-à-vis critical leadership analysis. That is, we look at power as an outcome of social relations, as well as constitutive of those social relations, in a codeterminant way. While Dahl (1957) represents a traditional definition of power as the ability of one individual to coerce another individual into doing something, we refrain from overprescribing what power is so as to avoid its instrumental deployment within assumed organizational parameters. In this sense, we refer to power as an "empty box." By that, we simply mean that we are avoiding an essentializing ontology of what power is. Instead, we look at it as a product of social relations. This is important because doing so is the basis of a critical analysis of the leader–follower arrangement that is often assumed as the starting point of inquiry in the field of leadership.

To draw a comparison from our transdisciplinary explorations, it is helpful to return to the notion of the alpha wolf. Hutchinson, Vickers, Jackson, and Wilkes (2006) and Meglich and Gumbus (2015) referred to people bullying in their workplaces as alpha wolves. That framing places responsibility on those individuals and conjures up a sense of savageness. Consider the knowledge briefly described in Chapter 5 about how wolves interact with members of their packs as cooperative family members and how they move collectively during hunts in complex ways following just two simple rules. The behavior of wolf pack individuals during a hunt had previously been assumed to require communication among them to direct individuals where to go and what to do. However, the research indicates that what looks like complex coordinated behavior requiring communication and direction results from each individual executing just two identical rules. That complex behavior requiring no communication nor coordination is exhibited not only by wolves, but other group hunting animals as well. Like the assumption that communication was occurring among the individual animals led to inaccurate understandings and models of group hunting behaviors, we argue that widespread assumption that power is an apparatus individual humans leverage while leading is misleading.

As we noted in our first tenet, oppression exists in all societies, and is a product of the social relations in those societies. Social relations create hegemony, which is a type of social power or energy because it is how

> dominant social groups achieve rulership or leadership on the basis of attaining social cohesion and consensus. It argues that the position of the ruling group is not automatically given, but rather that it requires the ruling group to attain consent to its leadership through the complex construction of political projects and social alliances. These allow for the unity of the ruling group and for the domination of this group over the rest of society. (Joseph, 2002, p. 1)

This fits our notion of power as an empty box, because "hegemony is not a thing or discrete social object but a series of mutually dependent social relations" (Joseph, 2002, p. 128). For Gramsci (1971) the question of hegemony is not *whether* it exists, but rather which groups determine it and benefit from it. Mirroring some of the threads in the first tenet, here too, is the notion that as a class-based analysis, it is not a matter of ethicized individual volition. That is, it is not a question of whether there are good or bad people who possess or do not possess power over other people. Rather, within the social contexts in which people operate, some sets of information are considered the received wisdom which guide and structure daily life of a society; the patterns of which are also reiteratively reproduced (Gramsci, 1971). What this means is that the ruling class stays the ruling class by enforcing and encoding certain norms, habits, and assumptions. Gramsci (1971) suggests this is a hegemony of thought and both he and Joseph (2002) would refer to it as cultural hegemony. Neither are referring to a conspiratorial cabal of elite individuals secretly meeting and plotting to maintain a stranglehold of thought, rather it is diffuse and collective actions through indirect means that results in each societies' unique set of belief structures and boundaries. We can use an everyday example to highlight the features. When people appeal to human nature as being cutthroat and competitive, or that the wealthy have more access to legislators, those are hegemonic modes of life in the societies where those seeming realities apply. Of course, it need not be that way, and at the core of Gramsci's (1971) project to highlight whose interests are served and why challenges that hegemony. Critical leadership studies, as we show in our transdisciplinary investigation, should challenge the cultural hegemony of such assumptions, such as the assumed leader-follower structure.

Hegemonic behaviors can also be examined within critical leadership projects by identifying the specific dominant social norms that are created and used within each specific project scope. The enactments of context-specific dominant norms will reflect the broader dominant social norms, but they will also reveal the particular ways in which the individuals included in the study are either consciously or unconsciously tapping into and using the invisible energy of the hegemony in an immediate particular instance. Such critical leadership research can also examine the contestations of those dominant social norms because resistance to dominant social norms contributes to the overall movement and direction of them—however slowly that materializes over time.

Our expectation that examining and disrupting hegemony be central in critical leadership projects also reiterates our finding in tenet one that accepting the institutional or organizational arrangements of society overlooks a critical analysis. In the case of power then, it is not enough to ask which group is able to exercise it but why. To answer this question and take the notion of power and challenging hegemony seriously, we suggest that the leader–follower dichotomy itself be subjected to critical scrutiny. In that sense, we suggest moving from the individual lens of power into a class-based analysis thus achieving our goal of paying attention to the broad social forces in which leadership might be best studied. If the leader–follower dichotomy remains fixed in a leadership analysis, then what both leaders and followers are doing in reinforcing and reproducing the hegemonic frame of hierarchies is never examined. It is this very reinforcing and reproduction that is a vital part of the problem of power in critical leadership studies because power is not the content or substance of the leader-follower interactions. However, their behaviors produce and reproduce the hegemonic common sense of these hierarchies at the outset. Challenging the leader-follower duality is thus not due to contrarianism but is rather a complement to the research that is done on the content and substance of the given leader-follower arrangements (Sturm & Antonakis, 2015).

Power is an illusion, or a myth, that papers over hierarchical structures. We are careful to note here that we do not say this to mean that power does not exist. Rather, we argue that an important critical analysis of power should encompass what produces leaders and followers in the first place, as well as how they interact. It is within this fundamental question that Baudrillard (2010) argues for abolishing the myth of power. He posits that a refusal to be dominated requires undoing power relations at a structural level. This is a massive undertaking, but it fits with our insistence of studying leadership versus cataloging what people labeled as leaders do. That is, what does leadership without leaders and followers look like? We think that question helps establish this new field of study, in the same way, that theoretical questions in other fields engage phenomena before doing empirical analysis. The reason for this is that if we limit our scope of analysis to people who are already designated as either leaders or followers, then leadership studies also reinforces the common sense hegemony of this hierarchy. The danger, of course, is that because hierarchy produces unjust and oppressive social relations, assuming them away as natural or unchallengeable precludes getting to the root of those oppressive social relations.

We realize that the task of adhering to this tenet is both incredibly large, and somewhat abstract. We are asking researchers to engage the scaffolding that produces the leader–follower dichotomy, and we understand that this broad view can be a difficult undertaking. But our transdisciplinary investigation provides a good logic for just such an analysis of power. As our exploration of the constructal law shows, a study of leadership that insists on rigid structures such as leader or follower insist on boundaries that are too rigid and not fluid enough for what actually occurs in interactions among people. Over various time frames and circumstances, people are simultaneously leading and following in small interpersonal flows of movement or in a large social context. Freezing certain behaviors at certain times and then ascribing a fixed personality trait as someone being a leader or follower does not account for those flows, and ignores the movement and direction of individuals, organizations, and society. Further, we connect the insight of this tenet back to our first. If the ceaseless flow that individuals operate in constantly changes their behaviors of leading or following, then we must ask ourselves how much of that is noise that does not investigate the phenomenon of leadership? We think this tenet orients the critical leadership researcher with an appropriately broad outlook for investigating the role of power within the concept of leadership itself.

Our explorations into research with nonhuman animals provide the backdrop for doing this kind of analysis. Describing the interactions among and between specific animals by classifying some as leaders and others as followers does not necessarily yield insights into essential qualities of those animals rather it illuminates processes yielding broader flows. Our second theme that emerged from our transdisciplinary survey emphasizes the environmental milieu in which people behave. Therefore, looking at behaviors within roles is certainly important, but the environmental architecture that emerges from the constructal analysis is just as important to understand to properly contextualize the behavior under investigation. In both the constructal and environmental frame, power becomes a phenomenon that explains social relations, rather than as a constitutive force of those relations. That is, instead of an individual possessing power and leveraging it against others in order to become a leader, the flows of a society and the hegemonic discourses provide the architecture whereby people become designated as leaders or followers with the essential categories, and their characteristics, assumed. Any analysis of power within leadership studies must account for the broad flows of power that go beyond particular organizations, or beyond interactions between individuals. In so doing, we hope that a critical leadership studies builds a broader analysis of power as it develops into a field of study.

Tenet 3

Critical leadership studies is not for teaching people how to lead or how to be better leaders or followers. Those who examine leadership critically eschew orthodox designations of *leader* or *follower* as the starting point of inquiry and focus on leadership as an emergent phenomenon of groups.   like Wilson

As we touched on in Chapter 3, our brains are wired to be distracted by the ubiquitous yet irrelevant human face. So, perhaps in ways similar to the distraction by human faces displaying emotion that Ambron and Foroni's (2015) examined in their work, those seeking to capitalize on a ready market are attracted to the field of leadership because they can take advantage of those tendencies. There is a vast amount of literature on this banal leadership as self-help; too numerous for us to review here. We note only that literature that promises to make people effective leaders , or to provide people with the right kinds of leadership from among all the kinds they might pick from, are not able to engage critical questions of what it means to analyze leadership in its broader contexts, and therefore preclude the critical engagement we lay out. To take only one anecdotal example, then, Kaufmann (2016) promises to give leaders the four virtues they need to be effective. The virtues that are listed are not grounded in any scholarly literature about the social situatedness of virtue ethics, and they make no room for critical analysis of the organizational contexts in which individuals are attempting to lead. The end of the text has an appeal to mindfulness, but not in any systematic way that seriously deals with the various cultural or historical traditions that inform this habit of mind. In other words, this is little more than a self-help book to let people give themselves a pep talk, flatter their self-importance, or otherwise reify the power relations that are already in place, already in violation of our first two tenets. Furthermore, this feeds the belief that there is some enchanted leadership knowledge or practices that one can discover or learn that will allow one to achieve everything one wants.

Instead, we stress that leadership in action looks fairly ordinary and commonplace. Over a decade ago others have emphasized that leadership in action is "fairly mundane, differing little from what other people do, at least at a behavioral level" (Alvesson & Sveningsson, 2003, p. 1454). And this was identified as a paradoxical challenge of conducting leadership research. This tenet stresses that this paradox is the result of framing leadership as a set of behaviors from an uncritical leadership taxonomy which individuals can practice and perfect according to a methodology or a blueprint. When leadership is conceptualized as an emergent property of groups it can be operationalized for measurement in numerous ways by focusing on the movement and direction, then this paradox fades.

The paradox is also maintained by concentrating on the intent of individuals. Some leadership research maintains a focus on efficiency by measuring what individuals labeled as leaders claimed they set out to accomplish (their intentions) compared to what was actually accomplished. Leadership researchers can stop overconcerning themselves with intent and instead critically focus on the impact of collective behavior developing attendant measures of movement and direction. Many examples of how to conduct such critical work focused on oppression based on race can be seen in *Measuring Racial Discrimination* (National Research Council, 2004). This work supplies any leadership researcher desiring to take a critical approach with the tools necessary for conceptualizing, defining, measuring, and examining oppression based on race within any social domain. Such a task can therefore readily be integrated within a larger critical leadership research investigation because the preparatory work has already been done.

In the lived experiences of individuals playing out second by second, minute-by-minute, each person's brain is engaged in the same processes of prediction and comparison in their attempts to achieve their own goals. So from an external viewpoint, a researcher could carve up each persons' seamless movements so that they can label some individuals as tending toward following more than leading or toward leading more than following similar to the designations as shy or bold that Nakayama, Stumpe, Manica, and Johnstone (2013) applied in their research with stickleback fish. Recall in their work, those designations were simply the starting point. They discovered that the following fish was more impacted by the rewards than the leading fish. And of course, people are not fish.

Examining leadership as an emergent phenomenon also means that the context is a full player in the action. And as we noted earlier in this chapter, changing the level of analysis to institutions, organizations, or society also comes with a challenge for critical leadership studies: we must also take it upon ourselves not only to study the systems of oppression, but also how and why they encourage the kind of behavior that they do, as well as how these systems are themselves reproduced. For an example of how this might be done, we can look at the subfields of some social sciences that have embraced institutionalism. Institutionalism emerged from the idea that institutions were the most resilient part of a society, because they have a longer lifespan than individuals, and reproduce social relations by reproducing themselves (Scott, 2014). In political science, institutionalism generally holds government is best understood by looking at the official institutions of governance (Scott, 2014). However, new institutionalists suggest that institutions do not need to be officially constituted by the state and show how individuals within communities identify shared needs and build capacity for collective action to best manage resources (Ostrom, 1990). In economics, the recognition that capitalism is a system of production that is historically determined and socially embedded led to a study of those institutions (Veblen, 1919). There are, of course, multiple other variants and deviations, but a common thread runs through each: the behaviors and choices of individuals are shaped by, encouraged, or precluded by the institutional arrangements with which those individuals choose to engage. With that in mind, we can claim that these institutions are oppressive, not because there are bad individuals (or individuals making bad choices) within those institutions, but institutions themselves perpetuate the oppressive relations and are responsible for their reproduction.

One of the most exciting things about leadership studies is that it is a relatively young field. It is certainly a newer field than many of the traditional disciplines, and as a result, we think there are novel opportunities to consciously guide the development of this field of study. We think it would be a misstep to insist on disciplinizing leadership studies; that is, building a stock of generally accepted theories, having a toolbox of the generally used methodologies of analysis, and fiercely protecting its intellectual space. Rather, we think that leadership studies should embrace its interdisciplinary endeavors, and invite a pluralism of perspective, theories, and methods into this field of study, as our themes show when we put our emphasis on the notion of movement and direction.

Tenet 4

Critical leadership researchers and theorists attend to the politico-economic milieu in which the leadership processes of interest function and employ a continually self-reflexive process.

Called to mind here are the problems caused when the researcher artificially ropes off a scope of inquiry as discussed by Pearl (2009) and explored in Chapter 4 as the main reason why causes cannot be truly discovered in most research. Considering this in conjunction with Miller and Clark's (2018) description of the human brain's predilection for prediction, and our capacity for seeing patterns that do not exist that Whitson and Galinsky's (2008) research revealed, attempting to cordon off and determine the specific causes of specific cases of oppressive outcomes that some individuals experienced in any specific organization in order to engineer a precise structural fix is a fool's errand. We note these initial conclusions to suggest that critical leadership scholars do not have

some external vantage from which to tinker with the institutional configurations under investigation or have some kind of privileged or enlight-
ened position when undertaking the analysis. This tenet instead invokes
a humility for researchers to see this interconnected complex web and
their own collusions with the structures and their resultant norms that
maintain it. Much like leadership, researchers are also embedded in
broad social contexts from which there is no outside, making analyzing the broad context in which individuals act all the more important.
Chapter 1 makes the case that a critical theory does not accept that logical positivism can always properly capture social phenomenon and argues
instead for envisioning a totality of lived experience. This totality is what
we mean when we suggest that the researcher needs to be aware of the
political-economic milieu. This milieu is undoubtedly multi-faceted with
many vectors of analysis, and while this does clearly establish that social
change is difficult, it is perhaps just as important to see that it is ongoing,
with the researcher being an observer *and* a participant. Social change
is a common way that movement and direction is conceptualized in the
social sciences and we believe our notion of movement and direction
intuits this, but to make it explicit, this tenet asks the critical leadership
scholar to consciously analyze the social relations of leadership in its contexts, how they are part of those contexts, and the impacts those social
relations have. We believe that this is the basis for a self-reflexive undertaking of research that more properly situates the researcher and values
intellectual humility on the part of a researcher to recognize that they
are just as much part of the problematic processes they are analyzing, to
some degree. This self-reflexive unfolding of the researcher as observer
as well as participant has no known endpoint, but in the enduring
struggle to be consciously aware of norms of oppression and collusion
within those norms, the critical leadership scholar is in a better position
to recognize and challenge oppression, as well as help build a vision of
non-oppressive leadership.

There are larger consequences for the uncritical reaffirmation of the
status quo that does not take stock of the political-economic context.
Taking the structures in which leadership takes place for granted allows
the uncritical researcher or leadership practitioner to advance the fallacy of presentism as explained by Stocking (1965). The fallacy of presentism suggests that while the past may not have been as good as it
could have been, the present is undoubtedly better, and a trajectory of
improvement will continue into the future, merely through the passage

of time, necessitating no fundamental actions to effect change (Chandler, 2016). There is surely an assumed movement when considering time as an experienced phenomenon, but this uncritical assumption highlights our argument above that not all examples of movement and direction are tied to a higher purpose. Instead, presentism is an example of how easily the observer can fallaciously assume that the chaotic vibrations of social churn are actual patterned meaningful movements showing a clear trajectory to somewhere or something better. This ties in with the one-dimensional thought laid out in our first tenet that assumes that since the social structure is unchangeable, we can only smooth out unfortunate kinks in a system that otherwise works. On a more concrete level, anyone relying on the false explanation of presentism downplays or even denies the social fact of oppression, by positioning it as a feature that is being resolved on its own during the inexorable march of progress. While we recognize the lure because it relieves people of having to confront oppression, obscuring, obliterating, excusing, or leaving intact the oppressive relations that keep marginalized groups marginalized is certainly no way to critically study leadership.

Within a framework of being continually self-reflexive, and with the cumulative effects of our other tenets in mind, we take up the idea of bad leadership. Within our thematic findings and our foundation of movement and direction, we note that there is a normative dimension to leadership and being aware of the political-economic situation in which individuals exhibit leadership intersects with those normative considerations. We will organize our discussion around Kellerman's *Bad Leadership* (2004) who stated that "it is my hope and intention that by discussing and distinguishing among the primary forms of bad leadership, we might ourselves avoid becoming entangled, both as bad leaders and as bad followers" (p. 48). The book starts by cleaving bad leadership into two subcategories, ineffective and unethical. It then describes several individuals grouped into seven types of bad leadership. The first assumptions that we tackle are the understandings or the definitions of what is examined. Kellerman's (2004) definition of leadership can be read as one in which certain people filling certain positions for a specific period of time are considered *leaders* and everything they did was *leadership*. The next definitional bundle is the understanding of *ineffective* that Kellerman (2004) applies. The one used seems to require identifying and measuring what people intended to accomplish and what was actually accomplished, and the degree of the difference is then their degree

[handwritten annotation: why does no one give examples or present where a case this applied?]

of effectiveness. Then somewhere along the continuum of effectiveness, someone can declare the demarcation between effective and ineffective. This is an example of the intent over impact emphasis that steers attention away from examining systemic social processes that perpetuate oppression that we addressed previously. The last definition issue is the essentialization of good versus bad leadership which we believe facilitates one-dimensional thought because the *good* leaders are the ones that reinforce neoliberal hegemonic rationality, and the *bad* leaders are illiberal. That is, to the extent that illiberal or bad leaders use their leadership to pursue those illiberal ends, they are bad; to the extent that leaders use leadership to reinforce the existing neoliberal hegemony, they are good. This dichotomy also violates the thematic findings from our transdisciplinary exploration, in particular, the constructal law, as well as the findings in tenet one, where we suggest that finding oppression requires a social-level analysis and should eschew essentializing individual behavior characteristics. In Kellerman's (2004) analysis the person deemed a *bad* leader has some sort of vice; they are evil, intemperate, or rigid. Those vices are then positioned as the causes or the reasons why the individuals were *bad* leaders. However, the argument is still advanced that it is possible to use the same techniques, strategies, that *bad* leaders have effectively used to accomplish bad things in the service of pursuing good things as long as one steers clear of the vices. Then one can be a *good* leader. This logic is similar to the argument that one can collude for years with dominant social norms that perpetuate oppression in order to achieve status and financial security and then detach unaffected from those norms as if one did not contribute to the suffering of marginalized people and then set off to "do good."

We are also concerned with the way Kellerman's (2004) analysis ignores the contributions of political and social theory as well as recent literature in neurosciences. One of those ideas is human nature. She asserts that human nature is not to do good, and some Enlightenment philosophers have argued the same. The problem with this analysis is that it pulls from a standard canon of Western liberal thought, the Hobbes-Locke-Rousseau nexus. Those writers were themselves trying to make sense of the liberal order emerging with market society. Their treatises on human nature, the state of nature, and government were, therefore, political exercises to make sense of their own movement and direction (Wolin, 2004). Also, in line with our third theme about the human brain, we find that there is no empirical evidence to support

what if good leaders are only good b/c they have good followers — which has been my experience the notion that humans have a legible nature that is external to society. Human behaviors are co-determinant with the social settings in which people live. So, there is little reason to try to dissociate individuals from their social settings (Fehr & Gintis, 2007). In other words, the question of whether it is human nature to try to do good or bad is empirically irrelevant, and more important, often says more about the political-economic system of the current context.

We did not single out Kellerman's (2004) text solely for criticism, however. Her position that we must not simply assume that leadership is when people do good things rings true, and we are well to heed that in leadership studies as well as in other fields of study. But as we have shown, essentializing the good-bad dichotomy as well as the hegemonic discourses that such a dichotomy reinforces does not help break the pattern of assuming that leadership is synonymous with good actions. We think that critical leadership scholars, by eschewing these moral assumptions, can move into a non-prescriptive realm of studying leadership. There are two upshots of this move. The first is that it relieves the researcher of trying to establish what kinds of leadership are good, or emancipatory, or democratic. This helps avoid uncritical taxonomizing and the assumptions of the social structures in which people designated as *leaders* act. The goal becomes less about what type of leadership leads to good outcomes that good people should adopt, but rather an intellectual engagement that people can avail themselves of as they look to understand and undo systems of oppression. We advise being wary of any leadership scholarship that has a kind, or a type of leadership that leads to emancipation; that kind of one-size-fits-all approach is one-dimensional and probably does not speak to the complex situations in which individuals act.

Tenet 5

The goal of critical leadership is human flourishing.

We realize that as we have established that there is no external vantage from which to conduct research and that we should avoid being prescriptive, essentialist, or overly normative when conducting research because of the chaotic movement and direction of large social flows, a critical leadership scholar may start to wonder if there is any particular goal of leadership upon which to start research. We think human flourishing should be that goal. We wish to avoid the critique that we elaborated on appreciate the collaboration of multiple sciences to make their point

188   J. L. S. CHANDLER AND R. E. KIRSCH

in tenet four, so we will establish how human flourishing is non-prescriptive, but nevertheless centers the goal of human flourishing as a starting point, while of course keeping its normative content up for debate.

Labeling the current epoch in which we live as the Anthropocene does not, it itself, accomplish anything. It does, however, center our collective responsibility because human flourishing as a goal binds us to the well-being of the Earth. Similarly, this tenet asks the critical leadership scholar to engage these big questions so as to better take into account the movement and direction toward a goal, and to act as a reflexive benchmark of that process. In explaining tenet four, we also described the chaotic vibrations that can be too magnified if we only look at individual behavior, and this tenet reinforces the need for a broad vision of a conscious movement toward a goal. In our transdisciplinary investigation, we find that human flourishing and the conscious movement toward a particular goal of flourishing is a common thread in many of the disciplines we analyzed. Perhaps aesthetics and the social sciences provided the most recognizable discussion of these goals. Philosophers from Plato to Hegel to Kant take up the goal of a good society and how to properly deploy reason to achieve it as their central questions. In the social sciences, too, we see how researchers strive for a better society by understanding how institutions and individual choices can be harnessed or changed. The direction is clearly toward a better world, and the movement is how to get there; this is most easily seen in a broad analysis. However, even in the animal sciences and engineering fields, we see that questions of movement and direction are still undertaken with the goal of human flourishing in mind. Animal sciences highlights the complex web of life that humans inhabit, and in the Anthropocene, reshape. Engineering takes up explicit questions of how the Earth that sustains us can be appropriated to facilitate the ease of existence. These are perhaps less explicit considerations than the fields of aesthetics or social sciences, but our theme of sustainability helps uncover how these fields undertake their analysis of movement and direction toward a goal that must take into account how humans interact with the environment.

Our emphasis on the ideas of movement and direction serve us well as we build out this tenet of human flourishing, because they allow us to avoid being prescriptive while still being nevertheless normative. What we mean by this is that we do not have an essentialized definition of what *flourishing* means, and it is part of a critical leadership researcher's agenda to make the case for what flourishing looks like. We maintain our skepticism of any research that claims to divine a standard set of things to do to achieve human flourishing. The discernment of movement and direction at a given place at a given time will inform the researcher what flourishing looks like. Avoiding that prescriptive element leaves the concept open to contestation, even if flourishing is generally understood to be the goal. The idea of flourishing ties back to our investigation of critical theory in Chapter 1. When the researcher understands that a society is at a critical juncture, that is, is in crisis, the researcher is compelled to attend to corrective action and that action should aim toward human flourishing.

Although we avoid essentializing the concept to keep it relevant and contestable, we nevertheless wish to establish how we envision it and how it can help build a critical leadership studies. Once again, going back to Chapter 1, we think that a critical disposition helps to envision alternatives to the current context. Indeed Marcuse (1968b) suggests that as humans consciously tend to the development of reason, there is the possibility of imagining transformative arrangements to the social order, and those alternatives should be fleshed out, debated, and acted upon. Some alternatives are wrong-headed, to be sure, and some are impractical. Nevertheless, we are excited by the prospect of critical research scholars contributing to such a vision.

Our own visions for human flourishing supported our analysis. We think the world is marred by oppressive social relations, but it need not be. In whatever ways we are able, we confront the norms that reinforce oppression, upset hierarchical assumptions, and hold an intellectual humility about the ways in which we are shaped by the very forces that we wish to analyze. We, too, are caught up in the movement and direction, but we hope a critical leadership studies tries to understand it in its totality and consciously work toward building a world where humans flourish.

How are you confronting the norms that reinforce oppression.

FINAL THOUGHTS

We believe that studying and theorizing leadership is an interdisciplinary enterprise, and its relation to other fields of study is a vital component to understanding leadership itself as a field of study. We are not seeking to disciplinize leadership studies, but we are grounding it in the broad normative questions that also exist in other areas to try to anchor where we think a critical perspective can be launched. We find that there is no cosmic determination of movement and direction in any particular field of inquiry. Rather, a human-centered approach places the onus of social change on an immanent critique of the researcher. Institutions and organizations exist within their broader societies only in as much as they were themselves created and perpetuated. Without taking institutional arrangements as given, nor that any movement or direction is necessarily progressing toward some idea of the good, a critical leadership scholar centers their analysis on the human effects and consequences of systems of oppression and how they might be otherwise.

Every discipline emerges as a broader interdisciplinary venture that eventually builds a body of knowledge that sustains itself (Foucault, 1982). However, that does not mean that the disciplinary structure is necessary or that it is unchangeable. Disciplines tell us how we organize our knowledge; what we value and what is important. We think, for this reason, keeping the disciplinary arrangements at the fore is part of an interdisciplinary investigation (Eley, 2005). To say that leadership is an interdisciplinary endeavor, then, speaks to its emergence on the intellectual landscape. We believe that rather than following the path to disciplinarity via theory, methods, and a canon, we think critical scholars should keep the investigation open to insights from multiple fields of study, sustain pluralism in methodology, and be open to epistemologies that may not come from traditional sources.

We realize that leaving this new area wide open might seem like too much to ask. To be sure, others in this new field have engaged with critical theory. To a large extent, our work here builds on the works of critical scholars in organization and management (Alvesson, Bridgman, & Willmott, 2011; Alvesson & Willmott, 2003; Alvesson & Spicer, 2014). Not only are there already some scholars at the boundaries of critical inquiry, we have elsewhere taken our approach to critical leadership studies to integrate critical race theory into analyzing traditional leadership studies (Chandler & Kirsch, 2018). There is no one critical approach for everyone for all time. But as the final section of these final thoughts will reveal, there are tangible ways of implementing a critical approach.

Keeping in mind the importance of recognizing crisis for the critical leadership scholar, we recommend looking for critical junctures in the societies in which they live. So, we offer a brief discussion as an example of how we envision critical leadership scholarship engaging in the current context. In the summer of 2018, a media firestorm emerged over the policy of separating family members of asylum seekers or undocumented migrants (Associated Press, 2018). Officials of the US government detained the families by taking the children from their parents or care-takers and sent them to separate detention facilities. News reports described the harrowing conditions, children packed into caged areas, and the lifelong psychological damage caused by such separations (CNN, 2018). Public reaction to these actions and the policy includes shock and outrage. A federal judge ordered a halt to the practice and ordered that families be reunified (Jarrett, 2018).

There are a number of ways to analyze the entire situation, but from a critical leadership perspective, for this brief example, we draw your draw attention to just the actions that individuals have taken to disassociate themselves or their organizations from the behavior of the US government officials. For example, American Airlines and Frontier Airlines both asked the US government not to use their airlines to transport separated children and at least one flight attendant stated publicly that they would not work on flights that included such children (Wootson, 2018). This behavior could be viewed as good and virtuous or it could be charac-terized as righteous indignation stemming from a desire to avoid accusations of complicity. Regardless, neither of those characterizations investigates the full context including why this particular policy exists, what attitudes it reinforces, and whom it serves. All these questions are part of researching what can change these oppressive social relations. Note the stark difference between looking at a critical situation and attempting to designate certain individuals as heroes or villains, good leaders or bad leaders. Rather, we ask the researcher to look at these crit-ical junctures and ask how the ongoing processes might be changed to be geared more toward human flourishing, and then provide a vision of leadership to achieve that goal. There are no easy answers, and no sure things. Nevertheless, critically engaged leadership scholars and practi-tioners can contribute to building a world with less oppression.

triggered!

REFERENCES

Alvesson, M., Bridgman, T., & Willmott, H. (2011). *The Oxford handbook of critical management studies.* Oxford: Oxford University Press.

Alvesson, M., & Spicer, A. (2014). Critical perspectives on leadership. In D. V. Day (Ed.), *The Oxford handbook of leadership and organizations* (pp. 40–57). New York, NY: Oxford University Press.

Alvesson, M., & Sveningsson, S. (2003). Managers doing leadership: The extra-ordinarization of the mundane. *Human Relations, 56*(12), 1435–1459.

192   J. L. S. CHANDLER AND R. E. KIRSCH

Alvesson, M., & Willmott, H. (Eds.). (2003). *Studying management critically*. London: Sage.

Ambron, E., & Foroni, F. (2015). The attraction of emotions: Irrelevant emotional information modulates motor actions. *Psychonomic Bulletin & Review, 22*(4), 1117–1123. https://doi.org/10.3758/s13423-014-0779-y.

Associated Press. (2018, June 29). *Hundreds of children wait in Border Patrol facility in Texas*. Retrieved from: https://www.apnews.com/9794 de32d39d4c6f89fbefaea3780769.

Bates, S., & Saint-Pierre, P. (2018). Adaptive policy framework through the lens of the viability theory: A theoretical contribution to sustainability in the Anthropocene Era. *Ecological Economics, 145*, 244–262. https://doi. org/10.1016/j.ecolecon.2017.09.007.

Baudrillard, J. (2010). *The agony of power* (A. Hodges, Trans.). Cambridge, MA: Semiotext.

Bejan, A. (1997). Constructal-theory network of conducting paths for cooling a heat generating volume. *International Journal of Heat and Mass Transfer, 40*(4), 799–811. https://doi.org/10.1016/0017-9310(96)00175-5.

Chandler, J. L. (2016). *Colluding, colliding, and contending with norms of whiteness*. Charlotte, NC: Information Age Publishing.

Chandler, J. L., & Kirsch, R. E. (2018). Addressing race and culture within a critical leadership approach. In J. L. Chin, J. E. Trimble, & J. E. Garcia (Eds.), *Global and culturally diverse leaders and leadership: New dimensions and challenges for business, education and society* (pp. 307–321). Bingley: Emerald.

Clark, A. (2016). *Surfing uncertainty: Prediction, action, and the embodied mind*. New York, NY: Oxford University Press.

CNN. (2018, June 29). *Doctors saw immigrant kids separated from their parents*. Now they're trying to stop it. Retrieved from: https://www.cnn. com/2018/06/14/health/immigrant-family-separation-doctors/index.html.

Dahl, R. A. (1957). The concept of power. *Behavioral Science, 2*(3), 201–205. https://doi.org/10.1002/bs.3830020303.

Eichinger, R. W. (2018). Should we get aboard the brain train? *Consulting Psychology Journal: Practice and Research, 70*(1), 89–94. https://doi. org/10.1037/cpb0000107.

Eley, G. (2005). *A crooked line: From cultural history to the history of society*. Ann Arbor: University of Michigan Press.

Fehr, E., & Gintis, H. (2007). Human motivation and social cooperation: Experimental and analytical foundations. *Annual Review of Sociology, 33*(1), 43–64. https://doi.org/10.1146/annurev.soc.33.040406.131812.

Foucault, M. (1982). *The archaeology of knowledge: And the discourse on language*. New York, NY: Vintage.

Gramsci, A. (1971). *Selections from the prison notebooks* (Q. Hoare & G. N. Smith, Eds.). New York, NY: International Publishers.

Hublin, J.-J., Ben-Ncer, A., Bailey, S. E., Freidline, S. E., Neubaur, S., Skinner, M. M., ... Gunz, P. (2017). New fossils from Jebel Irhoud, Morocco and the pan-African origin of Homo sapiens. *Nature, 546*, 289–292. https://doi.org/10.1038/nature22336.

Hutchinson, M., Vickers, M. H., Jackson, D., & Wilkes, L. (2006). Like wolves in a pack: Predatory alliances of bullies in nursing. *Journal of Management and Organization, 12*(3), 235–250. https://doi.org/10.1017/S1833367200003989.

International Chronostratigraphic Chart. (2017, February). Retrieved from International Commission on Stratigraphy: http://www.stratigraphy.org/ICSchart/ChronostratChart2017-02.jpg.

Jarrett, L. (2018, June 27). Federal judge orders reunification of parents and children, end to most family separations at border. *CNN.* Retrieved from: https://www.cnn.com/2018/06/26/politics/federal-court-order-family-separations/index.html.

Joseph, J. (2002). *Hegemony: A realist analysis.* New York, NY: Routledge.

Kaufman, E. J. (2016). *The four virtues of a leader: Navigating the hero's journey through risk to results.* Boulder, CO: Sounds True.

Kellerman, B. (2004). *Bad leadership: What it is, how it happens, why it matters.* Boston, MA: Harvard Business Review Press.

Kubrick, S. (Dir.). (1968). *2001: A Space Odyssey* [Motion Picture].

Kuhlmann, N., & Kadgien, C. A. (2018). Neuroleadership: Themes and limitations of an emerging interdisciplinary field. *Health Management Forum, 31*(3), 103–107. https://doi.org/10.1177/0840470417747004.

Lewis, S. L., & Maslin, M. A. (2015). Defining the anthropocene. *Nature, 519*, 171–180. https://doi.org/10.1038/nature14258.

Marcuse, H. (1968a). *One-dimensional man* (6th ed.). Boston, MA: Beacon.

Marcuse, H. (1968b). *Reason and revolution: Hegel and the rise of social theory* (2nd ed.). Boston, MA: Beacon Press.

Meglich, P. A., & Gumbus, A. (2015). Alpha and Omega: When bullies run in packs. *Journal of Leadership and Organizational Studies, 22*(4), 377–386. https://doi.org/10.1177/1548051815594008.

Merkx, G. W. (2007). Constructal models in social processes. In A. Bejan & G. W. Merkx (Eds.), *Constructal theory of social dynamics* (pp. 35–50). Cham: Springer.

Miller, M., & Clark, A. (2018). Happily entangled: Prediction, emotion, and the embodied mind. *Synthese, 195*, 2559–2575. https://doi.org/10.1007/s11229-017-1399-7.

Morgan, G. (2006). *Images of organization.* Thousand Oaks, CA: Sage.

Nakayama, S., Stumpe, M. C., Manica, A., & Johnstone, R. A. (2013). Experience overrides personality differences in the tendency to follow but not in the tendency to lead. *Proceedings of the Royal Society, 280.* https://doi. org/10.1098/rspb.2013.1724.

National Research Council. (2004). *Measuring racial discrimination* (R. M. Blank, M. Dabady, & C. F. Citro, Eds.). Washington, DC: The National Academies Press.

NeuroLeadership Institute. (2018). *NeuroLeadership Institute.* Retrieved from: https://neuroleadership.com/.

Ostrom, E. (1990). *Governing the commons: The evolution of institutions for collective action.* Cambridge: Cambridge University Press.

Pearl, J. (2009). *Causality: Models, reasoning, and inference* (2nd ed.). New York, NY: Cambridge University Press.

Scott, W. R. (2014). *Institutions and organizations: Ideas, interests, and identities.* Los Angeles, CA: Sage.

Stocking, G. W. (1965). On the limits of 'presentism' and 'historicism' in the historiography of the behavioral sciences. *Journal of the History of the Behavioral Sciences, 1*(3), 211–218. https://doi.org/10.1002/1520-6696 (196507)1:3<211:AID-JHBS2300010302>3.0.CO;2-W.

Sturm, R. E., & Antonakis, J. (2015). Interpersonal power: A review, critique, and research agenda. *Journal of Management, 41*(1), 136–163. https://doi. org/10.1177/0149206314555769.

Thompson, A., & Bendik-Keymer, J. (Eds.). (2012). *Ethical adaptation to climate change: Human virtues of the future.* Cambridge, MA: MIT Press.

Veblen, T. (1919). *The vested interests and the state of the industrial arts.* New York, NY: B. W. Huebsch.

Wall, M. (2014, August 26). How neuroscience is being used to spread quackery in business and education. *The Conversation.* Retrieved from: http://theconversation.com/how-neuroscience-is-being-used-to-spread-quackery-in-business-and-education-30342.

Whitson, J. A., & Galinsky, A. D. (2008). Lacking control increases illusory pattern perception. *Science, 322*(5898): 115–117. https://doi.org/10.1126/science.1159845.

Wolin, S. (2004). *Politics and vision: Continuity and innovation in Western political thought* (Expanded ed.). Princeton, NJ: Princeton University Press.

Wootson, C. L., Jr. (2018, June 20). Airlines demand feds stop using their flights to transport migrant children separated from parents. *Washington Post.* Retrieved from: https://www.washingtonpost.com/news/dr-gridlock/wp/2018/06/20/airlines-demand-feds-stop-using-their-flights-to-transport-migrant-children-separated-from-parents/.

INDEX

© The Editor(s) (if applicable) and The Author(s) 2018   195

J. L. S. Chandler and R. E. Kirsch, *Critical Leadership Theory*,

https://doi.org/10.1007/978-3-319-96472-0

Made in the USA
Las Vegas, NV
15 March 2025